It feels very strange to consider myself an author. I didn't set out to become a writer let alone achieve the impossible. Believe it or not, I actual wet myself as I sat my English GCSE exam during the endless summer of 1986. My exam paper resembled wet toilet paper that had been trampled on by a hedgehog, sweating like a dyslexic on countdown. Children who are subjected to neglect, physical and mental abuse inevitably have issues at school. I write because it heals the many wounds of childhood trauma. I write because it heals the scars of war, addiction and my endless struggle with mental health.

My life thus far, incomprehensible. I contemplate the simple question many times? how and why I am alive. My birth name I left in the sand dunes of Iraq, the man I became would be the personification of my tormented childhood. The individual I have struggled to be for decades is a man blessed beyond measure. Once you have turned the last page, you decide what you think about this author. My name is Auguste Knuckles, father, husband, friend, chef, soldier, recovered drug addict author and urban poet.

That little boy Justin who defied all odds

My soul mate and wife, it's because of you I am here today.
Our amazing children, the love I have for you both cannot be measured.
Phenomenal woman and the late DJ Breeze
A handful of beautiful souls I call family and friends.

Auguste Knuckles

HOT SOAPY WATER

A Bubble Bath Not For Kids

AUSTIN MACAULEY PUBLISHERS™

LONDON * CAMBRIDGE * NEW YORK * SHARJAH

A CIP catalogue record for this title is available from the British Library.

ISBN 9781398468559 (Paperback)
ISBN 9781398468566 (ePub e-book)

www.austinmacauley.com

First Published 2023
Austin Macauley Publishers Ltd®
1 Canada Square
Canary Wharf
London
E14 5AA

Talking Therapies Berkshire

Veterans UK

The lorry driver who stopped me from committing suicide

Crisis centre Berkshire

The forgotten souls

Emergency services Wexham hospital

My home economics teacher

Mental health UK

Austin Macauley Publishers

Guy Ritchie

Frankie Knuckles

Belongings BBC radio Suffolk

All my mentors Bilston community college Wolverhampton

Cancer research UK

The British army, thanks for turning me into a drug addict, "nice one"

The national society for the prevention of cruelty to children NSPCC

The late Anthony Bourdain

Gabriel Fernandez 20th February 2005 – 24th May 2013

To all those who are dealing with their demons, addictions and mental health problems day in day out, remember you are fucking legends, total respect.

Table of Contents

The inconceivable, incomprehensible life of the average fella trying to make sense of his past. One child abandoned, neglected, abused, beaten black and blue. A dyslexic punching bag who failed miserably at school but found a lifeline through and in the culinary underbelly of madness. Addicted to drugs and alcohol from the get-go with no comprehension of the aftermath in later life. A vulnerable individual trying to discover his identity and to navigate his way through the debris of family carnage.

A tsunami of mental health issues and trauma simmering on the back burner would lead to one inevitable outcome. Dead on the wrong side of the grass, or someone who would drag themselves out from hells gate and share their story. Well, it wasn't all hell. What you are about to read hasn't been filtered down, neither diluted. A demolition derby of a roller coaster train wreck. The hedonistic life of Auguste Knuckles said as it is. It's a pseudonym by the way.

Some readers might relate to *Hot Soapy Water*'s content. Some readers might think "yeah" whatever, what a load of bollocks. But truth may seem stranger than fiction. May I suggest you strap in, familiarise yourself with all exits. Pour yourself something strong, because this is a narrative of courage, determination, addiction, mental health, suicide, racism, willpower, resilience, humour, sadness and in some chapter's absolute bewilderment.

Amuse Bouche and Hard Liquor

Heart pounding, sweaty palms, agitated and excited, we wait in the alley. The sound of the hairdryer gets closer, time to show my boarding pass, 24 hours all-inclusive on the noodle train please brother.

We exchange glances hoping he doesn't see my beads of sweat and pulsating temples, the sound of the moped engine fades into the distance. Sketchy addicts disappear into the nights sky doing the four-legged octopus' shuffle. Shall I call in a rub to chaperone me on this journey, maybe not. I have no intention in waking up next to a corpse.

Large bottle of jack and 40 Marlborough lights please. No seatbelt, table tray down, flip flops kicked to the side, seat reclined. Welcome onboard, will you be traveling alone, most definitely. Any hand luggage sir? Yes, just 6 grams of cocaine.

Curtains closed, safety glasses on, it's time for take-off, no inflight meal for me thank you, its hard drugs and ferocious liquor for the duration of my flight. Pounding breaths and adult entertainment is my choice of inflight movie.

2 hours in, turbulent times, my heart stops and starts, I gather my trembling corpse, light two cigarettes and down a quadruple shot of jack, back on top. Time for my main course nose buffet, super large portion with all the trimmings and a cigarette laced with Pablo's finest.

The sun rises, bursting lasers of light through the cracks in my window seat blind. I fumble for my phone and call the hostess to slide a henry under my door mat. No need for glances or awkward exchanges, dirty cash is hidden in the letterbox.

I lace the side of a joint with crystal rocks and puff away, turning my plush booth into a 1st class crack den. Excuse me sir, a voice from the corner of the room echoes across my boiling flesh "are you aware this is a one-way flight" how foolish do they think I am. I know it's a one-way flight, I've been on it forever.

The scary calamity is I need to be bushy-tailed, bright-eyed, presentable in 2 hours before I start my shift as executive head chef of one of the largest and busiest hotels outside of London. Or I could just call sick like I did as a greenhorn custard-burning twat and leave the kitchen to a tsunami of unmanaged carnage? 2 hours to sort this carcass out, a fat line of Columbian, triple shot of vodka, cold shower and a blunt razor will suffice to pass for half a human.

By the way, this isn't the start of a demolition pig fucking orgy narrative. We need to go back to when this unidentified, unwanted object fell from his biological mother's cunt. Hot soapy water a bubble bath not for kids isn't just about "cocaine and cooking"; it's about the whole fucking nuclear fallout and the damage caused to a new-born half-breed born into a racist, dysfunctional anarchistic, tormented abusive family during the 70s.

Abandoned, neglected, beaten black and blue, discarded like a rusty old man's bike, subjected to physical, emotional and mental abuse. Then kicked out of the house at 17 only to fall into an establishment which I assumed would straighten me out, the British army; how fucking wrong was I.

Now when I said let's go back to the start, the cunt falling out thing. We just need to hold fire for a few chapters. Let's start with the cataclysmic psychotic physical and mental breakdown I suffered on the way home from work one winter's evening. This single gargantuan incident which prompted me to get my shit together and start the process of fixing my mind which resembled a frazzled unwanted meat kebab in the gutter at the age of 48 or inevitable suicide.

Just for the record, there are no welcome drinks, fancy canapes, nibbles, so to speak. It's just fucking carnage from here on. Welcome to the noodle train that is hot soapy water a bubble batch not for kids.

Who am I, what am I, why am I me, who the fuck is Auguste Knuckles?

Trying to hide a cocaine addiction is like wearing a clown costume and making out you're not a clown while everyone is laughing at you waiting for your next trick. Snorting cocaine off the bathroom floor wasn't a trick. it was me trying not to be blatantly obvious at 4am in the morning while my wife and children were sleeping. Do I flush the toilet even though I haven't pissed to suffocate the sound of me snorting a fat line with my boxers around my ankles?

I tiptoe back to the living room, my heart pounding. Blind twisted vision, porn on the plasma; another rush is on its way. Maybe my dick might respond to some nubile lesbian action. Not a chance; I'm beyond fucked, wasted. I'm a junkie, an addict. Cocaine is my life, my precious, you or nobody will convince me otherwise that she isn't.

As a child I remember the glue sniffers at the back of our council house. Heads in plastic shopping bags inhaling toxic fumes. Dizzy as kids, jelly legs, falling like new-born calves. Was it for fun, or were they trying to escape? Trying to escape the horrors of the four walls they slept in.

Addiction is real, it's a disease, a full-blown illness. A word which is frowned upon like the word paedophile. Sex predator, rapist, murderer, addict, junkie. Scum of the earth, "look at that piss head over there, kids, he's a waster". Apart from the glue sniffers I only witnessed a few lost souls staggering home on a Friday evening from my bedroom window in our welfare pig shit house of horrors.

The detrimental effect of alcohol, I witnessed in my own home as a kid in the 70s and 80s has had a lasting effect. Why would my legal parents say, "look at that loser over there, stinking of alcohol"? Which child knows the smell of alcohol? we did. What the fuck was happening within my four walls. Hate, regret, anger, frustration, addiction, abuse on all levels and neglect that's what was happening.

It wasn't the fella smelling of glue or cheap cider hanging around the subway laying into me when Boris or Doris lost it. The wrong look you were fucked. Chased down and beat with a fist.

Why point at someone else and assume authority and grandeur. The guy on the floor smashed might have had a bad day at the office. Lost a loved one or even diagnosed with a life-threatening illness. During the years before and after the years on that council estate did our parents stand on the back of others when it came to their addictions or issues. Always pointing at someone else. Passing the buck so to speak. Looking back, they were as far from the image they portrayed "respectable parents", it was just all so fucking wrong.

I'm fucked, mangled not because of matey boy staggering home, or the glue sniffer skin heads at the back of our council house. I'm not an addict because of life outside my own front door. I was fucked from day one. I was born into chaos, the domino of my age. Dozens off abused reckless dominos that had fallen before me. Only the dominos before me thought they were marbles.

Blame someone else, who do I blame, who do I turn to. All the dominos behind me have cleared off. Do I make out I inflicted my wounds and topple causing the cause-and-effect scenario? My children looking back at me as if I was that guy staggering home from work who my legal parents called a waster, a piss head, a nobody. "Kids you don't ever want to be like that toss pot over there when you grow up".

This journey is about the dog shit, this is the journey of me staggering home every day for 30 years. This narrative, there was no home, just wilderness, wilderness on my own doorstep and within its four walls. This is the true causation of that domino effect. Addiction unfiltered, and why addiction was as easy as putting on a clown costume. Just for the record I didn't dress myself as the big tops side kick. Addiction found me, for the vulnerable we don't know addiction until we are at death's door.

I became the manifestation of their dog shit gabble. I became the guy staggering around the streets all hours of the day. Not able to breath because I had in fact snorted to much cocaine. Drank too much net whisky. Why the fuck would I want to die on my own sofa while my wife and children were away visiting family. Well, there's more chance of someone finding a dead corpse on the street than locked In my own house for a week before the wife and kids come home and finding their daddy dead, green and smelling like a shit that did a shit. A manifestation of systemic racism, neglect, physical mental and emotional abuse. It wasn't going to end this fucking way, fuck no.

"You will only sleep when the dead faces allow you to sleep, until then the dead faces are not sleeping"

Back to the toilet, back to the bathroom floor. This is addiction, when you are this lost. You'll do anything to get this shit into you. If I had been alone and I have been on many occasions when the wife and kids had flown to Europe to visit family. I would we staggering around the house naked smoking and snorting cocaine. Paranoid beyond comprehension, drinking hard liquor from the bottle until I passed out.

I had lost my soul, all inhibitions. I could snort cocaine and stay in bed during the day pretending to be asleep. I lied, cheated, I did some outrageous and stupid things. I put myself in danger, I was promiscuous, I was a savage. Those individuals see us as dead beats, dropouts, wasters, junkies, a waste of taxpayers' money. I Was all that and a fish supper.

It's ironic that those individuals who don't understand addiction are the ones who have most likely driven their own children to the bottle or hard drugs. I was triple fucked, abandoned, physically mentally and emotionally abused. Not knowing fuck all about life and very vulnerable I was thrust into the army. Drugs and alcohol consumed me. Six-month active service during the 1st Gulf war was the catalyst, Fucked for life.

I'm not an author because of hate, I don't really consider myself an author. I'm Auguste Knuckles. A life lived like so many, so why have I been chosen to share my story. My guardian angel travelled across an ocean of stars through the eternity of space long before she was born, long before I was born. I held her close when death was close, alone, naked on the bathroom floor clinging to life itself. I suppose I had to die before I could live.

Is death the portal to eternity? after all death is eternal, life is just a moment in time, a moment in space. I, we have spent so many years in time, in spaces, in a pickle, in love. But I fucking hated myself, otherwise I wouldn't be trying to kill myself. Or was it just irony, a sick twisted game of irony.

Girl in a horror film hides in a closet where the killer just went, the audience knows the killer is there, but she doesn't, brown bread. In Romeo and Juliet, the audience knows that Juliet is only asleep-not dead-but Romeo does not, but he kills himself, is he a dick head?

Dyslexic kid beaten black and blue, school a car crash drags himself off the toilet floor covered in shit piss and vomit becomes an author. The domino cause and effect scenario, thought about that also. I drink too much wine, I need to take a piss, causality.

I suppose it's time to deep dive the cause of addiction. Before I try and do the impossible. When I shop at Lidl, I don't go back every minute, hour, day to get my rocks off. Even though there is a certain reward happening, going off in my brain when I procure snails, Wellington boots, a drill set, great cheese, sweet and sour peanuts and cheap wine from down under.

Why aren't I still jumping in and out of the same pool I first jumped into as a child? I mean, the buzz was off the charts, why am I not still chasing that pleasure seeking reward. "We splash". For the record, saying you're addicted to chocolate is bollocks, anyone who says eating chocolate is like an orgasm is full of shit. Most likely you're hungry, a salad dodger or halfway through a bottle of scotch.

The Beginning of the End

January 2020, the day my world came crashing down around me, the cold dark blanket of suicide once again having its day but this day he was all guns blazing. Thoughts so loud, thoughts so disturbing telling me it would be over quickly it would be quick easy and painless, nothing to worry about my thoughts were telling me, nothing to worry about.

I'd never experienced anything as powerful or overwhelming as what was going on in my head, a full blown lightspeed psychotic meltdown. Just pull the car over onto the hard shoulder, exit the car and walk head on into rush hour traffic on the M25. Quick easy and painless, I promise you Auguste this is as good as it gets, this is your time.

Leaving behind a world I had struggled so hard to build, a world that was my wife and our two beautiful children. My world that had given me so much love, something seldom I had experienced as a child.

I thought my war had ended when I returned from the middle east 1991 having served as a soldier, a dessert rat during the 1st gulf war. Awarded a commendation by the commanding chief of the allied forces, the gulf war medal and clasp and the liberation of Kuwait medal all of which I sold to feed my addiction.

Classically trained I went on to forge a career in the hospitality industry. Working my way up the ladder to executive head chef in some of the busiest and most prestigious hotels and restaurants in the UK, Dubai, across the Italian and French Alps, Mediterranean and as far as Vancouver.

When I had finally won the battle with drugs and alcohol another war had started, my war with mental health. It would have been easier to have put that bullet through my brain during the war. It's a war I'm still fighting to this day, diagnosed with, CPTSD, anxiety, OCD and all its side orders, I'm fucked but I'm a survivor. Miraculously I function in today's society.

Writing this book hasn't been easy but it has helped me put closure to some of my darkest flashbacks and nightmares. You see I'm just the average guy on the street trying to make his way through this complex labyrinth called life.

"I've a head like a smashed vase and a donkey is trying to put it back together"

4 Years Old

When I sit and ponder my life as a boy it brings tears to my eyes. When I think what I have achieved I can only but smile. What would I say if I could go back and speak with that scared frightened little fella? Run, hide, call the police, tell a family member, call a friend, tell a teacher. I find it hard to believe that no one saw the bruises the sadness the cry for help, the sadness behind my cheeky smile as a four-year-old boy.

I would say you will most certainly overcome the pain, but the biggest challenge will be dealing with the trauma as you grow through the decades into manhood and finally have children of your own.

It's been a turbulent journey, countless highs and lows, battling addiction, depression, anxiety and my demons within. It has in fact been brutal suffering in silence, but I'm no longer frightened or scared.

At the age I am today and still somewhat fragile I've finally found my voice. I've finally found a way to cope with the flashbacks, nightmares, the mental, emotional and physical abuse inflicted on me by the ones who should have protected me from harm. One could say I've found inner peace with the cold dark blanket of suicide, the last exist for so many lost souls.

I've finally willed the courage to speak out, I've finally confessed to loved ones, why I was disconnected, distant, fractured and lost. It wasn't meant to be this way, but others had a heavy hand that rained down on me.

If I could go back to speak with those abusers and the ones that stood silent in the shadows and did nothing, what would I say? I wouldn't say anything. It's all of you who have lived in my shadow, these past decades, you have all witnessed the beauty which I have created and it's all my abusers who have become silent knowing that my presence in theirs is me tolerating every breath they take.

70s Nigger Child

A rain cloud hovering above my head
Never warm, always cold, seldom fed
Nothing magical only pain
To many nights I cried myself to sleep
Looks like I'm walking home alone from school again tomorrow

I'm a lonely seventies nigger child
Not black enough to be black
Not white enough to be accepted
I feel your shame behind this child's back

To many memories of the fist and boot
Boot polish black, another wooden spoon broken across my sisters back
Always raining in this little man's world
Where is the sun upon my face?
locked in a room, a cold dark damp empty space
Mice and rats eat better than thee
I'm a nigger child your family will not embrace

My tears your laughter, it will soon be over
Torment and bullying, you think your so clever
The day will come when I Look down upon you
A child born; a nigger child much stronger
Did you really believe I would grow old but none the wiser?

My words bare my childhood trauma
This nigger child now much older
The sun shone down when I left you behind

My days are full of magical wonder
It's a shame the dead will never know my pain
It's a shame the living are full of rage and anger
To you I'm just a seventies nigger child.

Miraculously I rise and go on
I no longer feel shame, neither your toxic gain
Your grief, you will take to the grave
Remember my name, remember my name
A name I changed to rid myself of disgust
I'm free, this nigger child you all called crusty

I walk taller everyday
The wind in my hair the sun upon my face
My umbrella shields me from rain
My children will never walk home alone
Beside them on the merry go round
Remember me, do you remember me, I'm that nigger child you so easily gave
away.

A kettle between four, more like bathing in shite
Hot Soapy suds for the man in your life
Prime cuts of meat for the bully, such a delight
Tortured over a plate of sprouts until the sun was out of sight.

I don't ever want to be comfortable
I don't want to be content or tired
I want to be awake, on the edge
Restless with a sense of what next
If I owe you anything I owe you that.

Starters

Addicted to my craft, the brink of insanity

Where did it all start, my love for food, well that is simple, I remember the experience every time I eat homemade Indian food. Not Indian food eaten in an Indian restaurant, it must be home cooked by my good friends. My first food orgasm was not me on a beautiful barge slowly cruising through the French countryside eating exquisite French cuisine as a child.

Neither was it slurping hand dived oysters in Corsica, that came decades later. Neither was it diving into a seductive cheese fondue in the swizz alps, that also came decades later. No, absolutely nothing exotic, the day I feel in love with food and sharing a simple meal for pleasure was on the floor of a beat-up dilapidated coach. It was with the most random human, being driven through the roughest parts of the black country back in the early 80s.

Strawberry picking, during the summer break from school to earn some money, my only income during those crazy days as a kid. The coach driver would pick up a bunch of misfits from the local supermarket carpark. All walks of life, Indian, Pakistani, Asian, yobbo's, blacks, whites, half breeds, not just Jamaican white English half breeds. You name it, a multi-cultural mashup, a coach load of skint, destitute, broke, strawberry pickers.

It was a thirty-minute drive to Featherstone farms, next to Featherstone prison. Featherstone prison being the last stop for so many wasters, losers, rapist's, murders and strawberry pickers feeding their addiction. Yes, that is correct, strawberry pickers who would probably end upon the wrong side of the law sooner or later. A day strawberry picking would earn me £20, a day on my knees. I suppose there's worse jobs out there spending hours on your knees, if you know what I mean.

Now £20 was not bad considering the measly £4 per week I would get from my newspaper round. Unlike my fellow pickers, they would easily take home £40 for the day, easily. That's because they would and could pick at twice the

23

speed as I did. The coach home I would crash at the back, taking in the countryside a cheeky five-minute snooze before we reached our destination, and this is when it all happened.

The mind fuck of an experience, an old Indian lady who has most likely got £40 in her pocket lays out a pristine kitchen tea towel on the floor of the coach directly in front of me. She looks up and shakes her head but not that stupid English nod version, that Indian nod, as if to say, "are you ok, do you understand". Nope I do not understand, and I haven't a clue what is going on, but I role with it.

I never knew a nod could be so powerful without a spoken word, from her bag she pulls out a tiffin and pops it onto of the kitchen towel. Like a concubine making tea for her emperor, she opens the tiffin container. I am blown away with what this old lady is doing, practically between my legs.

The smell is mind bending for the lumpy mash and cold gravy kid, pilaf rice, sag aloo, Dahl and aloo Gobi, roti, and lime pickle. I did not know about these dishes at the time. The closest I got too foreign food was picking up a chicken curry from the Chinese for our next-door neighbour the lazy cow.

She looks up at me and offers me some of her food, I join my new companion on the floor of the coach and indulge myself. It is a cliché today, used by every celebrity chef or chef taking part in a mind-numbing cooking competition. "An explosion of flavours in one's mouth". Bollocks, this was a nuclear bomb going off, this was flavour genocide, mouth spit roasted, mouth gang bang central.

The experience was like coming up on ecstasy, eyes rolling in the back of my head, a warm fuzzy feeling, was this old lady coming on to me. Hypnotised by her culinary delights, was I to become her teen sex slave once I had followed her tiffin back to her place.

This simple offering, to share food with another human blew me away. Addicted, hooked, I was on that vibe, and I still am today. Cooking for close friends and family, small tight enclosed spaces, huddled together just enjoying each other's company and great food is a blessing it's a religion.

We ate in silence on the coach floor oblivious to time. My eyes watering as the lime pickle kicked the back of my throat in. The delicate flavours playing games with my senses. The rice perfectly cooked with a delicate creaminess of gee. "Right, everyone off" yelled the coach driver.

I waggled my head and thanked the lady; I walked the short walk home purchased snacks and pop with my £20 and chilled out in my shared room listening to PCRL the best pirate radio station in town. Still tasting those spicy mellow flavours in my mouth, I drifted off with my dick in my hand and dreamt that night about becoming an astronaut.

Fast forward a few full moons. 1992 I spent the night crashed on my mate's sofa, recovering from the drive back to the UK from Germany. I'm up early as I still need to drive back to the black country. The house is a fucking nightmare, it's worse than it was when I left 4 years ago. Boris and Doris are obviously at the end of their toxic marriage. The atmosphere was like what I had experienced during the war, chaos. I have been away for almost 4 years, I have returned an emotional wreck, an addict craving for a fix or a joint of some sort.

I'm in their house no more than 10 minutes, fuck this shit, I about face without saying a word to Doris and Boris, neither do they say a word to me, and leave. I make my way to the train station and catch the first train to Bristol.

Uncle Charlie was one of a few people I looked up to as a kid, tall, handsome, dressed like a dapper dan, always sharp and funny. Ex-military man who would most likely understand what his nephew was going through after leaving the forces.

A young man still dealing with the trauma of war without a purpose acclimatising to life on civilian street. It became clear as the driven snow, I wouldn't need identity in Bristol. I was a party boy who had a nose for good drugs, decent clubs with enough experience in my knife box that would land me my first posting as a pastry chef in one of the most prestigious hotels in Bristol.

I was young, unpredictable, I had no filter. It was obvious thinking about those years now as a parent, as an author, as a chef. There was something dark, unholy, eerie in my shadow looking back at me from the very first day I stepped off that train when I crashed landed at Bristol train station.

I moved in with Charlie and his wife Donna, party people then and still party people to this day. They hosted some of the maddest house parties in Bristol during the early eighties and 90s, Beautiful people, gay, straight, queens, black, white, Asian, everyone was equal, everyone on the same level. I settled in like a dick in a condom.

I was mad for it, Bristol and all her mysterious wonders. I started working at Donna's Cafe in town, cash in hand no questions asked. Simple fare nothing foreign, cook to order. The only thing that I was missing was drugs, I needed to score, anything, something and it could not have been any easier.

My butcher Roger, first day on the job, first delivery and introductions. Hi, I'm Auguste, "Hi I'm Roger", I asked if he knew a man about town? "Yes, me", who you? "Yes me", game on. Can you drop me an 8th of red seal and some hurry up next delivery, "when would that be", I will place an order today, for delivery tomorrow?

On the money 8am the following morning, 2 packets of sliced gammon, 2kg mince beef, 10 corn feed chicken breasts, 8 gammon steaks an 8th of red seal and a wrap of hurry up. "Credit or cash", credit, I will square the house Friday.

Stoned in the morning, stoned in the afternoon and stoned in the evening, stoned 24-7 on the bus off the bus to the cafe. Cheeky one skins out the back during work and a hot knife before we closed shop in the evening, stoned as a cave man in a cave, bombed off my chops.

Days soon turned into weeks, weeks turned into months, I started to cluck like a chicken, I needed the party, the underground scene. My uncle's house party scene was not doing it for me anymore. The young gay scene was off the charts in the city, clubs, drugs, fashion, music and beautiful up for it all day and all-night people. But this story is not about my sexual orientation during those crazy days. Although I must confess I did bat for both sides.

As I've always said, try everything once. More so when it's time to check out at the end of that obstacle course called life, you will not look back and say to yourself "I should have tried it once".

I needed a soul mate, I needed someone I could relate to, someone on the same level not just my drug dealing butcher. Long story short, after pissing my auntie Donna off most nights coming home with Charlie totally and utterly smashed. She knew I needed someone to party with, someone she did not want to divorce.

His name was shanty, handsome fella, tall mixed race with the sickest dress sense. John Paul Gauthier, John Richmond, Versace, D&G just for starters. He was the boyfriend of one of Donna's daughters work colleagues. Blind date is set, Temple meads Friday night 7pm. We clicked from the off, cheese and crackers with fig and liquorice chutney.

You must be shanty, "you must be Auguste, nice to meet you brother, do you like pills"? is a pig's pussy pork. Smashed off our eyeballs every weekend for the best part of 3 years. We smashed it all, we even shared hot cups of sweet tea, buzzing our chops off on the sweaty dance floor of Lakota.

We dropped bombs of speed into double shots of grey goose in every club in the west country. We got skunk fucked in every blues party known around Bristol. I lost count of the fine people we both dated. The drugs we consumed was mind boggling, as I reminisce, beautifully organised chaos. We also got pickled, peeled like bananas at both Prodigy concerts, hammered sideways, Astronauts on crack, living like there was no sun rise.

Anyways enough of the shenanigan's let's get back to the kitchen. 2nd interview of the day, crown plaza. I nailed it, only because I said they had made an offer at the park royal working alongside executive chef Johnny cheese straws Bananas. Bingo, I was employed as a pastry commis chef, 5* hotel, 2 rosettes pushing for a third. What could possibly go wrong? every fucking thing could go wrong, and everything did go fucking wrong. To this day the only thing I can put my finger on, my head wasn't straight. I had a head for every day of the week just like Wurzel the scarecrow. Only this chef did not know which head he was going to wake up with each morning.

Paul my chef de partie within the pastry section "my supervisor" was my Escoffier for the next 6 months, Paul was so talented his skill level was up there with some of the best pastry chefs in the country. After six months he had plans to move to London with his partner. I had every opportunity, if I worked hard to be promoted to CDP of the pastry section. Only I could fuck this up. 100% focused day in day out every shift, I was all over it, like a sponge. I partied hard but worked triple times harder.

Six months flew by, probably the only 6 months of my 35-year career that I took seriously, well that and my fat duck stagier years later. Once promoted for some inconceivable reason I turned into a full-blown kitchen terrorist. A lunatic, something upstairs clicked, a switch had been turned on. Was it the promotion or was it a bloody psychotic coincidence combined with some sort of delayed reaction to what I had witnessed during the gulf war or as a child?

I bought havoc to the kitchen, in a fun harmless way and by no means was it malicious or spiteful. I just drove everyone stir fucking crazy, but I cooked, and I bloody cooked well. During service I would be on the passé with my sous chef learning the sauce section, If I wasn't on sauce, I would be on the larder section. The cold section doing prep for the following day before my dessert orders came in.

I was in the kitchen at 7:30am every morning ready to start my shift. I would leave in the a:m the following day. I would dream about food, I was a food junkie not a foodie, a term the millennials like to call themselves today "I'm a foodie". A full-blown food junkie and that was before the competitions even started for me.

I was a walking repertoire, I would create jaw dropping desserts, petit fours, ice and fruit carvings, ice creams that some chefs today might think "um I don't think so". I was all over that kitchen like ratatouille the rat. I breathed and lived every day of the kitchen. I suppose that's why management turned a blind eye to my mischievous ways. Although I was a loose cannon, if anyone said a bad word towards the kitchen team, ban saw Bill would kick off, meaning me.

So, a brief walk around the kitchen and sections, let us start with Plug, the ugliest garnish chef from the roughest and ugliest part of Bristol. This poor chef didn't just fall from the ugly tree. He got thrown out an aircraft, landed in a tree on a huge hill. He then rolled down that hill hitting every boulder on the way down. Then feel into another tree in that creepy neighbour's garden. Then fell face first on to the pavement, ugly, funny mother fucker but he could cook.

If master chef the professionals had been invented back then, our kitchen team would have cleaned up, all day long. We would have the judges caressing our balls, stroking our shafts and swallowing our gravy. Plug loved that shit pop, panda, 10pence from the happy shopper store. We didn't have red bull, liquid speed, monster energy back in those days, we had shit pop and speed. If we did have such decadent hydration in a can, I guess Plug would be smacked up in the gents shooting that sit into his vein.

Pour that 10 pence pop into a pan, boil it, reduce it, what is left in the bottom of that pan is enough shit to make a sticky bomb, Google sticky bomb. My pastry section had every food colouring known to mankind, if there was a colour, I had it in small little alcohol type plastic bottles.

Plug always got it in the ass during service because he never bought anyone a can of that shit pop, not that I would accept it from him anyways. I still have a full set of teeth, Plug had two teeth on the top gum and 3 on the bottom. Some might call me a cunt, I was a cunt, every time Plug went out for a fag or to the toilet, I'd spike his can with a dab of speed and food colouring.

Not every night but most nights, but it worked both ways, we were the only two chefs in that kitchen who turned a blind eye to us spiking each other. If this fella missed the last bus home, he would run. Not only would he run home, but he would probably stop every person on the way for a quick chat. His jaw gnashing away they would probably wonder why this poor fella had blue teeth a yellow tongue and green gums.

The carnage did not stop there, oh no, service was play time, my playtime until I got hammered with checks, or wasn't covering the Jr sous on the passe who was another addict. He didn't dab from a baggie; he would shoot speed every day. His body at such a young age had been lynched and destroyed. Stew never wore a short-sleeved chef's jacket because of the scabs and train tracks in both arms. Looking back and knowing how well he cooked It was a sad story, a lot like mine. Word on the street he didn't make it past 30, RIP brother, we had some crazy services, and some unforgettable days and nights out in Bristol.

Back to Plug, my pastry section was about five meters from the garnish section, passed garnish would be the pot wash. During service on garnish there would be a huge pan of salted simmering water so that the chef "plug" could reheat his ingredients before tossing in butter seasoning and passing to the Jr sous on the passé. By the way if you are wondering what the passé is, it's the head of the kitchen where all plates are finished, garnished before they depart for the restaurant.

Bored, all my mise en place at the ready sat on my flour bin with a bunch of grapes at the ready. If basketball had been played with grapes, I would be Michael fucking grape Jordan. I had my shot down to a tee, I could launch a grape across the kitchen into a coffee cup. Grape invaders here we go.

1st check on, it's time to score some baskets. First grape launched into garnish air space, plop straight into the vat of salted water. The trick was to get the grape dead centre of the pot, this would cause a reverse swirl type plop splash out of the scalding pot. If plug was stood next to the pot reheating his vegetables, bulls' eye, dead centre of his ugly forehead, scolded for a day or two.

Plug wouldn't allow this to go down without launching whatever he had at his disposal back at me. He would often launch a half drunk can of panda pop into pastry air space. My pristine walls covered in all sorts of colours from my food colouring draw. "You fucking twat, stop with the fucking grapes, will you".

Who's next on the kitchen team tree? I have just been released from prison for armed robbery 4ft 10inc dish pig. Oldest man standing in the kitchen, proud, loved his pot wash but most of all he loved his hair. Imagine a beautiful head of black hair with a slight curl to it, Austin Powers sort of style on a dead man. Yes, Mick Jagger odd looking.

Every five minutes Donavan would be combing his hair, then tap the top of his head to reassure himself he had not combed it away. Health and safety, out the window with this one. I was super hyperactive; I was also super hyper vigilant every breathing hour of the day. Not good having this much adrenaline cursing through your body. Sonner or later you are going to pop, imploded or explode. Fight or flight mode every day.

By the way things went a little off-road living with Charlie and Donna. Donnas' eldest daughter is having her wicked way with me. The guy your procuring drugs from and playing football with every other weekend is Donnas eldest daughter's husband. This didn't go down to well when the family got wind through the toxic rumour mill.

I was summoned to the cafe and interrogated by every family member. In my defence it takes a bored housewife to tango. I was single who didn't tango, young somewhat irrational with a sprinkling of recklessness with more luggage than prince Akeem. She was a grown woman, married with kids who had bigger responsibilities than playing shag chase with a boy.

It's unfortunate that Charlie, someone I looked up to as a child when shit was going off back in the eighties has also turned out to be a person I can no longer relate too. Even after beating addiction, being clean for several years. I'm just a no good for nothing individual regardless of my achievements. Some individuals don't understand, they never will. They've all joined ranks to somehow justify their actions towards me. These dramas and experiences happened decades ago but they all found it funny back then. Somehow behind all the carnage and chaos that was going on, subconsciously I was in fact carving out a career.

Donavan the kitchen porter loved a clean kitchen, but after every job I would sprinkle flour everywhere. Not a handful, just a tiny sprinkle as If I were dusting my work service to roll out sweet pastry. The still room, flour, pot wash, flour, chef's office flour, breakfast fridge, flour, staff canteen, flour, sauce section, flour, loading bay flour and not forgetting the female changing rooms, flour.

Donavan would go ape, after a cruise ship daily deep clean. I would walk six feet behind him sprinkling flour on every clean surface and then sneak away like a ninja sniper flour assassin. You name a kitchen utensil I've had it launched at me, copper pots, shattered tiles in my section, sieves, all the coloured coded chopping boards and bins. Walls covered in demi-glace, vinaigrette and vegetable peelings. It was chaos, surprisingly no one got stabbed in the eye or electrocuted. We were the Adams family, the B-team of chefs, the most dysfunctional team in the hotel.

Before I get to the end of this chapter with me knocking out my sous chef, I cannot forget Water world and my head chef. Water world was another kitchen porter wannabe breakfast chef. Like flour for Donavan, it was water for water world. Everywhere this aquatic being ventured it was like a tsunami had ravaged the kitchen.

X-men, character explodes into a puddle of water; this is that guy, water world. And there is a valid reason, he loved to smoke in the none smoking areas around the hotel including the loading bay. Above the loading bay was a balcony which led out from the female changing rooms overlooking the delivery entrance.

"Just out for a fag chef" ok water world, several chefs armed to the teeth with pans of dish water, manky stock, left over soup that had been sat in the pot wash for a day. We depart the kitchen at speeds unknown to Jamaican sprinters. Upstairs into and out the female changing rooms. Drenched, soaked, it didn't make a difference how many changes of clothes water world bought to work. He would leave soaked to the bone covered in dish water, stock dribbles, meringue and left-over soup du jour.

We are pushing for 3 rosettes, film stars, rappers, producers, footballers, ballers we had everyone at that hotel, good times, crazy times. We were also mad for getting it on at competitions, saloon culinaire Bristol 1994.

We had practiced for several months for the competition, me, Steve the senior sous chef and the other salad squeezing larder chef, Steve. As a young teenager salad squeezing Steve had been run over by a lorry and that shit is 100% true. You get run down by a lorry during rush hour, let me rephrase that. You get run over by a lorry period; you are going to walk funny for the ever days of your life before death. That's if you don't perish by the 18 wheels and its load. This chef had the top of his body fused with the bottom half of his body with blue tac, super glue and a fucking miracle.

Countless operations, CPTSD sessions, he was the six-million-dollar man of our kitchen team. It's a fucking miracle how this guy survived, but he did and like every other fucked up chef in that team during that period during those years, we were living, we were chefs, and we were mad for the kitchen.

Play hard, cook harder, take drugs, drink even harder, fight harder, live harder. I didn't want to be anywhere else at that period of my career, we were walking on the moon wearing butchers' aprons. Salon culinaire 1994, cook off, black box 1hr 45minutes, 3 courses, starter, main, dessert. Steve the lorry on starters, Sr sous mains, me on dessert. The cook off took place in front of a packed house, judged by chefs who had peeled the big man's onions.

Peel, sizzle, bone, simmer, deglaze, sauté, steam, pickle, bake, grill, burn, cut, bleed, blue plaster, sweat, 1hr 45minutes stop cooking, poached fucking pears. WTF, I look down the cook's line, all I see are several poached fucking pears, cooked by Michelin starred chefs, poached fucking pears. All this talent, I was expecting eye watering, thumb in my mouth greatness, I have just wet my nappy, going for a wank top shelf porn, plates of pastry phenomenon.

Hop skip and a jump it is time for me to explain my dessert to the men in white. Tall chefs' hats held up with scaffolding with stars and stripes on top. No point bull shitting a bull shitter, these chefs were gods to me. Sable biscuit, baked in a mini brioche mould, filled with strawberry mousse, glazed strawberries, topped with a sugar cage, with confit pear pearls and fruit coulis chef. We went up against Michelin starred restaurants chefs. The swallow royal and a few future stars who after the cook off, I realised they must have been given a black box from happy shopper.

The grand fromage, "Chefs I have to say, I'm not impressed with the overall level of cooking during this year's competition. There are no team golds, silvers or bronzes, only merits, but for the record if I may say, no disrespect to the pastry chef". He looks over to me, tips his hat and winks, great dessert chef. Fuck me sideways, I had just won gold bronze and silver, one of the biggest highlights of my career. That afternoon I went out with the two Steve's, we all got paralytic only to be back in the kitchen early doors pickled as a Polish gherkin.

Hotel Olympia 94 was the year my life as a chef would change for ever. I truly believed it would be the year which would have the biggest impact towards the chef I would, not become. It was the year when it all went south. 17 hours per day on the hoof, two long services, lunch and dinner plus meeting and events. If you did get out during your split, it would be a few pints in the local battle cruiser scoring drugs. Or a snooze on the changing room floor using your apron as a blanket and you knife roll as a pillow.

It had been decided the same team from saloon culinaire Bristol would be entered to compete at hotel Olympia. Me and the two Steve's, super stoked beyond belief. I had been to hotel Olympia while studying at college in the 80s.

If a chef is going to be noticed it is going to be at hotel Olympia, the Olympics for chefs.

I fucking poured my heart into this competition, not only was I doing the static dessert display, 3 cold, 3 hot desserts I was in the cook off. 17hr days had turned into 19 hours, speed was the only answer. I was 23 6ft+, weighed 60kg just there or about, nothing to me but skin, bone and my undying passion for food which was my pastry section that I manned alone.

19hr days there's only 4 hours max to rest taking into consideration the commute. I looked like a zombie with dreads. Days off clubbing, drugs, coming into work to practice my dishes for Olympia and the odd spurt with a skirt and that wasn't often, neither in that order. You can also throw masturbating in there if I had the energy. During workdays I hardly saw daylight, only when I went out on to the loading bay to dab from my wrap of speed or have a cheeky pull-on water worlds skunk javelin.

Shortly after salon Culinaire Bristol the executive chef recruited a new commis chef to add support to all sections. The new commis over time would become a chef tournament. But only after working all sections and gaining experience.

First section for the new chef was my section, pastry. Debbie would spend two months with me. After those two months Debbie would manage the section for a week on her own. During that week I would start my training on sauce. The sauce section was also about managing the passé, the flow of service during lunch and dinner.

Monday and Tuesday, I would work the passé with the working head chef. Basically, I would be speed taught. Mise en place, ordering, presentation and managing the flow of diners into the restaurant. I had done a few hours here and there, so I had the basics in my locker. You had to move fucking quick during service and have a cool head. Think my executive chef thought it would be a good idea for me to channel my over hyperactive hypervigilant brain within the section that would either break me or break me even harder.

Mise en place for the sauce section was repetitive work. Nothing different to what I hadn't already done on pastry. Repetitive, easy for a young chef with a mild case of OCD. Lunch and dinner service, observe, document, process and execute when asked to repeat a dish from the vast menu. Two rosettes, I was all over it, but we wanted a 3rd so attention to detail, timing, presentation and calling away had to be flawless, fucking flawless. Unlike pastry service the chefs on sauce did not have time to refresh little pots for sauce and sauté pans for proteins.

They got launched into a huge pot wash dumpster at the end of the passé. It was down to the kp's to replenish the section while the chef could concentrate on service. "More fucking pots, more fucking sauté pans", "oui chef" all throughout service. Kp's had to move just as quick as the chefs, without a solid kitchen porter team you can forget a smooth service let alone a clean kitchen. The backbone to any successful kitchen.

Not only did I have to manage the kp's I had to manage the flow of service. Pre-service chats, we got briefed on bookings, special occasions, dietary, back in those days, vegetarian and celebrities every service without fail. Come 7pm the chefs on sauce knew who was coming in and when they were being seated. Every single table the restaurant manager would walk into the kitchen up to the passé and verbally let me know when a table had been sat. If it was busy, I would hold them back in the bar for five or ten minutes so that service flowed.

Wednesday it was my turn to manage the passé the restaurant and the entire kitchen. Pres-service chat boxed, time to crack on and to see if I had the apples the mentality and strength to run a service for 36 guests. 36, the head and executive chef didn't throw me in the deep end that night. It was nothing compared to the numbers we did Friday night and the weekends, bedlam.

My first service was like salon culinaire Bristol but for 3 hours. Loads of shouting, orders, direction and timings whilst cooking and plating 3 rosette plates of delicious food. Burnt, battered, bruised drenched in sweat with every sauce, demi-glace and reduction splattered against the wall next to the pot wash dumpster including my whites.

The head chef and sous came over after service and told me, "You had better get it together for Friday Knuckles". Considering the kitchen was a fucking bomb site and not one complaint from front of house my first service got the thumbs up. But I had to get my shit together and locked in tight for the big numbers.

Looking back years later I was giving 199% every day, it was obvious I was overlooking my wellbeing. Wellbeing back then was an evening off, which was spent getting blasted. The pressure pot cooking in the deepest parts of my soul where at boiling point. It just needed a trigger a spark, anything out of the ordinary would ignite the dynamite. Everything that was my world of food was normal. I considered myself normal.

Friday night and that weekend, I got hammered. From then on. I vaguely remember the flow of services during those days because it was decided after that first weekend I would stay on sauce for the foreseeable future while overseeing pastry. Debbie had decided she wanted to become a pastry chef, bitch.

As the weeks got closer, I would be in on my day off for 3 to 4 hours practicing for Olympia. Tik tock, tik tock, tik tock, eyes peeled downing double, triple, quadruple espressos. Amphetamines and weed were being consumed at a voracious pace. There was no filter; I would often find myself walking across the road with my eyes closed on the way home. The curtains to my bed sit never opened. Some days I would arrive home not having a clue what I had done that day, totally fucking spaced out.

My skill set was set at Michelin star level, I had my shit together on sauce, so much so I was coming in on Sundays. I would prepare, cook and serve plated Sunday carvery lunches. Starting my shift straight from an after party still buzzing.

Sundays I had the con, I ran the kitchen until lunch service was over. I traded pints of chilled come down beer with front of house for left over Sunday carvery. I would hide the beers under chefs' desk in the office. 2:30pm I would retire to the office, place orders eat my way through a plate of food that would have to sustain me until the next time I had time to eat, which was not often.

I staggered home every Sunday afternoon for months and months. If I weren't blind drunk unable to speak when I arrived home, I would order half a wrap of something fruity. It was a destructive routine, and I did not even know. It was killing myself; I was slowly killing myself. Blinded by my love for cooking and addiction which would last for decades. I was nailing my own nails into my own coffin with my forehead.

Check on, 2 duck both medium rare, two fillets both rare, 3 lamb cutlets medium, 1 buttered tagliatelle, 2 minted royals, 3 gratin, 7 seasonal vegetables, "oui chef". Alarm smashed against my bedroom wall, up showered off to work.

The duck dish on the menu was a fucking nightmare. Magret de canard duck breasts marinated in honey with ginger lime and lemons. A fucking nightmare when we had two dozen checks on. Hands or tongs into thick honey to retrieve a breast. Use fingers to remove excess honey then straight on to the char grill to scorch before it goes in the oven.

The lamb dish was another cunt to prepare. French trim best end of lamb. Cut into chops with only the eye of the meat attached to the bone. Sear the lamb on the solid top. Top with mushroom duxelles and a blanched leaf of spinach. Cover with lattice puff pastry egg wash and store until service. Grass fed angus beef fillet, served with rosti, fois gras, morrells, asparagus and baby carrots with a 48hr veal jus and shaved truffle. I was preparing cooking and sending these dishes in my sleep. If I could call it sleep.

It was the same while I was on pastry, all bar puff pastry, Danishes for breakfast, tart cases for meeting and events everything was made fresh. Petit fours, brandy snap baskets, ice creams and sorbets. All options for coffee breaks and banqueting 100% fresh. Unlike today so many establishments, chefs have the option of flicking through top shelf glossy brochures from several suppliers that supply high end products to high end establishments. I'm not complaining, it's how the industry is today, it's a money game. De-skill kitchens replace with convenient products it's a win-win situation if you have issues with payroll.

Days morphed into weeks, weeks into me being more mully mushed every month. I could sense something unsavoury was cooking in the chef's office. Basically, come competition time our executive chef would have departed the kitchen to set up his own business, leaving the head chef to take over.

This was the head chef's opportunity to bring me down a peg, the head chef who is stepping up to take the big man's office. Bring me down did he ever, there is always a brown-nosed cunt hiding in the shadows who wants to make his mark. I just wanted to cook; my nose was already brown.

"Auguste, office" yes chef, "we have decided you will not be part of the cook off team at hotel Olympia this year". What the fuck do you mean, who has decided this fucking dog shit, "me and the GM, we think you should concentrate on the static display competition". So, who the fuck is taking my place? "A chef from the Hilton, he will be joining us once he has worked his notice".

There are no words to express how I felt that day. I walked out of the just promoted chef's office, went up to the changing rooms and fucking destroyed the place. Mirrors, lockers, sinks, windows, toilets were smashed, toilet doors kicked through. I destroyed the entire changing room.

In a fit of rage and shock I went back downstairs, kicked open the chef's office door and knocked the fucker clean out. The cunt just collapsed in a heap on the office floor. I fucking went to town; a nuclear bomb had just gone off in the kitchen. I squared up to the general manger and called him a useless cunt.

I emptied my wrecked locker, cleared out my section, walked to my bed sit packed my bag and jumped on the first available train out of town. I left half my life behind including my sound system and never returned. My life had just been skull fucked, turned upside down. That day I decided from that day on I would have no respect for management.

I was a young man, a chef who had just returned from war. My first proper job on civilian street. If this is how life is fought and played, I am not going to play brown nose and suck dick. Neither was I going to be that go to chefs' little pet. I was going to live my life and forge my career my way.

Goldfish Bowl

Bent over backwards, twisted inside out, legs on back to front. The life inside your goldfish bowl is blackness, the only sound is the thudding of a broken windscreen wiper left to right on the outside. The only thing that makes sense is doing more cocaine. The world around you is plugged into a moon-sized speaker. Unable to string a sentence together you stand silent drinking yourself into a coma. AK

Auguste Escoffier

Georges Auguste Escoffier, born 28 October 1846, was a French chef, restaurateur and culinary writer who popularised and updated traditional French cooking methods. Much of Escoffier's technique was based on that of Marie-Antoine Carême, one of the codifiers of French haute cuisine; Escoffier's achievement was to simplify and modernise Carême's elaborate and ornate style.

In particular, he codified the recipes for the five mother sauces. Referred to by the French press as roi des cuisiniers et cuisinier des rois ("king of chefs and chef of kings" also previously said of Carême), Escoffier was a preeminent figure in London and Paris during the 1890s and the early part of the 20th century.

Alongside the recipes, Escoffier elevated the profession. Kitchens used to be loud and riotous where drinking on the job was commonplace. Escoffier demanded cleanliness, quiet and discipline from his staff. He worked in partnership with hotelier César Ritz. The two rose to prominence together at the Savoy in London serving the elite of society, and later at the Ritz Hotel in Paris and the Carlton in London.

Escoffier published Le Guide Culinaire, which is still used as a major reference work, both in the form of a cookbook and a textbook on cooking. Escoffier's recipes, techniques and approaches to kitchen management remain highly influential today and have been adopted by chefs and restaurants not only in France, but also throughout the world.

Escoffier was born in the village of Villeneuve-Loubet, today in Alpes-Maritimes, near Nice. The house where he was born is now the Musée de l'Art Culinaire, run by the Foundation Auguste Escoffier. At the age of twelve, despite showing early promise as an artist, his father took him out of school to start an apprenticeship in the kitchen of his uncle's restaurant, Le Restaurant Français, in Nice.

As an apprentice, August was bullied and swatted by his uncle and his small stature made him even more of a target, he was too short to safely open oven doors. Eventually, he wore boots with built up heels. Escoffier showed such an aptitude for cooking and kitchen management that he was soon hired by the nearby Hôtel Bellevue, where the owner of a fashionable Paris restaurant, Le Petit Moulin Rouge, offered him the position of commis-rôtisseur (apprentice roast cook) in 1865 at the age of 19. However, only months after arriving in Paris, Escoffier was called to active military duty, where he was given the position of army chef.

Escoffier spent nearly seven years in the army—at first stationed in various barracks throughout France (including five months in Villefranche-sur-Mer, coincidentally not three miles from his old home in Nice), and later at Metz as chef de cuisine of the Rhine Army after the outbreak of the Franco-Prussian War in 1870. His army experiences led him to study the technique of canning food.

Sometime before 1878, he opened his own restaurant, Le Faisan d'Or (The Golden Pheasant), in Cannes. On 28 August 1878, he married Delphine Daffis. She has been described as "a French poetess of some distinction and a member of the Academy". Escoffier apparently won her hand in a gamble with her father, publisher Paul Daffis, over a game of billiards. They had three children, Paul, Daniel (who was killed in World War I), and Germaine. She died on 6 February 1935.

In 1884, the couple moved to Monte Carlo, where Escoffier was employed by César Ritz, manager of the new Grand Hotel, to take control of the kitchens. At that time, the French Riviera was a winter resort: during the summers, Escoffier ran the kitchens of the Grand Hôtel National in Lucerne, also managed by Ritz.

In 1890, Ritz and Escoffier accepted an invitation from Richard D'Oyly Carte to transfer to his new Savoy Hotel in London, together with the third member of their team, the maître d'hôtel, Louis Echenard. Ritz put together what he described as "a little army of hotel men for the conquest of London", and Escoffier recruited French cooks and reorganised the kitchens.

The Savoy under Ritz and his partners was an immediate success, attracting a distinguished and moneyed clientele, headed by the Prince of Wales. Gregor von Görög, chef to the royal family, was an enthusiast of Escoffier's zealous organisation. Aristocratic women, hitherto unaccustomed to dining in public, were now "seen in full regalia in the Savoy dining and supper rooms".

Escoffier created many famous dishes at the Savoy. In 1893, he invented the pêche Melba in honour of the Australian singer Nellie Melba, and in 1897, Melba toast. Other Escoffier creations, famous in their time, were the bombe Néro (a flaming ice), fraises à la Sarah Bernhardt (strawberries with pineapple and Curaçao sorbet), baisers de Vierge (meringue with vanilla cream and crystallised white rose and violet petals) and suprêmes de volailles Jeannette (jellied chicken breasts with foie gras). He also created salad Réjane, after Gabrielle Réjane, and (although this is disputed) tournedos Rossini.

In 1897, the Savoy board of directors began noticing their revenues were falling despite business increasing. They discreetly hired an auditing company who in turn hired a private investigation company that began secretively tailing Ritz, Echenard and Escoffier. After a six-month investigation, they made a report to the board which detailed substantial evidence of fraud.

On 8 March 1898, Ritz, Echenard and Escoffier were brought in front of the board and dismissed from the Savoy "for…gross negligence and breaches of duty and mismanagement". They were to leave immediately that day.

Most of the kitchen and hotel staff were loyal to Ritz and Escoffier and as news spread disturbances in the Savoy kitchens reached the newspapers, with headlines such as "A Kitchen Revolt at The Savoy". The Star reported: "Three managers have been dismissed and 16 fiery French and Swiss cooks (some of them took their long knives and placed themselves in a position of defiance) have been bundled out by the aid of a strong force of Metropolitan police".

The real details of the dispute did not emerge at first. Ritz and his colleagues even prepared to sue for wrongful dismissal. Eventually, they settled the case privately: on 3 January 1900, Ritz, Echenard and Escoffier "made signed confessions" but their confessions "were never used or made public".

Escoffier's confession was the most serious admitting to an actual crime, taking kickbacks from the Savoy's food suppliers worth up to 5% of the resulting purchases. The scheme worked by Escoffier ordering for example 600 eggs from a supplier; the supplier would pay Escoffier a bribe and make up the difference by delivering a short count, for example 450 eggs, with Escoffier's complicity.

The Savoy's losses totalled more than £16,000 of which Escoffier was to repay £8,000 but he was allowed to settle his debt for £500 since that was all the money he possessed. The Ritz paid £4,173 but he denied taking part in any illegal activity, he confessed to being overly gratis with gifts to favoured guests and staff, the hotel paid for his home, food and laundry, and similar infractions.

Escoffier died on 12 February 1935, at the age of 88, less than a week after his wife Delphine. He is buried in the family vault at Villeneuve-Loubet.

Auguste Escoffier, Frankie Knuckles, Knuckles Frankie? Auguste Knuckles. Two of the most important inspiring figures that have helped shape my love for house music all things French mainly the French kitchen and the global culinary pantry. **(Sourced Wikipedia)**

Brussels Sprouts

I hate sprouts, yes sprouts, as a chef during the festive season having a good taste for a good sprout goes along way especially when cooking for thousands of Christmas party guests. I would get my commis chefs to check that they were cooked and seasoned well before plating. A well-cooked sprout can either break or make a Christmas dinner, during my childhood they would break me, every single time Doris served them.

When I initially began to write this book, I remember every 2nd, 3rd, 5th word would either be fuck, cunt, bastard, wanker or twat. Swear words just poured out of me with such venom, cursing through my veins and finally released via my fingertips. I just held my head in my hands thinking to myself why I am even thinking let alone trying to complete such a project, and the fact I'm dyslexic made me very anxious.

I suppose I wasn't mentally, emotionally or physically ready to embark on such a journey. If the truth be told I don't think I had truly processed the anger or the agony within. I don't think I will ever come to terms with my childhood, although I will have to process what has held me back all the years. All I pray for is that I find some sort of peace within myself and in a position whereby I can be a true inspiration to my children.

So, sprouts, what's the big deal with sprouts, my question to myself to this day is, if you have a child that doesn't like a certain food item then why go to all the trouble in persecuting them for hours on end at the dinner table in trying to force them to consume such an item.

I just didn't like sprouts, regardless of who cooked them or how they were cooked, I just had no love whatsoever for the humble baby cabbage. Over the decades of explaining the traumatic episode during my childhood to family and friends the only comparison is the Russian roulette scene in one the most epic movies ever made The Deer Hunter.

Sunday morning would start with our visit to church, Sunday school, I suppose it was the only chance for my parents to get a leg over living in such a small council house on the estate we lived during the 80s. 5 kids two adults cramped into a 3-bed semi-detached house like hundreds of other families living on the bread line.

One thing I did like about Sunday school is that I would always volunteer to go around and collect the collection. Main reason I would skim at least a fiver from the collection to spend on sweets, custard creams and crap during the school week. I'll go into that a bit later, savage I now robbing from the church.

Arrive home from to church then off to the corner shop to buy cider and barley wine for Doris and whatever else she needed to get through her day. I would make 2 or 3 journeys' before and after dinner, cider I say, yes, a 10-year-old off to buy alcohol for the grownups.

If the neighbours knew I was off to the shop they would shout over the garden fence, oi treacle can he pick 10 B&H and 4 cans of special brew for us. Procuring fags and alcohol at the ripe old age of 10, this had been going on for a few years, so do the math. Drink responsibly, fuck that shit back in the 80s, all you shabby parents should have procured responsibly.

So, she's in the kitchen preparing and cooking dinner smashed off her chops with a jaw at 9am. May I say for the record the kitchen on Sundays was out of bounds, if you did manage to get in, you would be meet with a scolding smash with a wooden spoon that had been sat in a pot of gravy for the best part of an hour.

Not only would you have a wooden spoon print across your chops for the remainder of the day you would be scalped with the most horrific verbal abuse. "Get the fuck out the kitchen you scroungy little bastard, go on fuck off, that's it get the fuck out of the kitchen" strange considering I didn't even get a foot in the door.

So, things are cooking up nicely before we go full wankered, full on abuse. Are we having sprouts for dinner? I've spent many years trying to put into perspective what was going on in the household kitchen every Sunday. Lines of coke a massive joint hanging out the kitchen window, were there other people in there having a party, maybe I'll never know, all I knew sprouts were being prepared and cooked with no respect.

I spent a lot of Sundays in someone else's kitchen during the 90s smashed off my chops on ecstasy, weed and speed. Thinking about it I didn't have a clue whose kitchen I was in half the time during the 90s let alone my own, but you'll always find me in the kitchen at parties.

Five minutes before service there is a mad panic around the place, like a dysfunctional kitchen before service, mayhem, carnage, kids pull the table out, get it laid. Mad panic, me and 4 siblings running around the gaff like headless waiters with 2 left feet. I mean mad panic, but who's got the balls to enter the kitchen to fetch the cutlery, black sheep of the family has, more like forced to enter the dreaded fortress.

I always used the think Doris was a decent chef but looking back I would be traumatised every other meal I was served. I remember sitting on a plastic chair food thrown in front of us like we had to be grateful for what we were about to consume. Grateful, grateful was beaten out of me every given chance, more like resentment for what I was forced to eat.

I don't ever remember meat being on my plate, but I always remember a juicy piece of meat being on Boris's plate. We've all witnessed a hungry dog attacking a bowl of dog meat, the dog goes bananas, well imagine 4 starving kids going off over a plate of veg, mash and lumpy gravy. My siblings would put a plate of food away in seconds while Boris lavished over his prime cut of whatever Doris happened to have purchased from the butchers.

Then the sprouts, food of the devil, this is when 2 bottles of cider and half a dozen cans of barley wine would kick in. I'd pushed the sprouts around the plate for the best part of 30 minutes, I sincerely didn't like them, eat those fucking sprouts or else, or else what another shaming for the black sheep, the hand the fist the belt, a saucepan maybe a gardening tool, may be mix it up this Sunday and use the boot, oh, they've already used that.

I've worked my ass off for you stinking kids to put food on the fucking table, like I knew what a hard day's work was like. It was totally irrelevant how hard she had worked for a child to comprehend. Why would she be so fixated in trying to force feed me something I couldn't stomach.

Four siblings have polished off their food, slurp, slurp Bosh, job done, please, I don't like the taste of sprouts, you're an ungrateful little bastard, you will not leave this table until those sprouts are eaten. Another 30 minutes have passed cold sprouts, Boris splayed out on the couch pushing out nasty z's as loud as a jet. Siblings out in the yard playing ball, another 30 minutes have passed, she's on me like a rat on a big mac, in my face, her eyes blazing with hatred, you fucking eat them now.

Sat at the table with a revolver at my temple, scared as a kid on a rollercoaster with a sick twisted Doris in my face sweating like a dyslexic on count down eyeballs glazed over. EAT THOSE FUCKING SPROUTS. Palm of her hand smashes on the table, she must be warming up, I've long pissed myself at the table, I'm frozen, crouching over a plate of cold sprouts unable to speak let alone breath.

I've started to hyper ventilate an asthma attack is clearly on its way, stressed beyond measure, whimpering, I don't like sprouts has no effect. This has probably turned into a mess of a come down for Doris, I'm now full blown in her vortex.

The mad crazed Vietnamese soldier is going off "Doris", a week in the bamboo cage submerged in a rat-infested waterway is looking inviting, I need to get off this table out of this nightmare. Before I know it, she screams, right fuck off to bed one nil to Doris. Playtime is long gone, siblings back in doors. It's in the bath, one boiled kettle between four of us.

I remove myself from the empty table Doris is slurping the last dregs from her cider bottle, mangled on the sofa. I haven't the energy to strip naked and climb into a bath of cold mud. I climb to the top bunk exhausted, shamed, lost, I cry myself to sleep knowing next Sunday will be the same barbaric insanity.

Daddy, yes son, I don't like sprouts, it's ok I haven't put any on your plate, thank you daddy I love you.

Head Fucked Boot Polish Black

During long summers back in the 80s, I couldn't sleep at night due to my asthma, it was difficult at times, we didn't get daily pollen reports like we do today on the news. Doris always insisted I go to bed with my younger siblings, my elder sister would be out and about hanging out with other teenagers her age. Black, white, mixed-race, Asian and ethnic kids, black like me, brown just like me.

Soon as my siblings fell asleep, I would sneak out of bed, crawl along the landing and hide or be as invisible as possible and watch TV from the top of the stairs. Haven't a clue what I'd be watching but I would sit there. Any decent mother would have known I was at the top of the stairs and most likely would have invited me down, if I was on my best behaviour and I didn't make a sound.

I could hear Boris and Doris talking, the thought today makes me sick, the pair of them plotting their assault on my sister when she returned home. The estate was multicultural, and my sister hung out with like-minded teenagers like herself most of her friends being black and mixed race.

Just for the record Boris and Doris white, 2 younger siblings "half siblings" white, older sister white, me black "half breed, mixed race", I hadn't a clue what my heritage was, so I can't go there at this stage. Knock at the door, I'm still watching whatever I was watching from the top of the stairs, it's not even 9am. I hear him say to Doris, "are you ready"; most likely he's given her a wink and a nod for confirmation that she's ok with the barbarian punishment about to be laid down on my sister.

Remember, Boris Doris white, siblings' blah blah blah, me half breed, black sheep you get it. My sister hasn't even stepped foot in the door, she's grabbed by the scruff of her neck and dragged through it two feet off the floor.

Dragged through the door, for the record I just need to mention this bully of a man Boris isn't even her father, the woman sat on her drunken twisted, sick and toxic ass is her "biological mother", Doris, who has given the go ahead for what is about to happen.

I didn't get it then and I will never get it now let alone understand how or why Doris would allow another man not even the fathers child to be beaten up on. What kind of woman would you have to be to allow this to happen, racism, pure unadulterated racism and I'm sat at the top of the stairs witnessing this in my own home.

I remember throughout the years later Doris would cower behind a large whisky or wine and blame him. She would blame Boris, no, she let this happen and to this day I'm convinced she probably got some sort of twisted pleasure witnessing her two children being battered. If not, why didn't she put herself between him me and my elder sister, why didn't she say, NO, don't you fucking dare touch my kids. I know why because when they first got together, they agreed they he would raise me as one of his own, and she feel for it.

My sister dragged into the kitchen, screaming let me go, I'm frozen still invisible at the top of the stairs. I still hear my sister's screams to this day, and I can still remember she did nothing, Doris did nothing she just sat on her ass, on her sofa pretending nothing was going on.

He would grab the black shoe polish from beneath the sink, sister screaming no, leave me alone, don't do it, please, please, Mum help me. Once he'd got a hold of the polish, my sister would be dragged into the living room still screaming, then he would rub black boot polish into her face.

I couldn't do anything I was battle shocked, totally and utterly frozen, should I have gone downstairs and pleaded with her for him to stop, guaranteed he would have laid into me, he had laid into me for less when I was a baby, for less.

You want to hang out with those black losers, he would shout, maybe we should paint you fucking black, so you can be like them. A wooden spoon would be broken over her back, boot polish all over her face, tears, so many tears, cries for help but she just sat there.

I'd run back to my bunk and try and hide under the bed sheets scared so scared that he would continue his rage and come up stairs. I lost count how many times this happened over the years, my sense of identity, it was surreal, but this was going on, it was going on. I started to have issues with my colour, I was having issues with being me, I began to hate myself for being black, because I saw what my sister was being subjected to because of boys like me, the ultimate head fuck.

Having children of my own with the most amazing wife, I just can't and will never understand why a parent would want to beat down on their kids, I know it happens, and its fucking wrong on all levels. Knowing full well they will be left with emotional, mental and physical scars for the remainder of their lives or was it just an 80's thing. No, it wasn't just an 80s thing, this was the result of generational abuse, passed down from mother to daughter and so on and so forth.

To want to hurt something born of their flesh and blood, to want to hurt something so beautiful, small, vulnerable, cheeky, funny and amazing, baffling. I'm not going to judge any of my children's future partners based on the colour of their skin, if they treat them with respect, love and care for them, then me and my wife are cool.

Now I'm not going to say I was an angle in my 30s and 40s, I was dealing with serious issues, so when I was given advice to seek help, I went and got help, you can lead a donkey to water but whether the donkey decides to drink that water it's down to the donkey. I drank the water, not the donkey's water, but you know where I'm coming from.

In later life, Doris would have the audacity to sit there crying most likely at a family get together with the biggest audience, obviously drunk, she would make out she was the victim. I couldn't do anything she would mumble from behind her glass, expecting all of us to feel sorry for her. She didn't do anything; Doris could have prevented the beatings and abuse when she knows full well that lying blatantly through her teeth doesn't cut it anymore because she was also the one dishing it out.

It's a bit late in life when you've been to hell and back and then went back for more to want to be subjected to more lies in having to be on the other end of a phone call, listening to someone wanting to tell you there sorry. Sorry, really, this boy is already baked, you can't go back and take out an ingredient, then re-bake and pretend everything is ok.

I see hundreds of thousands of people protesting for Black Lives Matter in the world we all live in today, racism today shouldn't exist, but it does. As a mixed-race man, I can't help but go back to the top of those stairs on that god forsaken estate we were dragged up on and not think about my sister. I was born into racism and have witnessed it first-hand, within a family that raised me so how can I not be affected.

21ˢᵗ Birthday Cocktail, Amsterdam

Recipe: 2grms PCP otherwise known as angel dust or apple juice, 2grms cocaine, 4 LSD tads Banana splits, 2grms Speed, 1 bottle Jack Daniels, 6 tumblers, 1oz of purple haze for the journey.

Method: Take all ingredients and crush on a mirror with a credit card. When all ingredients are combined, divide between tumblers, fill the glasses with Jack Daniels and consume. Please continue down the rabbit yellow brick road warren for the aftermath of such suicidal shenanigans.

Abandoned and Beaten

I'm a chef by trade, I've been cooking professionally since the age of 17 that's when I started my first proper paid Job within Her Majesties Forces, ACC, army catering Corp. The army catering corps no longer exists. The army bought in contractors, it's a shame although we were called slop jockeys, we cooked some seriously good quality food for the boys.

Considering there was never much about the household when we were kids and that number 2 always had different food than us kids at meals times, food seemed so appealing to me. My LOVE for food came about during my home economics classes at school, I would rock up to class with a bag of whatever I could scourge from around the house or shoplift from the local corner shop. At the end of class I would have made either spring rolls, some sort of Chinese stir fry, a gateau or sponge cake decorated with butter cream fresh fruit and chocolate garnishes.

long story short, my home economics teacher spoke with Doris during the school holidays then boom I was enrolled at catering college. I enrolled in 1985 and studied classical French cuisine, patisserie and food and beverage service for the hospitality industry.

GCSE'S
English: ungraded
History: ungraded
Maths: ungraded
Rural science: ungraded
Craft Design Technology: ungraded
Home economics, Theory: ungraded, practical (pass)

If you subject a child to extreme levels of mental, physical and emotional abuse there's going to be some serious issues with school. This showed in my school grades leaving school, in the words of so many teachers and my dysfunctional family I was going to be a loser a nobody when I finished school.

Makes me think out loud today my uncle Henry as flash as he was back then, the sports cars, the cool designer' labels, he was also one of the ones laughing about me being beaten black and blue. Where is Henry today staking shelves in a supermarket and I thought he was going to make it big time.

I had zero confidence throughout me teens as it had been beaten out of me for years, no self-esteem, I had no will power to do anything. If it wasn't for my home economics teacher Mrs Buxton, bless her soul I would have most likely drifted in and out of trouble, juvenile centres and most likely ended up in a young offender's centre, last stop prison and an early grave.

Mrs Buxton single handily changed the course of my destiny because the one and only thing I liked to do, she recognised it. She visited my home and spoke with Doris about my hidden talent the rest is history. Thinking about it back then she never encouraged me to do anything, nothing, and I mean fuck all. She might have dragged me up town a few times to carry shopping bags and forced me to join the sea cadets but apart from that, there wasn't much going on.

As a chef I've worked in some amazing restaurants with Michelin* chefs, stunning hotels across the globe, cruise ships and have been fortunate to have travelled extensively. I also ran my own restaurant in Spain for 2 years with 2 business partners I had meet working as a private chef in the Alps circa 2000 but there comes a time when we all need a time out.

In 2016, I was working at a beautiful hotel in Marlow as a pastry chef, something different than my usual line of employment as an executive head chef. I think I just needed a change to get out the office doing all the mundane jobs us executive head chefs hate and had to do and get back to some form of cooking.

The pay wasn't bad working through the agency but nothing like I've earned before, how I saw it if the bills and gym membership were covered, food on the table and I had change for petrol I was happy taking orders from someone else for a change. Not having much responsibility all bar to create beautiful desserts, afternoon teas and assist with weddings and functions across the estate, happy days.

I had been at the hotel for several months and our 2nd child was cooking nicely in the wife's belly oven due in August. I can't remember the exact date, but I received a phone call from a prestigious agency for chefs regarding a vacant position within a beautiful 4* deluxe hotel in Birmingham.

My resume was online on various social media platforms, one must keep themselves out there as you never know which general manager is looking for well-seasoned experienced, down to earth opened minded hands-on chef to revitalise their culinary department.

After several phone calls and 3 interviews later, plus several forth coming discussions with the wife about working away from home for a few years I was finally appointed the new executive head chef for the beautiful property, I started employment in the 3rd quarter 2016.

I travelled up the M40 from Berkshire to Birmingham first thing Monday morning, do what chefs do, meetings, strategize, menu development, forecasts and budgeting, rosters, face time with clients and suppliers and the odd bit of cooking. I would then travel back down the M40 Friday afternoon, sometimes I would cruise down the M1 mix the scenery up a little, M40 can be a drag, its flat as Belgium.

The one condition I was hesitant about was having to move back in with Doris, the house I had no love for when living there during my time at college as a catering student and the place I would finally leave when I joined the military.

Moving back into my old bedroom was going to have its challenges the main challenge getting on with Doris again, or maybe a chance for her to explain herself as to why I was battered left right and centre for so many years. How wrong was I, more chance of me swimming with mermaids, or having sex with a man lion?

The first few months flew by, Doris was now married to Alfred and was a carer for her mother the one and only evil SS leader back in the day's "Phillis". Into full blown dementia, wearing a nappy night and day in her designer clothes propped up in her chair sat in the naughty corner day in day out month after month year after year. Phillis would often call me her son, or she would say, look at the handsome young man who is he, what's he doing here, is it Christmas, dribble, dribble, dribble, she thought I was her father at one stage and a past lover, dirty stop out. Phillis is now with the angles, I've sat and thought on many occasions, was she full blown dementia, or did she really know who I actually was?

Doris and Alfred loved a drink, and I mean "drink" they would often be on the pop from the crack of dawn until they crashed in the afternoon. Arriving back home after an early shift It wasn't surprising if they were all tucked up by 5pm with a left-over takeaway in the dog bowl.

What I witnessed during my time back at that house absolutely set it in concrete how angry and sometimes evil Doris was. I often arrived home after work tired and needed to rest and she would be going off, going off the fucking rails, lost the plot, mental going off.

Shouting screaming abuse at Alfred, get away from me you fucking cunt, who the fuck are you, you fucking disgust me, you fucking horrible bastard. She would also lose it with Phillis, and I mean physically, mentally abusive, abusing an old woman regardless it's not on. She would also lose it with me, screaming up the stairs to my room, and your no fucking good either, fucking bastard just for walking in the house and minding my own business.

It's ironic after what Phillis did all those decades back, forcing her grown up matured daughter to give me up and I'm there stood between them both, shouting at mother to calm the fuck down and back off or I'll call the police and social services if the abuse doesn't stop. Phillis in a care home, one flew over the cuckoo's nest type places and Doris banged up in solitary for being a nutter.

Now what I'm about to say hasn't been dressed up like a beautiful line caught salmon poached and garnished ready for a million-dollar banquet, it's the truth. Just for the record I had no intention in writing a book during the time back with Doris, Alfred and Phillis. My only intention was to do well within my employment and embrace my wife and kids when I arrived home Friday afternoon.

Doris would mumble, "They made me do it, they fucking made me do it, fucking bastards", made you do what, what the fuck did they make you do, who made you do what. Tell him, tell him the truth Alfred would say, but she never did. This bullshit went on for months until one evening I sat with her and asked her face to face, drunk of cause because I couldn't have done it sober, what the fuck did they make you do?

Not having really dealt with my childhood and still ticking of the years I'm now 45 and sat face to face with her, what the fuck are you going on about. Made you do what? and out it came, when you were born, I had to take you to my parents' house because I had now where to go after I knifed him in the face with a kitchen knife. "What the fuck", knifed your then husband in the face, fuck me, talk about a psycho.

We just had to go there, you me and your sister but my parents your grandparents persecuted me every day about having a black baby in the house. They couldn't stand having you there, you were a shame on the family, this is just bonkers but considering the current climate in the UK in the early 70s mixed marriages and half-breed kids in some circles were not good for morale. Not good at all, I had been born into a family of Enock Powell supporters, BNP, you name it, it wouldn't surprise me if Phillis had a picture of the man himself hanging in the kitchen back in her hay day.

How can a baby be a shame on the family I mean seriously? this went on for months and months they fucking hated you being in there house, so they gave me an ultimatum. Can you fucking believe this? well this isn't Hollywood people, this isn't different strokes, we both leave, or you leave, leave me, leave me where, where would I leave to. Where would a baby go, nightclubbing, it's not like I could make a few sandwiches' wrap them in a handkerchief and head on out the door like Huckleberry Finn on one of his merry adventures through the red neck south.

My blood is starting to boil, my pulse erratic, beads of sweat pouring from my brow because the bitch who orchestrated this Phillis was sat in the next room. The woman I had defended from her own daughter not even a week ago the fucking SS commander, racist bitch was sat dribbling in the next room thinking I'm her ex-lover.

So, what did you do, **I ABANDONED YOU,** what do you mean you abandoned me? What like wrapped me in a blanket and left me outside a charity shop with a sign around my neck "please take to France" Your grandparents, stop, no, no, stop there, they couldn't be my grandparents their savages.

They just couldn't bear the thought of sharing their household with a baby who was black. We drove to Johnny's barracks, he was at the gates waiting and I just handed you to him and walked away, I'm fucking **GOBSMACKED.** I handed you, my baby to him like a packed fucking lunch, you were screaming, screaming so loud everyone was watching, you were trying to cling to me, it was horrible, you wouldn't let me go. I didn't have anyone all bar you, that day you threw me to wolves, threw your baby to the wolves and boy did they feast on me.

Now for the record I've seen the sunny snaps with them both in nice locations, me sat on laps all smiley happy, so what, I really don't care. I've seen pictures of Adolf Hitler with Eva Braun holidaying in the Austrian alps, but that doesn't change anything does it now, he's still a first-class genocidal maniac.

Now this wasn't your typical abandonment, drop him off with this selfish irresponsible fella, no, from what I've been told he then took me to his current wife's house, who he already had kids with. I believe somewhere in Scotland

and dropped me off like a dirty pair of football boots. I'm not her son, I'm the bastard he's just had with another woman behind her back, why on earth would she want a bastard about the house.

Abandoned for years, imagine that, imagine being told that as a grown man with children of my own. To this day I still haven't come to terms with it. The trauma alone as a baby is too much to endure. I've watched my son for hours playing with his toys being cheeky and getting up to mischief the lovable bundle of joy he is to us both and his big sister. It just doesn't compute that I could abandoned him let alone our daughter, wrap them up like a fish supper with a side order of mushy peas with pickled onions and leave them outside a stranger's house it just doesn't register anywhere.

Shortly after I resigned from my post in Birmingham which didn't end well due to my mental state. I couldn't bear to be within spitting distance of Doris let alone that toxic demented cunt of a woman who wanted me banished "Phillis".

Fast forward to 2020 a new decade, 2019, 2018 and 2017 were dreadful, adios, thank God that's over. Little did we know we would be slapped sideways with covid-19; I mean did God see that coming, maybe, did the chefs cooking up bat soup, pangolin stir fry with a side of crispy cats' ears and sweet and sour monkey chops, they should have, wrong on all levels.

After the most horrific lightning speed psychotic melt down driving home from work January 2020 and minutes away from ending my life on the M25 during rush hour it was time for me to get some serious help. I needed serious help, Gandalf the grey and white I need Obi-wan Kenobi I would have settled for nurse Ratchet.

Over the course of treatment, I spoke with my elder sister and her asked if we could talk about what she witnessed and if she knew about the abuse inflicted on me as a child, so we spoke, it crippled me, and it crippled her, it's has always crippled her.

We spoke openly for about 30 minutes about general covid-19 bollocks then I just dived in, are you sure you want to hear this, yes. Now I do not know the specifics, but I had been abandoned for some time, during this time Doris had moved up north from down south somewhere after divorcing Bob, the guy who thought I was his child when I popped out mother and linked up with Boris.

White dude, white women "Doris" maternity ward, out pops the wrong colour baby with an afro. They divorce because he can't bear the fact his wife has done the dirty and slept with a black chap, fare play, could you blame him.

I'm abandoned we've done that part, but now I'm about to be bought back to Doris because I'm being seriously abused. I'm finally reconnected with her and my sister and the man who is going to make the next 10 years of my life agonisingly painful Boris.

I'm rushed into the car, Doris is frantic, shouting get us out of her to her new man, sister on the back seat going bananas screaming. Boris is also having a meltdown thinking what the fuck am I getting into, I've just hooked up with this broad and I've inherited two fucking sprogs one of them being black.

Mother rips my clothes off in a panic, I can't possibly imagine what my sister is going through, but my sister said I was covered in bruises and bite marks, battered, not in good shape, not in good shape at all, looking back at photos I would say I was no older than 4. There are only two reasons I've surmised why I was in such a state, One, I was mauled by dog or two I was mauled by a human, who, why, what, were, when has never to this day been explained to me. Why would it, fuckers.

George Michael 97

The journey begins, "Good afternoon, everyone, and a huge welcome to Sardinia, I hope you all had a pleasant flight". "So wonderful people as you can see, we have blue skies in Sardinia today with a temperature of 35c". "Transfer time to the hotel today approximately 35 minutes". "I would also like to mention we have our new pizza chef traveling with us today. Welcome Auguste Knuckles". Golf claps from a coach load of ghostly white holiday makers gagging for some Sardinian sun, holiday shenanigans and sex.

Summer of 97 I was in a bullshit dead end relationship 60% my doing 40% their doing. I just wasn't feeling it, it wasn't like I was going to marry Georgie anyways. A large group of friends had just gone traveling around Asia then on to Australia to work for a year. I'm jealous stuck in England scratching my balls consuming to many drugs, bouncing from job to job, time to change this picture.

I was just one in a million young adults living the endless weekender during that decade. After Bristol I had nothing to show for myself all bar a lust for drugs and wasted talent. Caterer was the go-to website for chefs' jobs in the 90s. I organised my resume then started the process which hopefully would start the traveling bug. I applied for several jobs one being a vacant pizza chef role with a European leading holiday company out in Sardinia.

Suited, booted and totally hungover I head into London to lie through my teeth that I'm an experienced pizza chef with more experience than pappa Johns. I mean really, how hard is it to make a pizza with no pizza experience. "If you can piss you can paint" if you can make bread, roll it out like pastry, make a tomato sauce the rest is just toppings, cheese and oregano.

I'm on the coach, I'm in Sardinia, so I guess bullshit baffles brains thing worked. Destination Capo Testa located just a few kilometres west of Santa Teresa di Gallura. Capo Testa is the farthest point of North-eastern Sardinia in the province of Olbia. Its fucking paradise. Pizzas is what's putting money in the bank, but sun, sea and shenanigans is the agenda for the summer of 97.

Soon as I step foot from the coach, the head chef is in my face ready to get me in the pizza restaurant. No small talk, I'm chaperoned to my room, then whisked down to the kitchen at lighting speed soon as I've changed. The kitchen is a fucking bombsite, there's no other way to put it, a fucking shit tip. Dozens of chefs crammed into a small 5* beach resort hotel kitchen, its bedlam. Fish, seafood everywhere, on every section, chefs covered in fish mess, the kitchen floor had disappeared with off cuts, trimmings, innards, fish and shellfish shells.

No air-con, a fucked extraction hood, you can clearly see the chefs are all in a dehydrated zombie type frenzy to get the seafood buffet out on time for the arriving guests. "Oi you, are you the new pizza chef"? Yes, that's me, "you're with me over here". I follow Oi chef to a corner of the kitchen where she has cleared a space on the floor to make pizza dough.

The heat in the kitchen was unbearable, I had just started my shift, my Nike trainers fucked, bones, guts, fish on the soles of my chef's trainers. I'm sweating buckets; it is so uncomfortable in here. "Hi, my name is Trish I'm the outgoing pizza chef, I'll show you the setup, we'll make a few pizzas, then I'm fucking off". Fucking off were? "Fucking off out of this shit hole". "Just for the record what you see around you at this moment in time, it doesn't get any better, welcome to the arsehole end of the world".

Pizza dough, pizza sauce made on the floor as there was no visible prep space anywhere. We grab what we need from the walk-in fridge which was as hot as a sauna and make our way through the hotel reception to the air-conditioned pizza restaurant to begin our prep. "Before we start one word of warning, spend as little time as possible in that shithole of a kitchen and stay away from management". Now that is interesting, stay away from management.

Like I really had love for anyone in a suit or a manager wearing flip flops, shorts and Ray Bans. I'm no one special, I'm not one in a million. I'm like a lot of chefs who got used, abused and thrown to the gutter back in the 90s. It was brutal, it was savage back then. "Oh, if you dabble in cocaine, acid or weed the head bar man will sort you out, he's a local".

"Seven pizzas, seven toppings, there's the A4 colour printed SOP's, this is a pizza, these are the pizza oven settings, on, off, temperature, any questions"? No, "well it was nice meeting you, have a nice life". That my friends, was my 30-minute induction. I must say the view from the pizza restaurant was exceptional, blessed beyond measure to have such a view from my office. The restaurant overlooked the bay of Capo Testa with the valley of the moon as a magnificent back drop in the distance.

Seven pizzas, seven toppings, its seafood night in the main restaurant. I doubt anyone has flown out to Sardinia today to eat a pizza. Bonus Trish has forgotten her George Michael CD in the CD player, which is now my George Michael CD which would become my summer CD.

Pizza Margarita, no topping, maybe some basil.
Pizza Marinara, what seafood you could rob from the kitchen
Pizza Pugliese, forgot the topping with this one, can't be bothered to google.
Pizza Capricciosa, not sure, could be peppers
Pizza Prosciutto Crudo e Rucola, rocket
Pizza Melanzane, aubergine
Pizza Alla Salsiccia, sounds like a sausage, it's been a few years.

No sides, no fizzy drinks, no garlic bread, seven pizzas served with several gallons of Sardinian vino. 7pm service starts, 14 pizzas smashed out, section cleaned, toppings stored away, back to the bicycle shed to catch up with the head chef. The kitchen resembled a bull fighting arena with two dozen blood sodden matadors wearing chefs' whites.

Jugs of vino on every work bench which have now been cleared of fish detritus. The floor is made of red quarry tiles by the way. The temperature has dropped to a comfortable 20c, but the pot wash is a land fill site. Sodden white t-shirts, heavy duty aprons, rubber gauntlets, flip flops and shorts, the kitchen porter uniform.

"Sorry Auguste it's been a mad day, I'm Dom the head chef by the way". Looking over and past Dom's shoulder towards the back of the kitchen it appears a group of chefs are doing lines of cocaine behind a half-eaten swordfish which must have weighed 20kg. Dom why do all the kitchen porters have green on their left shoulder? "Fucking lunatics, its chafing gel, they rub a blob on their shoulder and inhale it during their shift, a cheap high, they earn pennies". Are you ok with that? "Yeah, so how many pizzas did you serve tonight"? A dozen.

"Ok, go shower change, meet me in the bar I will introduce you to the team". Team from the greatest showman, happy days. I might be a Sardinia virgin, but I'm no virgin to hard drugs and the party. I bump into the hotel manager, head nanny and the most important man in resort, the bar manager. A cheeky drug dealers' handshake I have in my possession a fat wrap of Sardinian quiver before I've arrived back to my room.

For the record here, the last place I "assumed" there would be nose candy, would be in a beautiful 5* beach resort for millionaires. I suppose I am the virgin after all. The night is quick, I'm sat with a dozen chefs, kitchen porters and waitresses who are grinding their jaws knocking back green beer. Recipe, half pint of beer, orange juice, blue curacao, double shot of vodka. Two pints of green beer and you will believe an uber fell on you.

Dom appears to be the only one who is not off his chops, fucked if I'm going to be easy pickings during my first night in Sardinia. My chop has been hidden in my suitcase. Dom what's the huge rock formation beyond the bay. "That my friend is the valley of the moon, Valley della Luna". "It's about an hour's walk, there is a full moon party next week, it's going to be awesome".

First night impressions, it's obvious that the staff are just as much on holiday here as the guests who are paying a small fortune for a week's all-inclusive holiday. A few drinks and idle banter I'm off to bed, "long day today". The following morning I'm up super early not on my own accord. Delivery lorries outside my window dropping off the day's orders.

Shit, shower, shave, I'm in the staff canteen eating an olive salami baguette. All bar the hotel manager who introduced himself to me everyone is hanging "red eye" smashed, hiding behind designer sunglasses. I swerve the kitchen, start my prep for service nice and early in the pizzeria hidden away so I can spend a morning and early afternoon on the beach. Prep is easy, sliced vegetables, pizza sauce, grated mozzarella, charcuterie. I've two dozen pizza bases from yesterday in my counter fridge, bonus.

I'm going to skip the sandcastles, snorkelling, sunbathing and sailing. 4pm it's back on shift, the main kitchen is in the same state as it was yesterday. Three whole lambs, stuffed with garlic, lemons, wild mint, shallots and rosemary. Trussed, rubbed with olive oil, balsamic, sugar, rock salt and crushed pepper ready for the spit looked heavenly.

From the outside looking in for guests the entire hotel had the calmness of a beautiful swan on a winter's lake. Gently gliding across the frosty waters, while underneath her legs are kicking like crazy. That was that kitchen in Sardinia, behind the scenes it was a plane crash. Delicious, delightful Sardinia cuisine prepared and cooked by a team of dust heads from Australia and the UK. At the end of the day because Sardinian produce was and is world class the chefs didn't have to do much. In super fresh, simple prep and served in a manner fit for a Sardinian king.

Don't get me wrong these Ozzy dust heads Could cook. I have travelled to Australia a few times, the dining scene in Sydney and Melbourne is up there, may be leading the way on the global diner's circuit. I ate out a lot in Sydney, my favourite restaurant being Longrain, in surrey hills owned by Martin Boetz. Exceptional modern Thai cuisine using the freshest of locally sourced produce. Also, Establishment in the heart of Sydney, sublime, sushi E out of this world, world class produce.

These chefs were travelling chefs mad for the party. I spoke with a few chefs over green beer who had travelled through southeast Asia, India and on to Europe, cooking all the way to cover their expenses. I have also travelled to Thailand a few times, I can see the attraction for chefs, although my visits to Thailand were to travel around at leisure and eat five-star Thai food for pennies.

Cocaine in Australia you pay top dollar, £100 per gram. It's not a drug easily smuggled across its boarders. In the UK and Europe cocaine starts at £40 depending on its strength. When in Rome party like a Roman. Travelling dust heads who have come from fine, all day Ozzy dining Michelin starred establishments, I 100% totally get the party mentality. I am no different to thousands of chefs out there doing their thing. Affordable cocaine unlike Oz unless your minted, what's there not to like about Europe and the UK.

A sous chef who I had the pleasure of working with in London many moons ago asked me. "Chef where do I go in the UK to learn how to make good Thai food". I replied there isn't any where to go in the UK, go to Thailand. A Year later he resigned and fucked off to Thailand with his girlfriend before heading out to Australia for a year.

I prepared, cooked and served seven pizzas with several toppings up until the full moon party in a somewhat sober state enjoying the sounds of my free George Michael CD. During that week, the main kitchen remained a war zone. The trick for me was to avoid it at all costs. I became friends with two kitchen porters a girlfriend boyfriend couple from Newcastle. They opted out from inhaling cheap chafing dish gel which was practically 100% alcohol. This couple preferred acid from the head bar man.

There are a few places on earth that have knocked me sideways with its stunning beauty. Valley of the moon capo Testa Sardinia is one of those places. As Dom mentioned the walk from the hotel takes approximately one hour. A tricky pathway must be navigated through caper bushes, olive trees, wild herbs and century old quarry boulders once you have left the main road. Once navigated the valley appears, cliff faces on either side with an opening the size of a football field. A dozen natural caves on either side. Throughout the summer months these caves would be occupied with travellers from all corners of the globe.

These travellers are not the type of travellers who would pay £2500 per night to stay in a 5-star London hotel. The hardcore of hardcore free spirited of travellers descending on the valley for a bongo bashing, acid dropping, barn dancing, soul searching love making party. Seven pizzas with seven toppings prepared and served for incoming guests. I had downed two litres of Sardinian vino while on shift. Showered, changed and out the door of my shared accommodation with a fat wrap, dons ma poche.

Navigation accomplished, no torches, we are guided by the light of the moon, destination, valley of the beautiful werewolf. A tab of acid was consumed with Charlie and Holly before we set off from the hotel staff accommodation with a dozen other staff members. I have done a full moon party twice, both times in Thailand 2007 and 08. Considering, the full moon parties in Thailand have become totally commercialised. Global DJs, booze buckets spiked with the date rape drug and the odd few casuals floating face down in the sea, brown bread dead. Beaches jam packed with westerners smashed off their melons on Yabba and mushroom shakes.

In the valley of the moon in Sardinia, no bars, no circus, no DJ's head lining spinning the deepest of soulful house tracks. All we had was the light of the moon and stars, a dozen bongo bashers and one didgeridoo. We laughed; we danced half naked tripping immaculate wading in warm Sardinian waters. We laughed so hard several hippie travellers wanted to charge us laughing taxes who were also intoxicated by our joyful childish mood.

The following morning, we strolled back to the hotel for a few hours' sleep before starting our shifts. Those few months of 97 went sideways. I downed so much Sardinia wine one evening I was rushed to hospital to be put on a drip due to alcohol poisoning. We snorted so much bar man cocaine and dropped so much acid my thinking became that of Scooby Doo. Like I didn't know this would happen, I became disinterested with pizza making and the working conditions of the kitchen which didn't improve. Half the guests one month went down with dysentery due to the hotel swimming pool being contaminated with raw hotel sewage. Stoned locals given the task of removing sewage from the hotel and cleaning the hotel guest pool something didn't smell right.

Staff members came and went, I believe for a few weeks paid holiday. I had shagged myself stupid on the beach in the early hours of the morning before ze Germans invaded. Doing the four-legged octopus rummage exchanging bodily fluids with several guests and staff. I had in fact had a great holiday.

So, after one drunken night in Santa Teresa waking up in a random doorway. In my drunken state I decide to rob some locals moped to make my way over the valley Back to the hotel. Leaving a stolen moped which I crashed into the hotel entrance in the early hours of the morning did not sit well with the hotel manager. The fact I had no recollection whatsoever was also of concern.

Being told I had to return the moped back to its rightful owner wasn't a gamble I was willing to take. Not if he was a budding mafia teenager wanting to gain respect. What better way to earn that by putting a bullet into an Englishman's kneecap? I rode the moped a mile away from the hotel and rode the fucker of a cliff. Luckily for me it didn't explode like in the movie fast and the furious moped part five staring Auguste Knuckles.

After my three-month orgy, I decided my seven pizzas with seven toppings summer season would come to an end. The following week, I gave the incoming pizza chef a 30-minute pizza induction. I ejected my George Michael CD from the sound system, packed my now bag and spent a week walking around Sardinia before returning to the UK with one hell of a suntan.

Another ambulance is on its way, I've lost count this year. Fucked on cocaine unable to breath like a human being. 24 hours in hospital on crazy meds to bring me down from another overdose.

Cheesy Puffs

Amsterdam to Germany, Germany to Amsterdam, 1991 before the big raid on military barracks across Germany after the gulf war, smuggling copious amounts of drugs into Germany as a squaddie was easy as putting a pair of drill boots on.

I lost count of the trips I made to Amsterdam during my 3-year posting but it was a lot, the crazy thing is I didn't even have a driving licence. Imagine that driving around Europe with no license, mental, proper mental, talk about my head being somewhere else, but my military pass sufficed Everyone else was doing it, it felt normal.

One evening me and a few chums had made a b-line for the Dam last minute dot come, the club named IT was the place to be, everything and anything was the norm. I had been to a dozen gay clubs In Germany during the early 90s. Hardcore Frankie goes to Hollywood with a dash of Priscilla queen of the desert. All the gay clubs had the best DJs, the music and yes, the best drugs.

Itinerary, arrive in Amsterdam get smashed, procure drugs get more smashed, go clubbing get more smashed. Sleep in the car smoking weed until we passed the fuck out. Wake up, public toilet, freshen up, breakfast, smoke weed, procure weed, solid and chemicals, coke, e's, PCP, speed and acid and whatever else the goody goody man is selling, pair of fake Ray Bons maybe a beach towel, don't mind if I do.

Smoke weed, begin the journey back to Germany, I've realised I'm carrying a load of olives and pickles "drugs" a lot more than I normally did. Panic doesn't set in as I'm peeled as a banana, up in smoke dusted. Pit stop a few clicks from the boarder, toilet break, super large coffee, mouth wash, munchies.

I've purchased a family size pack of cheesy puff, a huge fucking bag, almost at the boarder we start to get restless a tad, pockets full of delicious treats. The nutter on the back seat has a panic attack, "what if we get pulled over and we get searched, I'm smashed man I'm really fucking smashed". That will never happen bruv we are squaddies, fuck that bruv there's no way I'm doing 6 months in a military prison getting spit roast by to hairy wife, it just isn't going to happen. What isn't going to happen, the get nicked part of you having your back doors smashed in by a hairy locomotive engineer.

Ok fuck it lets take no chances, I empty the all the cheesy puffs into my foot well, right boys pass me all your stash, hide what you can down your pants. I fill the empty bag with our side orders then top it off with cheesy puffs and sling the rest out the window, bosh we are at the border.

Casual as a dog pissing on a garden fence we pull the car up to immigration and show our military passes. Now from a short distance what I've got in my hands is a bag of what appears to be cheesy puffs, and that's what I have, cheesy puffs. "Gutten morgan fellas where are you traveling from", football game in Hengelo, "good game", not too shabby.

I offer the immigration officer checking our passes my snacks, would you care for a cheese puff in my west country accent, "no thankyou I've just had breakfast", Passes handed back to us, a nod of the head and we are free to go about our business. As we leave Amsterdam behind as a celebration for our juvenile ways, we all pop two tabs of acid.

Years later after leaving the military we all meet at a rugby match in Twickenham, there was more cocaine being consumed that day than I've ever experienced, it was callosal. Walking around Tesco's buying booze for the game doing lines of the top of display freezers, it was nuts. We spoke about the time we all dropped the two acid tabs, looking back we were never the same fellas after that trip to the Dam as squaddies, acid that strong, bonkers, proper bonkers, fucked for ever days.

My Endless Summer

As far as irresponsible parents can push the boundaries of being irresponsible, sending your two children alone to parts of the UK on coaches to spend time with one's auntie and uncle and in my sister's case she would spend time with her dad Bob, yeah that fella is classed as being premier league of irresponsibleness, if that's even a word.

Before I continue, marching your children to the coach station at the ages of 8 and 6ish and then throwing them on a bus with a sandwich and a pound to Victoria station is mad. When we arrived at Victoria pockets full of random shit we robbed from the service station, my sister would put me on my coach then she would head off to Cornwall.

It doesn't happen today, it just doesn't happen, without a care in the world off we go so Boris and Doris could spend time together alone and with their new-born son without two bastards about the house. I've thought about this endlessly over the years did they care for us, well you're this far into the book so I guess the answer to that question, is no they didn't.

These shenanigans went on for years, every 6 weeks holiday from school and any other possible half term I'd be off. Bags packed dumped on a coach and sent to the switch. With regards to sister, she was sent away to spend time with her biological father, me I was sent away for one specific reason and the reason being I was black. I was the half-breed, black sheep the runt of the family sent away out of disgust.

I'm no psychologist and I don't have any experience whatsoever in psychology only what I've experienced in being treated by psychologists and various doctors in their profession that this being sent away whenever possible was having a serious impact on me and everything else I was being subjected to, I'm in fact the manifestation of their neglect, years of neglect.

A ticking time bomb had started during my first unmanned mission to the switch at that tender age of 6. I began to lose all sense of who or what I was, where I was going, why I was always being sent away. Basically, Doris wanted me out of her pathetic existence, but where did I belong. There was no father figure, there was no role model to look up to, no one I could call dad, pops, father, there was only and always will be my auntie, Stella.

Doris never mentioned anything about my biological father Johnny until I was 11 maybe 12, what I can remember from that failed attempt by her trying to explain I wasn't Boris's child went down like a failed souffle.

I really didn't give a fuck I really didn't care what she was trying to say I was beyond care; I was a child who had been systematically broken-down month after month year after year by her and everyone who had a heavy hand. I was a victim at the time of child abuse, relentless, none stop abuse on all levels and by all forms, Doris could have said my father was Father Christmas It wouldn't have made any difference I was beyond care.

Before I continue, I would just like to apologise to anyone reading this, If I could be more eloquent in explaining myself throughout this book this project I would, but I'm no Hunter S Thompson or Bret Easton Ellis. I'm just me, trying to tell my story to the best of my ability. So please excuse me if this comes across as if it's been written by a dyslexic 12-year-old who's just turned 48.

Yes, where was I, seemed to have gone off-piste there for a minute. That's it, I'm starting to contemplate who I was, where was I from, Africa, Mongolia, the Caribbean. I didn't know my heritage, I didn't have a clue and Doris didn't want to tell me, I started contemplating the fact I could have been adopted, I would have taken that on the chin any day.

I had spent time with my biological father Johnny as a baby, but I have no recollection of the time. Even she didn't know where he was from no one did, she didn't even know his proper name. I was in no man's land, "no child's land" drifting up and down the country during holidays and half term, or were all the coach drivers my dad, dads, I was a kid in a serious pickle.

When I turned 24, I meet him for the first time Johnny, "no rush there then" the first question I asked him was, where the fuck he had been and where the fuck he was from. I'm from Jamaica son, happy days a rubber stamp on my forehead "I'm from Jamaica", finally after spending 2 decades thinking I was from Barbados I have some form of I'D. When I was born and up until I changed my name Doris registered me with Bobs surname and couldn't even be bothered to tell me.

Where I belonged was a simple fact in my undeveloped way of thinking. My auntie Stella she was white, her vivacious charismatic out going handsome husband was black and both their children "my cousins", my beautiful cousins where the same colour as me, mixed race, dual heritage, half cast, toffee caramel brown and I fitted beautifully into the mix, so why wouldn't I call this home.

I had some sort of belonging, I truly felt part of the family, I was part of the family and that middle England never really existed only in my worst nightmares, but I'm fully aware it was not a nightmare it was reality. From as young as I can remember we did family things together with auntie Stella, my first life experiences and I'm mean good healthy experiences were in the switch. Everything was meaningful, I felt part of something I felt free to be me without repercussions, or a slap for laughing out loud.

I can remember like it was yesterday, spending long hot summers with my auntie Stella, she would buy me and my cousins easy riders. Access to all public transport across town, we would travel all over, visiting sports centres, parks, museums, outdoor swimming pools. Out all-day meeting friends doing all the great stuff kids love to do, I had friends not like the wankers I hung out with on that dreadful estate, well maybe one or two were ok, the rest were wankers.

During the evenings we would hang out with other kids on the street playing games listening to music, lose ends was my favourite band during the 80s and just generally have a good time. Returning home to middle England a few days before school opened after the summer holidays was awful, I fucking hated it. Back to being soul destroyed, the black kid within a family that beyond doubt was proper fucked.

So here we go and here it begins, in the most sarcastic of half-drunk voices Doris would say what have you been up too all summer, fuck all I bet. Like she really cared, I mean really cared, what I had been up to. It was her chance, her opportunity to ridicule me, embarrass me in front of everyone and I mean everyone, she loved it, even my snivelling little half siblings would join in.

Even if Phillis was or wasn't there or the neighbour's happened to have popped in for a drink, it was her sick and twisted sense of power over me, toxic then and still toxic now. She even embarrassed me at my wedding, my wedding was her opportunity to spend time with her eldest daughter as opposed to spend time with me, my new wife and her grandkids. If its ok Auguste I would like to sit and spend time with your sister as I don't see her often.

69

I remember having jerk style chicken wings for lunch during one summer with my auntie Stella, I had never tasted anything like this before. Well, which mixed race kid would have tasted or heard of jerk spice growing up with the mashed potato and lumpy gravy sprout family.

This was something new something different, So I told Doris, 5, 4, 3, 2, 1, lift off, fucking chicken wings LMFAO, it was like I had told the world's best joke, LOL chicken fucking wings, have you fucking heard this you lot. She was hysterical every 2nd word was fucking, ended with chicken wings, or chicken wings fucking.

Imagine Oliver twist receiving a full-on roast chicken dinner, could you imagine the look on his face, could imagine the smile he would have, it would be a smile too big for his face, well that was those chicken wings for me, and she fucking killed it. Food of my real heritage, she fucking destroyed me as if to say, "what the fuck is it with all that nigger loving shit those fuckers eat". Soul destroyed with nothing to say back as I knew what the repercussions would be.

Shadow

Neighbours separated by a wooden fence
Their garden still rubble and cement
A house not built
A fortress for abuse will soon be finished

Kerby out front fights around the back
Kids jumping friends on makeshift ramps
Conkers and marbles games of summer
Parents arguing was our endless winter

Our noise was the sound of children
Screaming running falling on the playground
British bulldog one two three
We were safe we protected each other

Rumbling bellies school dinners were a delight
Arts and crafts blue tac and glue
Rockets and boats we built from shoe boxes
A puppet on a string colourful and bright

The school bell rings time for neglect
How I long for that protection amongst you all
Sad faces as we walk to the gate
Who will be there to collect me not my best mate

You are my superhero a child I shall never forget
You are the bravest boy bravest of them all
Walking home alone with the sun on your face
Smiling skipping whistling chasing my shadow
The shadow of me looking back at you

AK

Terrorists Everywhere

Being a chef with a mild addiction for great British and French cheeses I get a great buzz from educating diners to some new cheese they might not have eaten. Before I continue, we are not talking about a handful of mouldy grapes. Out of date crackers served on a freezing cold plate with an onion and balsamic chutney cooked by a fucking twat. I'm just as passionate about putting a cheese plate on the menu which costs as much as rib-eye steak. Two of my all-time favourite cheeses, Oxford ISIS and Lancashire bomb. I never knew cheese could cause such a pickle. A brief run down on both cheeses.

Oxford Isis is a sticky, strong washed-rind cheese made in Oxfordshire. Named after the alternative name for the river Thames where it flows from the Cotswolds to Oxfordshire. Oxford Isis is washed regularly in honey mead, which gives it a sticky rind and pungent aroma.

The Lancashire Bomb, sometime referred to as the Black Lancashire Bomb is rather self-explanatory it's wrapped in muslin and dipped in black wax, shaped like a bomb, and yep, you've got it, made in Lancashire.

The Lancashire Black Bomb Cheese is the creation of the Shorrock family run dairy, which has operated out of Goosnargh, near Preston in Lancashire since 1923. All Lancashire Bomb Cheese are handmade and matured for a minimum of two years. A strong mature flavour with a crumbly texture, it goes great with most fruit chutneys.

During my decades of cooking, I've come across all kinds of guests who just love to complain. Serial complainers who have every intention to complain wherever they go regardless. Serial complainers have got their shit locked so tight they should be awarded Oscars. Serial complainers know how to work the system. They use the right words, long important words that terrifies the shirt out of inexperienced vulnerable service staff.

Gizmos, paraphernalia, props and costumes geared up for complaint action. "Excuse me, there appears to be a taxi in my soup", money back guaranteed. I have dealt with every complaint and have witnessed diners that have been given a weekends all-inclusive stay. They've also been upgraded with gym access because they were served the wrong dish "claim they were served the wrong dish" or waited to long for a main course.

The easiest money back shit scaring complaint, "I and my partner dined in your restaurant yesterday evening, unfortunately my partner experienced chronic diarrhoea and vomiting throughout the night". They've most likely forgot to mention the 12 pints of beer, several bottles of wine they also consumed plus 2 grams of cocaine. Money back guaranteed plus upgrade.

When a complaint goes straight to the top regarding food a chef's insides can fall out their arse. It must be serious; heads must roll someone must be made an example. "Chef we need to change the cheese board or rename the cheeses, a guest dined in a few weeks ago and was highly offended with the cheese course". Highly offended is an understatement, this guest went fucking berserk. The fact that they were American ripples of this complaint were felt across the pond, literally. Straight to head office, direct to the CEO of the company.

They assumed I was an egotistical stuck up individual with no moral fibre. They stated in their correspondence that putting Oxford **ISIS** and Lancashire **bomb** on a cheese menu I should be fired with immediate effect. The cheese menu be removed, and the hotels integrity bought into question. The certain guest also stated that they will no longer use the hotel and opt for another brand.

I don't know if this certain individual was FBI, CIA, ex-military, someone who may have got blown up or knew someone that got blown up by an IED, or all the above. All I do know is that ISIS and bomb on a cheese menu didn't sit well with them; they assumed it was a sick joke. The cheese menu changed; the whole commotion was a management joke months later.

I never could find a cheese with Taliban let alone terrorist within its name. It would have been a great sounding cheese offering. Mature Taliban goats cheese accompanied with tangy terrorist apricot chutney, sourdough Daesh crackers served on a plate made by an Afghanistan opium smuggler who uses the drug money to fund their love for making world class cheese. That would certainly be a different pre-service chat. I mean really, at the end of the day, it's only fucking cheese you silly cunt, I have no intention in starting a cheese war.

Shit Is Fucking Real

Being told by your therapist that her findings after a few sessions that I was most definitely sexually abused as a child most likely an infant isn't something I will ever live with. I have obsessive thoughts being armed to the teeth with guns going full Rambo, as a child soldier. I would massacre every fucking living individual who has preyed on innocent children.

"The causes of hypersexual behaviour are not well understood. Some children or adolescents may engage in increased or developmentally inappropriate sexual behaviour as a result of traumatic experiences. Adults who have buried their history of child abuse can continue to suffer in ways that can include post-traumatic stress disorder (PTSD), eating disorders, substance misuse, depression, anxiety, low self-esteem, anger, guilt, learning disabilities, physical illness, disturbing memories and dissociation".

While this can often be the case, a review of the research on childhood sexual abuse (from the American Academy of Experts in Traumatic Stress, or AAETS) confirms that many survivors engage in promiscuous behaviours, even those who turn away close relationships.

My behaviour as a child wasn't normal. Sexually active, what the fuck. A child can't be sexually active. Reliving the early days at infant school has made me question the carnage inflicted on me. I haven't written about the sexual journey that was to become as addictive as drugs and alcohol. All the issues I have dealt with that have caused me to attempt in taking my own life are the conscious actions of vermin.

It would be the perpetrators who set my sails. Individuals who cannot be called human. Monsters, molesters, paedophiles. The distressing flashbacks I relive today during decades of promiscuous behaviour there was no emotion attached with any relationship or sexual encounter. It was just an act being played out. Role play, loveless and cold. Love was a lifeless, soulless physical act, acted out by an individual who was reliving sexual abusive trauma. Sitting here amongst the grass in my yard the whole fucking programme was utterly overwhelmingly fucking twisted. I will explain a little more later within this psychedelic narrative.

"Hey, you, yeah you, how's it going, you, ok, are you ok?"

Main Course 1986

It's not the easiest things adapting to the outside world when you've had the wind constantly knocked out your sails for the past decade. Wipe that smile from your face or I'll wipe it off for you, why are you so fucking happy, if you don't stop crying, I'll give you something to cry for.

Every waking hour was the opportunity to put me down, happy mood slapped out of you, crying because you had the happy mood slapped out of you another slap for crying. It never stopped; confidence knocked out of you. It got to the point in my teens where I was physically shit scared to ask either of them for anything. I had to ask my friends if they would ask Boris if I could go swimming while Doris was out.

So, in a nutshell was I ready for the outside world? no I wasn't, I had been enrolled at college at a young age, it was just how my birthday fell in the year, 15. During the 1st year of college all students had to complete a two-week work experience placement part of our studies to experience life in a working kitchen.

My two weeks work experience was at the prestigious 4* Opera hotel, every celebrity who stared in any pantomime in town would stay there during the 80s and probably still to this day. I was mad nervous, proper nervous, I was doing well at my studies practical and theory, when you made a good stock or sauce or trussed a bird for the pot you receive good praise from your tutor. The more praise I got the harder I worked, the harder I worked the better my craft with that my confidence started to grow.

My first shift was Monday morning 8am, I had all weekend to get prepared, pressed my whites sharpened my knives. I can't remember specifically the dates like a lot of things today, but this work experience was going to be a fucking game changer during winter 1986.

Yeah, I know I may swear from time to time, some may say I swear because of a poor education, no, the education wasn't poor I just didn't get it. The bullshit home life, how the fuck could I concentrate at school not knowing what was install when I got home or the mood of the household, it was play your cards right every other day.

Monday morning I'm up early brush my teeth grab my clobber out the door, no good luck son or anything like that. They knew it was only a matter of time before I was going to leave home and out of there miserable lives.

What the hell was a good luck son going to do for me any way, this work experience is either going to make me or break me, break me my future would have been so much more different. Wanting to prove my family and every scumbag who wanted to see me fail was my doing and maybe my downfall

This is where my mind begins to wonder as I reminisce at the life I've managed to forge for myself, I can only but smile. The guys I would look up to who, had the cool gear, the bikes, the family stand. Even the local shoplifters up town were cool, the guys that would fight on bond street outside pubs and clubs on a Friday or Saturday I thought they were so cool.

In fact, every reprobate around town during the 8os I thought was cool probably because they were in there moment at that given time and I was that lost soul who hadn't a clue where the fuck he was going. I just followed them, half the time getting up to no good, I started shop lifting, robbing bikes, people's luggage off trains, If I thought I could rob it, I'd have it and I didn't even consider the consequences.

I robbed a bag of a rain once with 2 two other losers from a train station In Middle England, we ended up being chased by the Britch transport police. So where do we run, only through a tunnel, a mile long out of the station we shut down the entire train service in the West Midlands for 2 hours, what a dick head. If we would have fallen on the tracks, brown bread dead, hit by a rain the fucking obvious.

It's a million miles away and a million reasons how I made it, someone upstairs must have known a child born into so much abuse, carnage, destruction might deserve an opportunity in life. I suppose it's why I use the phrase kissed by God, am I religious, yes. Do I wear sandals and socks knocking on people's doors 9am on a Saturday morning preaching the word of the son, the father and the holy ghost, no.

Maybe an opportunity to be sat here in my kitchen today when the house is silent the wife and kids in bed sipping a nice glass of wine writing this book, maybe. If this book reaches out to a few people and those individuals speak out about mental health, addiction, child abuse or suicide and other challenges then that's the proverbial ripple effect.

I jumped on the bus headed into town made my connection and off to the other side of town, the posh part of town. Having worked with UCB the catering college in Birmingham I know how it is with students. You take two on show them the ropes then put them on the shit section for the duration of their apprenticeship. Not me the chefs who had worked under me from UCB I made sure they worked all sections. Larder, sauce, banqueting, breakfast, staff canteen, pastry and service.

I enter the kitchen via the staff entrance this instruction was on my brief from college "1st day on the job back doors", and I don't mean your mum. I'm greeted by the executive chef, a mean looking fella.

Change in my office I'll be back in 5 to show you the ins and outs of my domain. The office consisted of a wooden table and chair, an ash tray, 20 B&H, dirty chefs whites on the floor and a poster of Sam Fox pinned to the wall, tits out of cause.

Starters, mains, pastry, pot wash, fridges, fire exit my office, first job prep broccoli for a function, wasn't told which function just prep. I'm dwarfed by 6 crates of broccoli, no sweat let's crack on, florets in the container stalks in the bin.

Beacon radio playing in the background, I'm stood practically outside as the prep area is situated to the rear of the kitchen "back doors". Within the hour I'm done, florets in the container stalks in the bin, clean my section, empty the bin.

Now I didn't think anything of prepping the broccoli that quick, I just did it. A few more chefs arrive on shift. I'm whisked around the kitchen during lunch service. Its Willy Wonka I'm in my element or so I thought I was.

Executive chef screams across the kitchen where the fuck are the broccoli stalks, chef I threw them out the florets are in the prep fridge. Ever seen a silver back on PCP, ape I mean, yeah, a silver back ape on PCP with an erection. Well, that's what this chef had turned into chef Ramsey hasn't got shit on this chef.

If he'd have said stalks in that container then I would have done the obvious, now I thought the verbal abuse at home was bad. This was on another level, another level on top of that level at the top of the Burj Khalifa.

In my face mustard in the eye sockets petrified, the ape on PCP with his lipstick poking out his chefs' trousers was going off. FUCKINBIN get your black fuck ass out there and get me those fucking broccoli stalks you fucking,

78

spellcheck gollywog "Hollywood" umm gollywog, get out there and fetch me those stalks.

The day had turned to a bleak winter's afternoon, artic winds swirling around the yard, bins the size of a garden shed. No recycling back in those days, every department just dumping their shit in any bin. Get in those fucking bins and get me those broccoli stalks, "oui chef", by the way this book isn't based on a true story, it is a true story, it's how shit went down back in those days, just another fucking racist in my face.

In I go full chefs' whites, apron, hat neckerchief etc, frozen to the bone and believe me there wasn't much meat on me back in those days. knee deep in hotel waste, the smell is something else, I'm ripping bags apart throwing out every stalk.

Before long I'm back in the kitchen a total mess, the broccoli stalks covered in all sorts of detritus. Good lad now get them fucking washed and bring them to me on the sauce section when you're ready, "yes chef, wee chef, oui chef".

Cream of broccoli and blue cheese soup topped with garlic herb croutons finished with creme and garnished with the classic 80s garnish "chopped parsley". 6pm I was told to fuck off home and come back tomorrow If I dared. I Cried all the way home, destroyed wounded broken, fuck this chef malarkey for a living.

I arrive home battered, I smell bad, proper nasty, hotel waste nasty, no sympathy, why would there be, snivelling like a child lost in Woolworths I attempt to explain my day. I can't go back there, this cooking thing is not for me, you better get your fucking arse back there tomorrow or else. That's the day that my future as a chef was set in stone, those words, "you better get back there or else", it's the only piece of encouragement I need to get me out of that god forsaken house.

First job that following morning was to melt chocolate and make garnishes for the pastry chef, nuclear powered microwave, chocolate in 2 minutes, not good, not good at all, black chocolate smoke covered half the kitchen. I went back every day for 2 weeks regardless, battered broken shattered mentally physically exhausted.

For me to have become the chef I am today I had to experience the dog shit, I had to experience the brutal ways of the kitchen in the 80s. Hr go fuck yourself, don't like my racists remarks go fuck yourself self, fuck shit crap wank go fuck yourself, Hr go fuck yourself some more, Human resources back then "go fuck yourself".

Plenty of Time

I had made several trips up to Birmingham for interviews with various managers for the vacant executive chef role within Birmingham's most prestigious hotel. A beautiful 4-star deluxe hotel which needed a strong, well-travelled experience chef. During this period, I was working as a pastry chef near Henley on Thames with a 2* Michelin chef whose kitchen brigade was solid.

All though I was working at the hotel and spa on a temporary basis taking some much-needed time out from management and a bad spell within my career. I knew it wouldn't be long before a respected establishment would be on my case to offer me a position I could not refuse. Before the final interview with the reginal director of this prestigious hotel I was invited to do a cook off.

The chef who would oversee my cook off was the executive head chef of one of London's finest 5* hotels. This chef's resume was on another level to that of mine. Peter had managed some huge 5* establishments across the globe for the company that I hoped would employ me. As always for a vacant role such as this and being Infront of some big personalities within this company's flagship hotel in London I dusted off my best suite willed all my experience and charisma which hopefully would tick the right boxes.

Chefs whites ironed, knife roll under my arm, I headed into London for the beast of all cook offs. The hotel boasted a 2* Michelin French restaurant, its clientele, were some of the most influential people from across the globe. Arriving at the hotel I was meet by Peter the executive head chef along with the food and beverage director. After brief introductions Peter gave me the grand tour of his stunning hotel. Peter was courteous, graceful, very polite and cool as a cucumber. I could tell how his team of chefs, kitchen porters and front of house responded to him that he had them all in his pocket. 100% respect for such a giant of a chef.

The staff canteen wasn't a canteen as such, it was practically a two-rosette restaurant with several chefs preparing breakfast, lunch, dinner and night meal for 150+ staff members who dressed and walked the floor like models. I had a simple brief regarding the morning from the operations manager in Birmingham that I would have a cook lasting roughly two hours. Plenty of time to knock out a two-course menu for Peter using anything from his fridges that morning.

Two hours later into my walk around with Peter I've got my eye on the clock as I need to get changed into whites and start cracking on with my prep. Brief to myself when I left home that morning was to leave it all on the chopping board. Everyone who had interviewed me in Birmingham had given me the green light. I know I can cook, so do not fuck it up.

I was the front runner, the horse way out in front to be appointed, all roads were leading to me. "Ok chef Auguste let's start your cook off, 1hr three courses, starter, main, dessert". What the fuck, 1hr, I better start moving, and move I did. Leave it all on the chopping board. Peter did say, "you can use whatever is in the prep fridges", oui chef.

Starter, salmon tartare, asparagus tips, soft boiled quail's eggs, dressed pea shoots, citrus dressing. Main course, pressed belly pork, pork fillet, heritage roast carrots, fondant potato, roast apple pearls, thyme reduction (I forgot the garnish). Dessert, apple tart Tatin, poached pear, sticky apple puree, shortbread crumb, vanilla bean ice cream, blackcurrant and raspberry halves.

During this headless 1hr, I had managed to have a few brief chats with several chefs on shift within what can only be described as a state-of-the-art shiny new kitchen. Demonstrating not only could I cook under pressure, but I could also communicate in a calm approachable manner. I had taken a few bits and bobs from various sections and prep fridges to complete my cook off within the hour.

Chef, ready when you are, Peter was joined by two of the Michelin starred chefs from the French restaurant which was just one of several outlets within the hotel. "Ok Auguste please explain the menu which you have prepared today, by the way presentation, spot on". Thank you, chef.

Starter, wild salmon tartare bound with a light citrus and caper mayonnaise, soft runny boiled quail's eggs "how long did you boil the quails eggs"? two and a half minutes chef then plunged into iced water. Asparagus tips quickly sauteed in clarified butter and seasoned. Pea shoots dressed with a few drops of olive oil and squeeze of lemon and sea salt. "Great looking dish, totally classic combination, asparagus soft runny eggs and asparagus" delicious chef. Starter plate practically licked clean.

"Main course please chef", well as you can see, I pinched a few bits from your prep fridge. "Auguste, it's a stunning plate of food, cooked and presented well, not too many ingredients on the plate, great tasting sauce, excellent".

"Before you explain the dessert, in all my years of conducting cook offs I've never witnessed such a stunning dessert". Well chef I'm currently working as a pastry chef near Henley and on Thames, "I know the chef Auguste, it's a stunning property, very swanky". Three plates of food demolished, licked clean, me shattered. Both Michelin chefs gave me a pat on the back and a wink "great food chef".

As well as the human resources and operations director in Birmingham I had now been given the green light by Pater who said, "I'll be seeing you very soon in Birmingham". The interview process had been incredibly positive. Just an hours Skype call with the food and beverage director who managed Europe and north Africa. My Skype interview was an interrogation, if they need a chef to sort a kitchen out, who can cook and communicate at many levels, this job, I'm good to go.

If they want to employ a chef who looks and sounds good in front of a camera, I'm not that guy, this is what I sensed from a two-hour grilling by the food and beverage director. Physically, mentally exhausted with mustard squirted in my eyes, after a full day, what must an applicant go through to be successful in today's culinary industry.

You are dragged to hell and back, indoctrinated to the company's values. Bamboozled with distant company targets, battered eloquently senseless buy the smiling army, then shit out. Soon as I'm outside in the fresh air I take 10 minutes to compose myself before I call my agent who has done a fantastic job thus far in managing me through what has now been a 2-month process which is far from over.

Two beers and a sushi takeaway I'm on the train heading out of London on my way home. The phone call with my agent Tim is extremely positive, He congratulates me for a strong cookoff as he has just come off the phone with Peter. He also praises me on how I have conducted myself thus far. Everyone is keen to get me onboard and orientated in time for the conservative conference party in two months' time. Super stoked I can only but hold my head high as I know that cook off was on point. Classic, cooked well, not over complicated and packed full of flavour. I left it all on the chopping board.

The following morning, I receive a call from Birmingham, the operation director congratulating me on an outstanding cook off. "Auguste you will hear from us tomorrow with hopefully positive news and a start date". I respond eloquently and thank all parties. Two bottles of wine, I think it's time to celebrate. Now it's my agent's best interest to sell me and I mean sell me well as they pocket 15% of the gross salary as their rate, not too shabby considering the proposed salary.

On the money, the following morning I receive a phone call from Tim, my agent. "Good morning, Auguste how's tricks"? All good Tim, any news from Birmingham? "Yes, there is, but unfortunately it's not good news I'm afraid mate" What's happened I reply? "They have given the role to a chef already employed within the company who is going to relocate from Spain". What a fucking dick punch. "Listen buddy I know how hard you have worked and how much time you have put into this, leave it with me I will have something for you in a week or two".

Cheeky fucking wankers, I'm minding my own business in a role I'm enjoying as pastry chef within a super prestigious establishment. All bar the money it's a great gig. The agency contacted me; I didn't contact them, let alone the hotel in Birmingham. I have spent hard earned money on traveling halfway across the country. Everyone who has interviewed me has given the thumbs up. At the end of the day what a waste of fucking time. Why didn't they just employ this chef from Spain in the first place and not waste my fucking time and play on people's emotions.

What doesn't start well does not end well. Two weeks later after licking my wounds dusting myself down again, I receive a call from Tim. "Hi Auguste how's life my friend"? Not too shabby how can I help you, Tim? "Listen fella, are you sat down at this moment in time"? Nope, but I can be. "I've just had a call from Birmingham, they want to offer you the vacant position as head chef. One condition they want you to meet the regional director first in Birmingham" Fuck off, are you fucking kidding me, who are these people? "I know it's fucked but it's a cracking opportunity to get back on the horse Auguste".

Long story made extremely short, the following week I meet with the regional director. I negotiate an extra 10k plus bonus and start the following week. The operations director apologised during my first day of orientation for fucking me around. Everyone is apologising to me all the bar the general manager for such a shabby application process. The thing is, I never applied for the role, but they want you to feel like you owe them a pound of flesh. Regardless of being head hunted today, such a buzz word "head hunted" if they're going to treat you like a cunt, they'll treat you like a cunt, it all depends, if you're going to let them treat you like a cunt.

This is what we all must go through not just as chefs, all executive management posts. You are pulled from pillow to post, treated with such disregard. Application and interview processes are not going to get any easier. I'm witnessing the shocking behaviour and standards now being implemented during covid-19 by global hospitality brands. Salaries which were once 50k for a strong experienced executive chef, now being advertised at 35k. It's happening because these companies are taking advantage of the current situation.

These brands know they will have hundreds of chefs applying for that one job which will keep their family out of poverty. These brands also know these experienced applicants will take it in the ass and have the moral compass fucked with. At a time when the hospitality industry is on its knees, lets know really fuck over the chefs that have dedicated their lives to their craft by paying them less.

Filthy Maggots

"You three get in here now, quick fucking sharpish, come on, chop fucking chop". "Do you filthy maggots know why you're all in here, standing before me"? No sergeant. "You horrible fucking liars". "It's come to my attention, one of you, two of you, or all three of you horrible little wankers have been smoking cannabis". "Fucking cannabis, well, I'm sure you've all heard of the glass house, you stupid ignorant cunts".

The glass house is the military prison, any prison in South America times it by 10, add the jungle, you still are nowhere near the monstrosity of the place that it is. There is no time to ponder how the fuck do I get out of this sticky situation; I am in it. I'm done, finished, this is it, the day I get booted out of the army for smoking drugs, yea fucking drugs. I do not know of an army chef in the history of the army catering Corp who has been dishonourably discharged in this fashion. Drugs did not sit well with the British army.

"Corporal search these fucking animals" yes Sargent. My legs have gone weak at the knees, busted with a lump of solid in my pants. It's not going to pass for shit, not in a mini pink keyring backpack with king size rizla, not today.

"Private smith step forward and empty the contents of your fucking pockets on the table". Weed, rizla, 20 Marlborough reds and 110 Dutch mark. "Umm, do you understand the magnitude of the shit storm you're in private Smith", yes Sargent. "You my son are fucked, you horrible little wanker, about face and stand facing the wall you stupid fucking cunt".

"Private Gray step forward and empty the contents of your pockets on the table along with private smiths little stash" yes Sargent. My insides have fallen out my ass, not good considering the chances of getting a job on civvy street are all but fucked, that is if I survive the glass house.

"What do we have here private Gray marijuana and what appears to be ecstasy, you dirty little bastard, you my son are proper fucked". I'm up next, I feel like crying, calling out for my auntie. The phone on the sergeant's desk rings.

"Right, you three, you dirty rotten maggots fuck off and wait outside, corporal guard these animals" yes Sargent.

We are marched into the corridor and held at gun point. corporal please may I go to the toilet, I'm about to piss myself. "Quick fucking sharpish Knuckles and no fucking funny business" Absolutely corporal, no funny business.

As soon as my back is facing the Corporal on duty my hand dives into my pants to retrieve my little bag of willy Wonka sweets. "Leave the door open Knuckles". I can feel his breath on my neck, I turn to the corporal and ask if he would like to shake my dick for me when I'm done. "Do you know the shit storm you boys are in, do you, less of the small talk you cocky black cunt".

I'm holding my mini bag of goodies squashed in the palm of my left hand. "Ok Knuckles let's go". The corporal leads me out of the toilet, as I exit, I throw the contents in my hand behind me as far as I could without making out, I've just thrown a javelin into the four-man dorm and follow the corporal back out into the corridor.

"Ok you horrible little maggots get in here now". We are quick marched back into the room. The sergeant is going bananas, he's not a happy bunny. "Ok Knuckles contents of your pockets on the fucking table" yes Sargent. 60 Dutch mark half a packet of Marlborough lights, the kitchen keys and a zippo lighter. "Right corporal search him". All bar a hand up my ass I'm searched as If this corporal has just got lucky with a hairy Bavarian woman in the local village.

"Nothing Sergeant", "Knuckles fuck off out of my sight. As I exit the guard room the sergeant is going fucking bonkers at my two mates who are about to be flown back to the UK to spend 6 months in the glass house in Colchester, then dishonourably discharged, traumatised for life".

Fuck knows who made that phone call, but it could not have come at a perfect time or else it would have been three losers on that military flight. That night I dodged a bullet, the closest I ever came to being pinched in the military. I had smuggled copious amounts of drugs across the Dutch boarder into Germany. I had sold drugs to 50% of the squaddies on camp. I was in fact the camps Pablo Escobar.

The following morning, I was up early to prepare breakfast for my squadron. "Oi Knuckles does this belong to you, you lucky fucking cunt". Geoff an engineer who I had partied with in so many raves across Germany throws me my little key ring backpack and says, "you must have dropped your girlfriend's purse last night, you lucky cunt". Yes, I was, the luckiest squaddie chef who had just gotten away with murder.

That evening after service and kitchen cleaned down, I retire to my room to lay low. That night I ate a gob stopper size piece of red seal and span the fuck out on my bunk bed for several hours. I whited like I had never whited before, at one stage I thought I was going to die. Harsher than any hash cake I had eaten in Amsterdam in one of a dozen coffee shops. But there was no way I was going to flush it down the toilet no fucking way.

Dementia Plum Crumble

Hands down if I'm playing a game of dice or cards today, the hand of all hands is going to be a full house, sprouts over plum crumble. I have no love in the world for tinned plums, no love whatsoever. Bullet to the head or tinned plum crumble, bullet to the head, skin peeled from my body with a blunt spoon or tinned plum crumble, the skin peeling thing. Molested by a giraffe and a whale over plum crumble, the molesting thing, I would rather take it up the arse by a rhino than eat Phillis's dementia crumble.

Ok kids it's off to your grandparents "not my grandparents, Fascists" she's made her lovely crumble for us all "what a treat" two fingers to the back of the throat already retching before we've made it to the car for the journey across town for dog shit dementia crumble with cold lumpy fox vomit custard.

No disrespect but my she isn't no Italian granny chef; the crumble topping resembled the glue you used at infant school to stick fairy liquid bottles together with green garden sticks to make a sail and gravel for sand. Yes, warm gravel type burnt topping then the gluey glop in between that and the filling.

The whole dish presented like a Joel Robuchon masterpiece in a battered Pyrex dish we all had to marvel at it, then sit there and consume it like it was a warm triple chocolate fudge cake, with more fudge on top of the fudge, caramel filling with vanilla bean ice cream and marshmallows, and then fudge sauce poured on top, with more sprinkles and garnished with chocolate wafers.

Fuck that shit, I was more than prepared to be at the table for 2 weeks, I knew Phillis didn't have a shotgun so what's the worst that can happen, I don't get a blue ribbon for being a good boy because I ate all my pudding, you can stick that blue ribbon where the sun has never shined.

Tears And Toys

All I know and all experienced during the early years with Boris and Doris and my sister we both lived in absolute fear. I was about still a baby, but this is the age I really started to remember things. I can close my eyes as a man today and go back to how shit life was, living in fear day in day out not knowing what was in store for us pesky kids.

Quick kids she would shout as Boris pulled onto the driveway, well it wasn't a drive as such, just the front garden, your dads' home she would shout, we would literally run for cover. We would both hide under tables, beds, in cupboards, anywhere we thought we were safe. Anywhere we could hide we'd fucking hide, and mother would make it 100 times worse, quick kids he's coming, quickly go and hide before he sees you, this wasn't playful shenanigans, this was her putting the fear of God in us.

We would scarper, our little hearts beating out our little chests, quick, he's at the door, the only reason I can come up with, for this kind of terror, well there's probably a dozen, one being that she totally fucking resented the air we breathed, the ground we walked on, total resentment, the sheer sound of those footsteps walking through the house still sends shivers down my spine to this day.

The love I have for my son is breath-taking every waking hour he reminds me of all the beauty in the world, he reminds me why I must be better and overcome my demons. I have the same love for my daughter **Love** is what defines us **Love** is what holds our family together, it's what I try to embrace every day regardless of if it's a good or bad day.

I never felt the slightest ounce of love as a child growing up in that god forsaken house. Every day was filled with screaming, fights between her and him. Every day was a misery, the house was invested with mice and rats running freely during the night. I could hear them beneath my bed scratching around, vile, damp and depressing.

The garden was always overgrown, there were trees at the bottom, we often built dens me and my sister. There was also a waste ground through and beyond the fence at the bottom of the garden. Slag heaps from old building sites, weeds and boulders, during the summer miraculously wild mint grew. How would I know this because as a chef my favourite herb is mint?

If I'm having a bad day at work, I would walk into the vegetable fridge grab a bunch of mint hold it to my nose and take a deep breath. It would take me back to the only time I found some sort of normality, scratching around on the waste land at the back of our crumbling house, tearing at wild mint holding it to my young nose and smelling something beautiful.

Most weekends Boris and Doris would leave us to fend for ourselves while they went out, my sister would have been no older than 7, I would have been 5ish. Mother would put their firstborn as a couple to bed, 18 months old at a push and leave my sister and me to it.

This is how they rolled, they'd fuck off out without a care in the world leaving 2 vulnerable children and a baby alone. During adulthood my sister would tell me how at the age of 7 she would try and deal with baby's night terrors, imagine that a 7-year-old looking after me and an 18-month-old baby bringing the house down with night terrors.

It really hasn't been easy writing this, I've been tapping away on my keypad words sentences flowing for the past few days and I'm feeling physically sick with the neglect. My sister would panic, the only option would be to bang on the neighbour's door screaming crying traumatised asking for help.

Where's your mum and dad, the neighbour would ask, they've left us, they went out, neglect on a scale that would have parents banged away today. When they finally arrived home, they would be intoxicated, we would be punished for not dealing with baby number one, smacked about told we were useless. Useless fucking kids you are, fuck knows why I had you fucking pair, fucking waste of space.

There isn't one night whereby I didn't physically cry myself to sleep as a kid, I just cried out the pain, shivering in a cold bed under an itchy blanket, no heating through the house all bar a shitty little coal fire down stairs. I would cry until finally the world I was living in disappeared, disappeared until woken by the sheer cold.

Some nights I would wake up due to the noise of the mice scratching under my bed. I remember vividly to this day I would get out of my bed with just my pants on walk along the landing to mothers' room and crawl under her bed and fall asleep on the floorboards as I would be too scared to climb into her bed and ask for attention and warmth.

There were nights I would wake up, or be woken up, the side of my face burning as if I had been slapped in the face by someone. I would be so scared to move an inch I would be frozen in time staring at the figure in the doorway to my room, I fucking knew it was him, I just knew, the fucking coward not only is it enough to be fucked over while awake this abuse was going on while I was asleep, you cold-hearted bastard.

As a father today, there's nothing more rewarding than taking my kids to bed and making sure they are tucked in and cosy. Before I go to bed I must tuck them in maybe a cheeky kiss on the cheek while they both sleep, reasons for being cheerful.

Back then when I had knobbly knees and wore nothing but pants and a t-shirt around the house I can't recall ever playing with toys it was bricks and sticks. The one time I did was Christmas circa 1976 I was bought a train set, a single track with a train pulling a carriage around in a circle. I remember playing with my Christmas present that train set once that same day it disappeared.

The following Christmas I got the same train set, the batteries must have leaked in the box throughout the year because I can remember silver foil crammed into to where the batteries sat, didn't even work.

He was my friend, and he lived a few doors up from us, haven't a clue how we started hanging out together, most likely his mother would baby sit me. My friend had some amazing toys, a figure of eight Scalextric, so many types of cars with a garage, action men with vehicles it was like Santa's grotto.

I truly loved being at Miguel's house playing for hours on end in his bedroom, toy story personified. This is the first time I remember my first beating; I know there was others before this, but this is the first beating I know happened in my little brain. I would always make my own back and forth to Miguel's house. I arrived home after an awesome afternoon at my friend's house, huge smile from ear to ear beaming from my face as I walked in the house. What the fuck are you smiling for, you better wipe that smile of your face before your dad sees you. Fucking dad, Hitler more like, the fucking audacity to call him my dad, he was a bully who prayed on me and my sister.

He walked into the living room stood next to Doris and asked why I was smiling and so cheerful. She said did you have a nice time, yes, I loved it he's got so many toys we played drank squash it was awesome. She says in such a sarcastic voice would you like to live with your friend, yes, just because he has nice toys.

Well, you've asked for it now, I was dragged upstairs by that man, I was stripped naked and beaten, fucking beaten. My screams and cries for help could be heard out in the garden by my sister. Doris was nowhere to be seen, that evil woman didn't raise a finger to protect me, she stood by and let it all happen, raise me as one of his own, it makes me laugh out loud today "one of his own", the hatred that filled that dungeon was on another level.

A week later I was back at Miguel's house again, I strolled back down the road, gleaming smile. I'm convinced they were waiting for me because as I entered the house I was summoned to the kitchen and asked the same question.

My answer was the same, yes, I would love to live with my friend, Boris told me to go upstairs and strip naked. My sister was in kitchen kicking off yelling, screaming don't you touch him. Don't you lay a finger on him or else I will run away, this went on for some time because I could clearly hear my sister desperately pleading with her to help me.

My sister pleading with her while I was upstairs cowering behind the door in my pants petrified, shaking, whimpering knowing only one thing I was minutes away from another beating. He never came up stairs that afternoon my sister had saved me, saved me today but who knew what was in store the following day.

What I fail to understand in later life is that she went through so much trouble in getting me back from my previous abusers. Once my wounds had healed from one experience, I was then battered **black and blue** regularly, a phrase one of my uncles used to describe what he witnessed on several occasions but did nothing, absolutely nothing to intervene, nothing.

All of them, each single member of that family did nothing, they all had a hand in the abuse all bar auntie Stella. There isn't much in life that I hate, I love my wife and children that's a given, I love diversity, my profession, all sports, music, the arts, fashion, political debate, music, good wine, socialising with friends, eating out, golf, keeping fit.

I would say there wasn't much I disliked until I started this project, and I wouldn't go as far as calling it hatred more like disgust. Do I have closure knowing he's no longer here, dead in the ground, no, in a strange way no and I don't have a clue why, for some strange reason I still remember the date of his birthday.

All those children, teenagers, men and women out there that don't have a voice or the courage to speak with someone about the damage inflicted on them due to the impact of prolonged childhood abuse across all forms emotional physical mental we are not alone, **we are not alone**.

Some of us survivors although permanently scared who have managed to carve a life out for ourselves only know one thing, feeling the warm breeze on our faces on a summers day or the laughter of our own children and the warmth of their love is healing in itself, for they will never feel a heavy fist, they will never know hatred or resentment, they will only know love, our love and that is peace within, Amen to that.

A Chef with no Filter

Seasonal work objectives, shag as many chalet girls or chalet boys as humanly possible. Spend all your earnings on the most expensive ski or snowboarding gear, irrespective if you cannot get down the mountain, you just had to look good. Max all credit cards, drink more, fuck more, nail more 360s 720s back flips than Shaun White in the park. Risk life and limb riding the most insane off-piste in the world.

Bags packed; snowboarding gear squared away ready for the mammoth coach journey to the Alps. I arrive at Victoria Street coach station drowned in jack Daniels and lemonade I consumed on the train down from Scotland and make my way to the meeting place "le bar". I found it funny why the food and beverage director for the company wanted the meeting place to be a gay bar. I once asked him what his first experience of an oyster tasted like. He replied, "it tasted like young boys' semen".

No messing around, I head straight to the off license to buy as much alcohol as I can cram into my funky new Oakley rucksack I purchased from snow and rock. Then it's off to the "meeting place" to meet up with old faces. Hopefully, they'll be no nannies in attendance that I smashed in the crèche during previous seasons.

The place is awash with hordes of seasonairs donning the finest winter wear ready to start or continue their life in the mountains for six whole months of face licking shenanigans, fresh powder, drugs and fisting.

"Nice one mate, yeah mate, how you are doing mate, off to do a season mate", St Anton sausage, "sausage, sausage yeah like it mate, new word for the season mate". Sausage, yeah nice, "yeah mate, there last season mate, do you know matey girl and matey boy ran Scotty's", yeah mate, wicked mate.

"What do you ride mate", your mum, "laugh out loud mate". Ride timeless, last year's model fella, wicked off-piste, pops like a fucker in the park. "What size mate", 159, "wicked". "Fanny everywhere mate, fancy a pint sausage",

Yeah mate, "what's your name" Auguste Knuckles, "Oh shit, Auguste Knuckles I've heard about you". You're that crazy fucker, they had a picture of you up in the Morris pub in Val snowboarding on the moon a few years back", yeah mate that's me. "Jesus' fella the fucking Astronaut", let's get on it.

Two hours of mate this, mate that, milking my prostate mate is exhausting, thank fuck I'm not traveling with matey boy to the mountains. Full English, 10 pints of Stella, it's time to board the coach.

I arrive at terminal 10, the bottles in my rucksack jangling like Santa's sack. I hustle my way through a dozen chalet girls smelling like Debenhams. Dump my bags in the under carriage and head to the back of the coach.

The coach pulls out of Victoria station like Thomas the tank engine setting off on an adventure through the valleys or was that Ivor the engine. The banter is dormant till we are out of London. A few teenagers start whispering, "I'm going to smash the granny out of anything that's breaths this season, do you know what I mean", "yeah I do know what you mean, in it, on it, all fucking over it".

Time to get involved, see what kind of badgers are on board. let's crack open Santa's sack even though drinking on board is totally against company policy. Jingle jangle, ears prick up and down the coach, heads start to turn my way to the sound of guzzling vodka.

A wink and a finger to the nose, before I can say avalanche, I'm surrounded by vodka fans on cold turkey. "How you are doing mate, where you from mate, seen you before mate, what you ride mate, what you are doing in the Alps fella", I'm a chef, "me too fella, you got a dribble of that love potion for uncle Demon".

12 of us getting involved on the back seats in some serious seasonair banter, chatting endlessly about previous seasons. Everyone is in high spirits now the proverbial ice has been broken and a bottle consumed. Even a few toffee-nosed managers get on it, at the end of the day they are just up for it like everyone else on the winter bus.

Exchanging glances, passing thoughts, boy girl, girl boy, boy boy, girl girl, Touchy feely. I'm going to drill the back side out of you on the training course you feel me, "yes big boy" she gives him the nod that they are fuck buddies for the season. Bad move for so many seasonairs.

Trick is, to get out to resort before you commit to such heart ache. Mated for life fuck that Avatar bollocks, not for the astronaut. A chef with no filter, in the alps blessed with seasonal work. OCD, super hypervigilant plus hyperactive it's going to get extremely naughty and extremely messy.

Girls are on it, just like the lads, up for it, mad for it, away from home for the first time. Gagging mad for it, like a frenzied rabbit on a crunchy lettuce. Crazy for some alfresco action with a hunky ski instructor flicking snow up their home counties virgin bottom with their European shaved ball sack.

Or hopefully being smashed in every part of the hotel, maybe over a car bonnet outside bar Cuba before they start their briefcase life working in the city. They might be posh girls living off daddy's credit card for the season. Guaranteed they will all at some point during their season be stroking the shaft, caressing those marbles and swallowing the hollandaise.

We all have the same mentality, seasonal workers, we all want to work hard and play harder. It's amazing what a few bottles of absolute and a dozen cans of red bull can do. Obliging to a palm shandy under my new Bonfire jacket is only the start of the shenanigans to come. Booze refill, Dover to Calais is standard procedure for the merry bus. Back on the coach, Idle chat continues for a few hours into France then I pop several sleeping pills, its lights out. Arrive at our location 17 hours later, the mood is somewhat to that of dying on an easy jet flight from Cyprus to London. Five hours of easy jet torture, 6ft 3" squashed into a child's go-kart.

Ice breakers, training courses are two a penny, ecstasy, shagging nannies and drinking black sambuca till the snow stops falling. let us move forward. Although it's a little different for me, I've got the job of training a dozen chefs on menu development, ordering, budgets, local produce and not to get persuaded into procuring Japanese sake from the local vegetable supplier in resort.

Training courses are a proper giggle though, hotel managers getting drilled by resort ski reps. Top brass making out their well-behaved shining examples of the company but there just as crazy. Sneaking off with head nannies receiving blow jobs in two feet of fresh snow on the nursery slope. Ironic, a blow job by a head nanny on the nursery slopes.

Training course over, I've got to make my way to Geneva, then a train journey to my hotel. I'm with three other chefs working in the same resort. So, what to do? head straight to the train bar to get skull fucked on elephant beer for the next three hours as we cruise through the beautiful alps.

"I understood myself only after I destroyed myself and in the process of fixing myself did, I know who I truly was"

Pork Neck

Head chef's winter objectives: get as many chefs and kitchen porters as possible involved in the secret extreme drinking club. Cook authentic local cuisine, have the craziest season without being hospitalised. Hotel ready, suppliers dialled in, kitchen blitzed and ready for arriving staff and guests. Part of the management teams pre-season resort orientation is, we eat out at all the top restaurants and bars before the rest of the team arrive. Local resort knowledge when advising guests to dine out during chalet day off.

I have a strong kitchen team this season, my number two is a good friend, so we've got each other's back. Fast forward to the best bits, the prime cuts, the 12oz prime fillet with fois gras and morrell mushrooms. The gold leaf covered lobster claws with hollandaise sauce. The sauteed sweet breads with sweet potato puree. The parts that are stranger than fiction. The parts we like to mop up with a fresh warm piece of baguette after devouring a Swiss cheese fondue with a dozen bottles of vino calapso.

The menu that evening was not your average chalet hotel menu. I had worked my budgets well and was way under and on course for my bonus. The menu was a mix of contemporary French brasserie style fare. Frogs' legs with pastis and cherry tomatoes. Snails served in their shell with garlic butter. Roast pear and brie, fillet steak and fois gras, confit duck with puy lentils and garlic creamed mash. Lobster with mushy peas and fat chips, ratatouille strudel. Chocolate fondant, petit fours, local cheese plate with dried fruits and sour dough crackers.

My team of chefs that season were a bunch of hoodlums, drinkers and druggies mostly northerners. As mentioned, I had a strong team regardless of their devious habits and addictions.

Preservice chat: Ok guys its New Year's Eve we are all away from home thank fuck, so let's make it a special one. When you hear me shout pork neck dash to my office down the shot on the desk and continue working. Also, every time the plate wash machine opens you down an egg cup of house red. I have also placed an egg cup and jug of red on all sections. You will be notified of the plate wash opening when you hear me shout Morris, Morris please, "Mousey", everybody cool, "cool chef".

The restaurant manager was an easy-going guy called Brendan. He didn't care much what me and my team got up to during service. If it was smooth, the food went out with no delays and piping hot, he turned a blind eye. "Pork neck, pork neck, porn neck".

The shots in the office where Absinth and orange juice, poured out, all on parade to get us totally and absolutely smashed. My sous chef was feeling the pinch due to several beers during Après ski, we hadn't even started service. The washing machine was already in action with a few early kids' meals. The kitchen porters had decorated the washing machine with fairy lights and tinsel, priceless.

I turn to my team of chefs and kitchen porters, faces beaming with joy as they all know something special was about to happen. Some chefs already with dribbles of red wine absinthe and orange juice down the fronts of their jackets giggling like kids, winks all round, may the carnage begin, "pork neck".

Starters begin to fly across the passe and out into the restaurant. It's only a matter of time before we all know the washing machine will be in full swing. Let's brace ourselves for action, it's going to be beautiful.

"Here we go chef, check on, 2 duck, 4 fillet, 1 lobster", fuck, main course, where was the heads up, "pork neck", washing machine is in 4th gear. "Pork neck". Here comes forty minutes of sweat and concentration. "Pork neck, pork neck".

The first and second tables go out quick time, the kitchen cooking up nicely. "Pork neck" we all stumble to my office, "PORKNECK", YEAH, I FUCKING KNOW. It wasn't the greatest move, but I had done worse, far worse before in similar settings. Close the door chefs, ecstasy anyone, "Oh my days chefs got beans, you're a fuckin diamond". Chop, chop let's get a move on chefs, beans on the tongue swilled down with a shot of absinth.

The kitchen was about to become a whole different "kitchen" once these beans kicked in. Quick pork neck, we all step from my office and head to our sections. It could have only been me who walked straight into the brat pan and fell in it. "Hold it down Chef" whispers my sous chef.

If you have heard of the compilation Yoshieque by deep dish, then you have an established ear for house music. It's a mix of the most uplifting soulful, deep house I have ever listened to or purchased. Another great album hard times Vol

1 by Roger Sanchez. Check 3, check 4, check 5, "PORKNECK", the plate wash is going ballistic. "And a partridge in a pear tree" screams my sous chef.

Service is now in full swing, my eyelids start to tremble, my saddle sack starts to tingle. Looking out across the passé I see a haze of bodies, a black and white mist buzzing around, psychedelic people covered in streamers wearing Christmas cracker hats.

"PORKFUCKINGMERRYCHRISTMASNECK, come on boys let's get bang on it", Danny the dog screams out "4 calling birds, 3 pork necks, 2 startled doves and a pork neck in a pear tree". Shots in the office are almost done, my insides are swirling around like a witch's caldron. The music is background noise being drowned out by the clutter of pots and pans, echoes of waitresses trying to communicate feedback.

My walnut sack is on fire as if a waitress is behind me on her knees rimming the living strawberries out of my pandoras box. Caressing my sausage like a puppy's head then stroking the insides of my legs with a feather duster. A deep breath comes from deep inside my stomach which sends shivers up my spine. My eyeballs start to roll, bolts of lightning tickle my forehead frying my brain easy over.

"I spunk all over the place", shouts Kevin, I turn to my wingman, you ok sausage, "I need two more duck and three fillets chef", Kevin's jaw is working overtime, a stick of wriggles mate, "that would be super nice chef". He starts giving me a back rub. have you seen the state of your eyes, stop with the back rub, not right now, maybe later darling? Dig deep my man eight more minutes and where home free.

We dig deep, extra deep and get the few remaining tables out, the entire kitchen team are buzzing. Lucky these beans were not the old school variety, or we would have all been in a proper pickle. I shake and gently stroke Kevin and Brendan's hand while trying to hold down my buzz. Great service, I stagger to the kitchen office my number two behind me making monkey sounds. Jaw trembling, twisted eyes, buzzing like a fruit machine ready to drop the jackpot. It's not over yet sausage, double, triple, quadruple parked a dozen egg cups lined out ready for consumption.

At the end of service during New Year's Eve it's tradition for all chefs to help kitchen porters with the clean down. So, buzzing our tits off we grab our snowboards from the ski room and stow them in the pastry section. When all other managers have left for the evening it's time to crank up the music. Make a huge punch for the team remaining and get blasted.

Indoor Ski Slope

Drench the entire kitchen floor with the fire hose, spray washing up liquid everywhere. The kitchen in the hotel was a weird set up, it was long and narrow from the pastry section through to the pot wash about 40meters.

The party was truly underway, topless chefs on tables dancing, downing dregs from the caldron, house music pumping. Waitresses twerking mad for some snowball action. Kevin and I strip down to our pants, place our boards at the entrance of the pastry section and stroll to the back wall.

We have a maximum a 4-meter run up; fat man stretches I'm off. I sprint, jump on to my snowboard and slide the entire length of the kitchen only to crash headfirst into the pot wash. Covered in angle lights and tinsel the head kitchen porter walks over and shouts "pork neck, a triple shot for you chef".

The festivities continued in resort, miraculously we all managed to finally sort ourselves out which was early morning. It was a mad crazy sight for the entire resort watching a dozen wasted chefs, kitchen porters and waitresses playing naked ice hockey on the resort ice rink.

G-Strings

Pre-service drinks
5th floor outside room 512
Tomorrow night 7.45pm
Dress Code
G strings

Late afternoon, after après ski before service, several chalet girls approached me saying chefs had been asking them for their slips and G strings. I might have forgot to mention the drinking club was top secret shit. No one could know what we were up to, faggots, sausage jockeys the lot of them I replied.

7pm, we start to get ready for service, 8am we start to receive our first orders. I turn to half a dozen confused chefs all pondering how the fuck they were going to get out of the kitchen. Get changed into their G strings and up to the fifth floor by 7.45pm? not my problem.

7.30pm we start sending food out for the kid's buffet, hold the fort Kevin I'm just popping to the toilet. "YOU CUNT" he replies. I stroll out the kitchen, catch the lift to my room which is on the fifth floor and slide my G string on. What a sight for sore eyes, my cock and balls hanging out from one side like a slaughtered squirrel. Two bottles of Absolute vodka split six ways into plastic bottles, 5 Ibuprofen popped into each bottle, a large splash of tequila topped off with lemonade.

7.44pm I wander out into the corridor like a rat on a big mac, hoping some yummy mummy is going to catch me and give me a good spanking. Imagine that, yeah bonkers I know. 7.45pm from the far end of corridor the laundry lift doors open. Out scramble six hairy chefs crashing towards me wearing G strings, white bodies and suntanned faces. Meat and potatoes slapping around from side to side. If only a guest had walked out from their hotel room and witnessed what I was seeing, customer feedback for that week might have been quite different. Dear General Manager

"It's with deep regret I write such a devastating account of the scene I and my wife witnessed on the given date". "Our lives have been traumatised beyond recognition, several grown men, downing what can only be described as loopy juice wearing only G strings". "I can no longer look at my wife in sexy underwear due to the mental and emotional trauma we both were subjected to". "I would like a full refund and a bottle of whatever those hairy beats were drinking that evening".

It's dark, it's wrong any which way you look at it, this is the sort of shenanigans Freddie Mercury would have been up for. Half a dozen hunks in G strings ready for a foot fisting orgy. We were there to get wasted, no touchy feely aloud, that behaviour was for later.

Fellas, cocks and hairy ball sacks of the extreme drinking club welcome to our first mission. We have only minutes to consume the contents of these bottles before we change and return safely to the kitchen. I nominate Roger to conduct the next meeting. Wherever you choose to meet, whatever it is you wish us to drink we must obey the rules or forfeit.

We return safely to the kitchen, greeted angrily by waiting staff, "where the fuck have you lot been", cock feast, "what did you say to me"? toilet. Trick is to hold it down as best as humanly possible without falling face first into your mise en place tray. Let alone keeling over into the Brat pan because you cannot feel your legs. Consuming this amount of alcohol within such a short space of time is not for kids. So please do not try this at home, unless the kids are in bed or with their grandparents.

Service was a fucking shambles, half a dozen telly tubbies smashed on cheap booze and pharmaceuticals trying to hold service down. Food went out all over the place, for what it was worth at least every hotel guest received a hot meal that evening. If it hadn't been for half the restaurant team turning up for their shift totally wasted after getting legless during Après ski us chefs would have received a good telling off from the hotel manager.

Service boxed off, myself, my team showered changed we headed out to see what trouble we could get up to in resort that evening. Little did we know the entire cast from the most off world TV show dirty Sanchez had descended on our resort that evening to get blind, battered, obscenely fucking wasted drunk.

Half a dozen battered chefs plus the dirty Sanchez boys, it ended in absolute chaos. Stunt men tequila shots snort a line of salt, squeeze lemon juice in your eye and down the tequila. Break dancing naked in the red grouse pub, human darts, cock hockey. Downing half pints of top shelf mixers were just for starters.

The drugs we consumed that evening were off the chart's carnage, chefs vomiting all over resort, waiters passing out face first in yellow snow. Kitchen porters shagging nannies in shop doorways. Chefs smashing pint glasses over each other's heads, pool cues being broken across shins. Unless someone got killed that evening anything and everything got the green light, until someone got killed or killed themselves no one blinked an eye lid.

Binge Drinking and Ski Boots

That morning was a white out in resort, drizzle in the air, guaranteed the snow would be like porridge on the mountain. Chalet day off and fuck all to do but get up to no good. A docile knock at my door, who is it? "este bon", who? "este bon, no este bon". Head kitchen porter who liked to be called este bon due to his summer seasons in Magaluf. He walks into my accommodation holding two pints of vodka OJ 50/50 mix.

"Morning chef bought you breakfast", cheers mate what's the occasion, "well its chalet day off and there's porridge everywhere. Staff are talking about a pub crawl around resort, you in"? does a horse trot? yeah, I'm in. The kitchen team pour into my room with a few chalet girls. Bastards must had been hiding around the corner. If my reply had been no, it would have resulted in a murderous forfeit. Probably sitting naked in 4ft of snow downing a bottle of warm garlic and chili rum. Not good for morale, especially if you are not a warm garlic and chili rum drinking kind of person.

We sit chatting, drinking, smoking a few joints watching snowboarding DVDs. "Right fellas the grouse pub it is", este bon. Up, shower, change and it's out the door. We crunch through the snow a dozen stoned chefs a handful of kitchen porters with a few chalet girl's hell bent on the inevitable. We pile into the grouse pub at 10am and order 12 pints of sauce.

The pub is bustling with several groups of skiers and snowboarders with the same agenda, get merry, live life and love the company you are with. "If you can't be with the one you love, love the one you're with" is the song of the morning.

If you have ever visited the resort of Flaine, you will know it's a small, tiny village most likely designed for a Star Wars movie. Nestled in a fruit bowl with weird and wonderful architecture. It was too early for grown up chat, so that morning we decided on the ultimate binge session. last man standing will be crowned king Kong of the piss heads.

I would not dream of drinking 8 pints today, not for breakfast anyways, divorce written all over it. 1pm comes around like a half smoked joint and we all stagger to the flying Dutch man. A small bar ran by a Dutch man funny enough. We order our drinks and make our way to the back of the bar. The conversation is relaxed, chatting about sex, cooking, our back grounds, which chefs we had worked for, where we had travelled to and what bought us to the Alps. The most common response was drugs and relationships, unfuckingbelievable, we are all here to get away from fucked up relationships and our love for drugs.

The chalet girls are mangled faces in bowls of crisps with rosy cheeks falling off the stools. I noticed directly above our table the owner had screwed a pair of old 1970s stormtrooper ski boots into the ceiling. Ok fellas whose first, "first for what"? I raise my head, that's what, "your fucking joking", nope. Right fellas hold me up, upside down. I'll fix my feet into the boots and hopefully they'll hold my weight. Five minutes later of man jostling and a finger in the eye I'm suspended from the ceiling like a fancy lampshade.

Well, the piss heads, they couldn't hold back the temptation, they pulled my trousers up and poured their drinks over my private parts, up my mush, they nearly fucking drowned me. Everyone gagging to get into the boots, "my turn cunt", "fuck off me next".

After being unhung from the ceiling I had a word with Erikson my new Dutch mate, the owner. He thought we were the best thing he had ever witnessed in his bar. "You guys are fucking bonkers" Anyways just like all crazy Dutch man up for giggles he got involved and organised a punch that would inevitably kill us all.

1, 2, 3, 4, 5, 6, hoisted and jostled into the boots, every orifice filled with punch. Eye sockets, bum holes, ears, japs eyes, breasts, you name it, filled. A dozen crazed chefs and kitchen porters dancing like Belgians on it's a knockout gagging for a second go.

Dutch Man Cocktail

Recipe

2 bottles Eristoff vodka, 1 bottle absinthe, red bull to taste.

8 diazepam, Larry's idea of a sick joke, but we fucking loved anything sick.

Method

Mix all together with lots of ice ready for the funnel

No cooking involved.

Hoist your fellow man into ski boots, if they fall unlucky, they would be dragged to the resort hospital. 10 seconds on the funnel, lovely jubley. If you are going to try this at home, I would suggest doing it in the garden using a sturdy branch to hang oneself upside down from. Please don't use a noose, the neighbours might call social services.

Day had turned into late afternoon, skiers were heading back to the resort to party, Après ski. We had been on it for 8 straight hours, we had turned into savages. We had suffered several casualties to the plight of the ski boots. My sous chef was on it, I could see that look in his eyes. He was mad for it, he was prepared to go all the way, Colonel Kurtz Apocalypse now all the way. He whispers in my ear "YOU'RE MINE BITCH" and smashes a pint glass over my head.

Yes, I was, I was my sous chefs bitch, he was crowned king of Kong of the piss heads. I had passed out in the wrong bed in the wrong hotel with some dragon from Sweden.

Leaving Mousse

Ingredients

Flour, French corn flakes, eggs, out of date double cream, coco pops, dish water, D2 D10 (sanitiser and degreaser), the urine from three chefs, cocoa powder, food colouring optional, glitter and sprinkles from the creche.

Method

Mix all ingredients together in a container that you will never use in the kitchen again, store in the bin area for 2–3 days.

Brendan the restaurant manager had decided he was going to cut the season short and return to England. So, after his last service I invited him to my office for a glass of champagne. "Great service again chef" cheers my man, we chatted for about 15 minutes about the politics of the hotel.

Outside my office two chefs were preparing for his exit, either side of the door with a bucket each of leaving mousse. All I can say sausage its lucky you didn't have long hair Brendan. Well, it has been nice working with you mate hope to see you again soon. I bumped into Brendan several years later in Spinneys car park on the Al Washal road in Dubai. He introduced me to his wife and told me he was working at the Dusit Dubai hotel, the conversation was brief to say the least.

Take it easy mate, I swiftly closed the door to the office, two chefs caught him square on. He must have got a mouth full of the mousse because the look on his face was that of shear horror. Head to toe saturated, he was not amused. Brendan looked like a human chocolate, coco pop, cornflake cupcake with silver sprinkles with a warning sign, do not eat.

"There are certain truths, holy truths, that enlighten man about his past, present and future conditions, these truths most certainly exist".

Who is Auguste Knuckles?

Frankie Knuckles the godfather of house

Frankie Knuckles born in The Bronx, Knuckles and his friend Larry Levan began frequenting discos as teenagers during the 1970s. While studying textile design at the FIT, Knuckles and Levan began working as DJs, playing soul, disco, and R&B at two of the most important early discos. The Continental Baths and The Gallery.

In the late 1970s, Knuckles moved from New York City to Chicago, where his old friend, Robert Williams, was opening what became the nightclub called Warehouse. When the club opened in Chicago in 1977, he was invited to play on a regular basis, which enabled him to hone his skills and style. This style was a mixture of disco classics, unusual indie-label soul, the occasional rock track, European synth-disco and all manner of rarities, which would all eventually codify as "House Music". The style of music now known as house was named after a shortened version of the Warehouse.

Knuckles was so popular that the Warehouse, initially a members-only club for largely black gay men, began attracting straighter, whiter crowds, leading its owner, Robert Williams, to eschew membership. Knuckles continued DJing at the Warehouse until November 1982, when he started his own club in Chicago, The Power Plant.

Around 1983, Knuckles bought his first drum machine to enhance his mixes from Derrick May, a young DJ who regularly made the trip from Detroit to see Knuckles at the Warehouse and Ron Hardy at the Music Box, both in Chicago.

The combination of bare, insistent drum machine pulses and an overlay of cult disco classics defined the sound of early Chicago house music, a sound which many local producers began to mimic in the studios by 1985.

When his next club the Powerhouse closed in 1987, Knuckles moved to the UK for four months and DJ-ed at DELIRIUM!, a Thursday night party at Heaven (nightclub) in London. Chicago house artists were in high demand and having major success in the UK with this new genre of music.

Knuckles also had a stint in New York, where he continued to immerse himself in producing, remixing, and recording. 1988 saw the release of Pet Shop Boys' third album, Introspective, which featured Knuckles as a co-producer of the song "I Want a Dog".

In 1982, Knuckles was introduced to then-unknown Jamie Principle by mutual friend Jose "Louie" Gomez, who had recorded the original vocal-dub of "Your Love" to reel-to-reel tape. Louie Gomez met up with Frankie at the local record pool (I.R.S.) and gave him a tape copy of the track.

Knuckles played Gomez's unreleased dub mix for an entire year in his sets during which it became a crowd favourite. Knuckles later went into the studio to re-record the track with Principle, and in 1987 helped put Your Love and Baby Wants to Ride out on vinyl after these tunes had been regulars on his reel-to-reel player at the Warehouse for a year.

As house music was developing in Chicago, producer Chip E. took Knuckles under his tutelage and produced Knuckles' first recording, "You Can't Hide from Yourself". Then came more production work, including Jamie Principle's "Baby Wants to Ride", and later "Tears" with Robert Owens (of Fingers Inc.) and (Knuckles' protégé and future Def Mix associate) Satoshi Tomiie.

Knuckles made numerous popular Def Classic Mixes with John Poppo as sound engineer, Knuckles partnered with David Morales on Def Mix Productions. His debut album Beyond the Mix (1991), released on Virgin Records, contained what would be considered his seminal work, "The Whistle Song",] which was the first of four number ones on the US dance chart.

The Def Classic mix of Lisa Stansfield's "Change", released in the same year, also featured the whistle-like motif. Another track from the album, "Rain Falls", featured vocals from Lisa Michaelis. Eight thousand copies of the album had sold by 2004. Other key remixes from this time include his rework of the Electribe 101 anthem "Talking with Myself" and Alison Limerick's "Where Love Lives".

When Junior Vasquez took a sabbatical from The Sound Factory in Manhattan, Knuckles took over and launched a successful run as resident DJHe continued to work as a remixer through the 1990s and into the next decade, reworking tracks from Michael Jackson, Luther Vandross, Diana Ross, Eternal and Toni Braxton.

He released several new singles, including *"Keep on Movin"* and a reissue of an earlier hit, *Bac N Da Day* with Definity Records. In 1995, he released his second album titled Welcome to the Real World. By 2004, 13,000 copies had sold. Openly gay, Knuckles was inducted into the Chicago Gay and Lesbian Hall of Fame in 1996.

In 2004, Knuckles released a 13-track album of original materialhis first in over a decade titled A New Reality. In October 2004, "Your Love" appeared in the videogame Grand Theft Auto: San Andreas, playing on house music radio station, SF-UR.

In the mid-2000s, Knuckles developed Type II diabetes. He developed osteomyelitis after breaking his foot snowboarding, and had it amputated after declining to take time off for treatment. On 31 March 2014, he died in Chicago at the age of 59 due to the complications from his diabetes. **(Sourced Wikipedia)**

When Mental Health Said
Go Fuck Yourself

I'll always remember that day, that fucking day, the first day mental health said hello to me and introduced itself like a nuclear explosion. I was in Australia circa 2007 with my partner at the time. Her parents had given us their holiday home for the week. It was a 3hr drive north of Sydney. The holiday site was a small collection of exclusive chalets within a private gated area. The place was stunning, her parent's chalet was proper bling, spacious, well stocked, all the mod cons, "all the mod cons".

The first evening we settled in, BBQ drinks and shenanigans, slept in the following morning, late breakfast, large espresso, bacon and eggs then a walk into the local seaside resort no bigger than a small village. It was no stroll up the garden pathway and a gentle knock at the door when MH introduced himself to me, no no no.

It was violent like a bullet to the head, an axe to the face, a shovel up my ass, we both literally had walked out of a beautiful souvenir shop and BANG, the big bang went off, lemon juice and salt on the brain.

I had sheer anger, horror, murder running through my veins, I wanted to kill everyone in sight. I had visions of myself walking through that village killing everything and everyone, women children old folk anything that moved. I had guns, knives, machetes the whole fucking nuclear fallout playing out like some fucking horror movie while I'm walking hand in hand with the girl I loved at the time. "You ok babe" yeah, I'm fine babe.

Fine, how far from the fucking truth, what am I going to say? That I'm the grim reaper on speed, fine was a silk bath robe with me wearing fluffy slippers a G&T in one hand with other on the top of my partners head playing with her hair while she's kneeling between my legs playing the theme tune to the A-team.

This played out for the best part of 2 hours lemon juice in my eyes and nails in my brain, scotch bonnets lodged in the back of my throat. I was fucking drowning I didn't know what to do, what was going on, I was scared, frightened and it was the first time I felt the presence of the cold dark blanket, "suicide". Killing myself would have been the easy option that day, back to the villa, rusty box cuter across the wrists and throat, job done.

I'd just been mined raped, and it didn't feel good the only way I was going to suppress this is with booze and loads of booze until I passed the fuck out. Welcome home UK, dealer drugs booze and I hide away for three days. Hello, it's me again, Christmas 2009 I'm driving to the switch to be with my cousins, and it was the first time my wife is going to meet the fam.

Christmas day, its crisp and fresh outside blue skies picture perfect, as I walk into the kitchen pumped for our Christmas breakfast, I picture myself smashing my now wife's face into the sink and cutting her head off with a carving knife. I've sliced both her breast off and have volleyed her head through the window.

Yet again out of the fucking blue "BOOM" scrambled brain and smoked salmon for breakfast. I'm sat at the table and I'm hacking at my cousin's throat with a blunt dinner knife, hacking at it like some ravaged cannibal, writing merry crimbo on the table with her warm blood. I've cooked the little one in the microwave and hanged everyone else from the Christmas tree, peeled flesh covered in marmite and sprinkles, on with dinner preparation.

Please God this can't be happening Christmas day, my head is screaming from the Inside, black and grey dark shadows shroud my racing thoughts. why was it I had these thoughts, thoughts about hurting my loved ones hurting the ones I love, I was well and truly messed up, messed up is putting it lightly considering the rage.

It being Christmas the only way to deal with this was to drink, and drink I did, I always cook Christmas day so soon as breakfast was over, I put on my chefs' jacket on and began prep. I had three large glasses of wine positioned around the kitchen in case I forgot where I had put one plus a can of beer open in the fridge plus standard hourly triple vodka shots. If I was standing when dinner had finished, I would be upstairs chopping out a fat line of cocaine, this would just accelerate everything and make the mood inside my head triple worse, more booze, more hard booze.

After years of self-inflicted abuse, I could handle my booze and drugs, LOL, sorry hold on, handle my booze and drugs, the booze and drugs were handling me. When I came down from a session the thoughts were on another level. I'd have thoughts and visions of walking to the local train station in the village literally a 5-minute walk from our house and stepping in front of the first train to Paddington.

Flying was a nightmare, I believed I had Goliath strength and could take down anyone, even a plane full of passages. I would casually stroll to the door look around, pretend to stretch and yawn then a mad scramble to open it. Fucking chairs people trolley dolly's been sucked out. Then I would snap out of it distracted or something and order two small plastic bottles of wine.

I had mutilated my wife a hundred different ways slaughtered all my neighbours in the most horrific ways. Burnt my friends alive suffocated my daughter and raped and murdered countless victims. I decapitated more people than I can remember, chopped up and buried countless people. The more aggressive the thoughts the more drugs and alcohol I consumed the more I consumed the stronger the come downs the stronger desire to kill myself.

I was not only addicted to drugs and alcohol I was also addicted to sex, porn, strip clubs the whole fucking buffet I wanted it all and I took it all. Every fucking piece of cake, I smashed the lot, to this day I cringe, I cringe at some of things I did and some of the situations I put myself in.

To this day I haven't had the stomach to tell anyone, my wife, family members, closest friends let alone psychologists or any of the doctors I have recently had assessments with regarding the actual thoughts I was having for fear of being sectioned or a risk, so please forgive me if what you are reading has bought tears to your eyes, I'm sorry but these visions were the awake version of my nightmare's.

"BUT" and this is no ordinary, "BUT" All my thoughts thank God and heaven on earth and all above, my thoughts and everything I was thinking were passive. The slightest thought of thinking I was in a mental state to have committed any such act of horror towards anyone, my life would have been the price, I would easily have taken it.

What I do remember most about the times I was sat with my physiologist or doctor during one of the many visits to A&E for overdosing, by the way there is a banging rave tune from the early 90s called overdose. It goes something like this "Mr Smith your son is dead, how did he die, he died of an overdose, oooooverdose" and then the most insane break beat.

Apologies, totally went off-piste there again, let's try and remain focused as I would like to finish this project. Yes, my childhood would always come up, pieces of the puzzle the pattern somehow somewhere the subject would always come up.

I remember once I said to Doris at a family birthday, I think it was hers that I had problems with cocaine, she looked at me and said sorry son that was never my thing and walked off. Not one solitary member of that family ever, not once even a phone call, a text, nothing with regards to warm words of support. When I did bring it up all those years back about how I was suffering they ignored it and didn't want to know, changed the subject, even Johnny didn't want to know.

All they wanted from me was to cling to me like leeches, like blood sucking swamp leeches, so that maybe I would become one of them. A father with too many kids to mention, a parent that would do nothing and watch their flesh and blood beaten by other people. That somehow, I would continue the abuse that had been a part of their heritage for decades before me, well it didn't turn out that, thank God.

Fat Duck

I doubt many chefs can say they have worked three Michelin stars, not only 3* but gained valuable experience within a restaurant awarded the best restaurant in the world 2005. I have got the upmost respect for this establishment. So why the Fat Duck by Heston Blumenthal. I needed to test myself, push myself, to see after all my worldly shenanigans and globetrotting if I could I mix it up, and cook with the elite. The astronauts of the industry.

There have only been a few places whereby I've switched on, tuned in, put all the chaos and tomfoolery on the back burner to concentrate all my energy during my time on the pans with the best chefs on the planet. No nonsense, head down, ears pinned, eyes peeled 24/7.

2008 I applied on the fat duck website for a one month stagier, a straightforward process If you can work a laptop. I knew there would probably be hundreds of chefs all applying for a stagier at such a prestigious restaurant. I was already employed as executive chef at a huge hotel just outside London. It took me some time to persuade my GM if I could take time out if my application were successful.

We agreed that if I got the placement, I would have to be in the office one day per week to make sure the kitchen was in good shape and that my head chefs were on top of the culinary department.

2nd quarter 2009 I received an email from the human resource department at the fat duck with the good news, I was offered a one-month placement. I just had to choose a start date in their schedule which suited both parties, and it was game on. My hotel just outside London was in good shape, I had a strong brigade which would make one month less stressful for me. Managing four kitchens within a 900+ room hotel with two conference centres, a team of 45 chefs and kitchen porters. I didn't want to be micromanage my boys, time for them to step up and earn their stripes.

First day at the fat duck was like the first day I walked into my first work experience during college, super nervous. I had my entire knife set ready for action. I buzz the door to the prep kitchen; I'm greeted by a young chef with a deep American accent. "Morning chef, you must be Auguste Knuckles" yes chef that's me. "Huge fucking suitcase chef, this morning and every morning you will just need a paring knife, cooks' knife, peeler and steal".

Yes chef, "oh and stop with the chef thing my names Gavin". "I'm not the executive chef here my friend, you are". I dump my knife set in the car and headed back to the prep kitchen. "Ok chef, you're with me this week, crazy prep, day in day out".

"Upstairs is the pastry kitchen and experimental lab, where chef Heston creates his magic". "Right let's crack on", the prep list was something I have never seen before. The entire white board was filled with items that needed preparing. The prep list didn't change until chef Heston had created a new dish or wanted to tweak an existing one.

"First job, prep for snail porridge". Brunoise small dice, 100gms shallots and 50gms garlic. The prep kitchen was a small workspace. Sinks and water baths situated at the back, several work benches and several chefs. Talk about mise en place on a surgical level.

Everything had to be precise, weighed and prepared to perfection. No room for era, you fucked up, you started again. Time was precious, you fucked up twice, or thought that you were bigger than the establishment, regardless of your experience, you were out. I got it and I loved it. The discipline was that of the military, the respect the energy was overwhelming.

Lunch service begins at 12:30pm on the dot. Everything on the prep list had to be ready and ferried across to the finishing kitchen before all chefs sat down for lunch in the garden, located at the rear of the restaurant. Soon as staff lunch was done, prep chefs would return to the prep kitchen to prep for evening service. The prep kitchen was the hub, it prepared everything for the finishing kitchen, the restaurant, the fat duck.

That evening I was invited by the head chef to the finishing kitchen. The main restaurant where I would be a spectator and watch the entire service from the passé. What an honour, service was astronomical, every course that went out an extra dish was prepared and served to me with wine pairing for that dish.

My first evening I was given the ultimate fat duck experience. Willy Wonka, Alice in wonderland, the Matrix all smashed into an experience I still talk about to this day with friends. Its why I'm smiling from ear to ear while I write about this wonderful chapter.

The job of a stagier, is a prep chef, there is no pay you are paid in other ways. Experiencing life in a three Michelin starred kitchen which is priceless. But at the end of the day what could I take back and implement into my own kitchen, nothing. There isn't much apart from presentation techniques and being introduced to new suppliers. Besides one months it was for me and me alone. This was me experiencing a world I had loved since my days at college. long before I had become an executive chef with a crippling addiction.

Over the weeks myself and Gavin became good mates, he knew I could cut it when it came to prep. So, besides the mundane boring stuff we did during the day, in the evening he cut me lose. I started to prepare key items, butchery, fish prep, preparing meat and poultry for the water baths, garnishes and marinades. I was truly in my element, I belonged to this world. I did what was asked, I was humble, respectful to the chefs, internships and placements.

Where did it all go wrong, was I ever a straight arrow. I used to dream about this style of cooking as a teenager in Bristol. Where did my wheels fall off, did I have wheels in the first place? No time for juvenile behaviour in such an esteemed establishment. Although during prep time and getting ready for service funky beats echoed through the sections. Service, heads down for open heart surgery. Being a chef's chef, I could gather by the look in a few chefs' eyes they were struggling with similar issues to that of mine.

I spent my stagier mixing it up, working all sections in the restaurant and prep kitchen. Managing a large business, corporate leisure hotel seemed a million miles away. I met Heston a couple of times during my stagier. Hands down for me he is the best chef I have ever had the privilege of meeting and working for in a sort of way. Personally, I rate Heston within my three top chefs globally to this day.

My final shift at the fat duck I bought the chefs a case of beer. I was asked by the head chef if I was interested in coming on full time as a chef de partie, totally made up. Besides the point, on the day of my daughter's birthday I had to refuse. My salary at the hotel was 60K plus bonus and a few garnishes. Salary for a chef de partie working three stars back then 16k plus service charge. If it had been an offer earlier in my career, I would have bitten the chefs arm off.

After one months off the gear, hard booze and smelling like garlic and onions every other day, I got straight back into my routine. The average working chef in today's culinary world, back on the battle bus.

"I never knew I was addicted, until I tried to stop"

Tasty Pussy

I asked one of my Kenyan chefs the other day if he ate pussy, I only asked because I knew his girlfriend had flown over from Kenya for the weekend to visit. Mostly to get her rocks off and to see how here honey monster was fairing in the ever-evolving sand pit slash Lego city of Dubai.

So, I asked him a question, do you eat pussy chef, "what, eat pussy, fuck no chef". You don't eat pussy man? what is up with you, I take it you have never eaten an oyster let alone savoured the flavour of a sea urchin or seared fois gras. "An oyster chef", no, a fucking Klondike, an oyster man, "eh, no chef".

Listen to me big fella, there is three things in life which are standard, and I mean standard, fine wine, great food, and a woman's holy place. "But it's not clean, chef", so you're telling me, I and all your fellow chefs including your good self that we were spawned from dirty pussies, "no chef".

A few of the guys were having a chuckle, "pussy, you don't eat pussy, man I'm sure Mary Magdalena had her pussy chomped by Joseph back in the days", chuckles Ronnie. Aye I reckon that rapper what's his name, 50 Pence he must eat pussy right. Jim frowned, turned his back, head slumped down and continued his mis en place.

Just for the record, myself and Jim are still in contact to this day, he knew it was kitchen banter. He tells me he pulls the same shit today with his own commis chefs.

Jim came into work the next day with a grin on his face from ear-to-ear walking on air "aye chef", what? "I went down on my girlfriend's pussy last night, the holy place". Did she let you, did she like it? "Yes chef", what did it taste like "tasted sweet chef, really fucking sweet, better than your banoffee cheesecake". "Even better than my triple chocolate brownie", easy tiger I don't want to know about your triple chocolate Kenyan brownie thank you.

You should try everything at least once in life I replied. If you haven't eaten pussy yet you're missing out on the finer things in life, "yes chef". Hey, remember even lesbians eat pussy, vegetarians, vegans too, "oui chef". "What about pescatarian chefs", what do you mean what about pescatarian? "Do they eat pussy". Pescatarians don't know what side of the fence there sitting on. They don't eat meat but eat fish, that's like saying you're a devout Muslim but you eat pork. "Yeah, I get what you're saying chef, I suppose a pescatarian is the same as saying you're a lesbian, but you still suck dick" I suppose so, I never looked at it like that before.

I myself Jim, I'm a flexitarian, "What the fuck is a flexitarian chef"? someone who has a flexible diet. One week I'm a vegetarian, the other I'm a full-blown vampire, the following week a vegan. Hey, but Jim don't tell anyone I'm a flexitarian I've got enough shit on my plate as it is.

I was in no position to give Jim a warning when I caught Jim going down on a Josephine a fine-looking waitress a few months later in the dry store after service. I just closed the door and chuckled to myself, stay out of the dry store chefs big Jim is doing a stock take.

Beaujolais Nouveau

After storming out of Bristol in what can only be summed up as a psychotic mental emotional and destructive rage, I moved in with my cousin. I had moved to Ipswich a place I had always called my second home. Within no time I had a dozen interviews lined up for jobs in town. The first being a pasta bar. Word on the street the food was authentic Italian, ran by an Italian who treated his staff well. I arrive at my interview early; I enter the restaurant to the sound of the God Father theme tune playing in the background.

Sat at the back of the restaurant was Alex the boss, "Come sit with me please", he ushers me forward with two fingers like Don Corleone. I park myself opposite the boss who is nursing a mug of something stronger than coffee, because I can hear the ice cubes clanking around. I notice two chefs, two waiters peering through the passe pulling faces at me. Giving me the bird pointing to Alex giving him the wanker sign.

I try to focus on the boss, who isn't Italian by the way, Alex was Algerian. "So, tell me where you have worked"? I've just moved from Bristol; I was working within a 4* hotel. Chef de partie, working hot section and pastry. Before that, the British Army, "can you cook Italian food"? I glance across to the passe, the boys are nodding their heads with a praying motion. Yes, I can cook Italian food, "when can you start"? tomorrow, "Bellissima, £300 a week cash in hand, do you have whites"? yes, "fantastico".

All the boys come out into the restaurant and welcome me to the family. There was Mario head chef, Enrico kitchen porter and starter chef. Rambo, Massimo front of house. Jenny, Alex's wife did the books and walked the restaurant dog. Jenny liked to finish everyone's name with an O, so I became Augusto. I had a quick tour of the kitchen which was the size of my bedsit and no bigger than a 12 by 12 army cooks tent. It was a shit hole, fifteen steps back to what I had just come from. It was doable, plus I didn't want the headache of a ball breaking corporate business set up.

The next day I arrive at 9am to the same scenario as the day before, God Father theme tune with Alex sat in the same place nursing his mug of 45% coffee. Morning boss, "call me Alex please", yes Alex. Mario was already in the kitchen, change, coffee, what to do chef. "Call me Mario please, we need to cook allada pasta for today, makeada sauces, stuff the mushrooms, okeydokey mate"? okeydokey. "I will makeada lasagna, the cannelloni and smokeada fags, you Italiano speak no"? no, "no problemo I teach my mate no speakada Italiano".

Mario was from Naples, big drug dealer in his day, we got on like a bolognaise on spaghetti. It's interesting how life plays out, almost every Italian chef I have had the pleasure of working with these past decades, who have relocated to the UK were either dealers or drug runners. When you are into the same boat you break the ice quickly, language is just a learning curve. Massimo the long-haired waiter loved himself, most of all he loved his hair like Donovan the kitchen porter. He was also from Naples. Massimo also had the biggest nose I have ever seen on a human face, he looked like a rhino.

Enrico like the boss Alex was also from Algeria, all Enrico did was smoke fags and laugh, laugh all day. He would laugh at anything and everything, got run over by a bus, fits of laughter, head fell off, house burnt down, pissed himself. Fucked over by a gang of starving hyenas he fell off his chair in fits of laughter. For me, his laughter and humour kind of obscured the shit working conditions I had decided to work in.

First shift I cooked several types of pasta before you could say tiramisu, stuffed all the mushrooms, finished the cannelloni, lasagne and even helped Mario with the sauces. Compared to what I was doing in Bristol the mise en place for service was like drinking frosty pints of beer and dabbing from a wrap of wizz.

Before my first lunch service Mario showed me around. Above the restaurant were three apartments, dry store and wine loft, not wine cellar. He also showed me the back alley to the Market Bar and kitchen. A funky brasserie where all the faces around town would hang out during the week. My first day at the pasta bar, I never thought for the life of me that one day I was going to run the market bar and kitchen and put it on the dining scene map in town.

Friday night came to quick, the Pasta bar soon got going, full to the rafters. I and Mario throwing shit through the passé all night, authentic Italian food, bullshit. This was slapstick cuisine cooked by jail breakers from Italy. My journey and love for Italian food would begin several years later as a chef on the island of Sardinia for several months during the summer.

Everything basically went into the juke box (microwave) finished in sauté pans or under the grill. Enrico was busy doing starters and desserts on the pot wash draining board next to the bins. Prawn cocktail, salad caprese, minestrone soup, banoffee pie, pavlova, tiramisu, fruit salad, it all came from the pot wash.

The kitchen porter who came in on the weekends to wash up, had a tattoo of his face on his arm with a dick for a nose. Under the tattoo was tattooed, FUCKNOSE. If you wanted cigarettes from the cigarette machine during the weekend, he was the man to go to, fuck nose. Fuck knows where he got the key for the cigarette machine, "pack of Marley reds mate", yes please, "no worries man". Every now and then he would give you some money from the machine. Enough for a few pints after work. The restaurant was good fellas, in through the front door and out through the back door.

If Mario needed the toilet during service, he would piss next to the chest freezer into an empty chopped tomato tin. Yeah, whatever some might say, no seriously, this place had no filter, fucking pirates of the Caribbean, pirates of the pasta bar. Something I never understood, during split shifts Jenny would leave the takings in the till. I didn't think it strange when Mario handed me £50 that Friday during my first week. "That's a bonus mate", Fuck fifteen steps backwards I had to make a quick move. I was young, unpredictable with a few loose rivets, but this was dogshit on the pans.

"Oi, who's there, hello, anybody there, hey chef". I walk out the kitchen through the back door to find this huge black guy standing there. Fucking huge, a huge handsome black man with a bold cockney accent. "How are you doing mate, who are you"? I was going to ask the same thing.

My name is Auguste Knuckles I'm the new chef, "wicked fella, the new chef, wicked grub mate I was in here last week with me misses, fancy a line"? is a pig's pussy pork? "what, pigs' pussy pork, oh yeah". You just mentioned the food was wicked, was that a serious comment. "It was ok but not top of the pops if you know what I mean". Yeah, I know what you mean.

This fella pulls out from his jacket pocket a bag of cocaine the size of cue ball, sticks the corner of his credit card in, scopes out a fat one and holds it to my nostril. "You got alight chef", yeah, I have as it happens, here you go, "cheers", what is your name by the way my man? "Lenny, I'm Lenny, pop by the Market bar for a drink later if you fancy one". Yeah sure, cheers and off he strolls back down the alley. Back to the Italian garage to chuck more slapstick shit across the passé with Mario, "a one, a two a three, service over you fuckers" shouts Mario.

With service over it's a quick clean down with a soapy sponge of washing up liquid. Kitchen, pot wash and starters cleaned with a dirty mop and cold bucket of water. Quick squaddie bath, arm pits and face, I pop into the market bar to make new friends. Relocating from Bristol and having lived in Germany, being part of the scene, I always dressed sharp.

I enter the market bar; I'm meet with a wave from Lenny. "Grab a beer put it on my tab, come join us". "This is Geoff and George they own the bar and need a chef for their new brasserie upstairs, you interested, before you answer, that cunt next door will rip you off, plus he's a piss head".

"The boys are cool but he's a dick, thinks he's Italian the Moroccan, Algerian, Libyan fucker". "You interested asks Geoff, yes or no"? George requests I give him a quick overview of my career. Simple request with a brief answer as I haven't done much, I respond with enthusiasm.

I take a quick look around the bar, full of beautiful people, smiley happy faces. Young trendsetters hanging out, drinking, chatting, funky beats being played on the Bose system in the background. The bar girls obviously selected for the super model looks. "So, what's your answer chef", Yes 100%. The following day I handed in my notice after working a few weeks at the Italian, Algerian, Libyan, Mexican pasta bar and started at the market bar and kitchen Monday morning.

Head chef: Auguste Knuckles "me"

Addicted to drugs, but does not do smack or crack, has a huge dependency for sex with a multitude of partners. Maintains no control whatsoever when it comes to drink. Doesn't have got a clue that CPTSD is simmering within the depths of his chef's locker. Neither does he know he has OCD and suffering with childhood trauma. The average working chef in the 90s.

Assistant chef: Mr Butts

Well educated within Cambridge, degree in cosmic physics. Also has a dependency for everything I have a dependency for. A naturally gifted chef who talks like a university lecturer who should be an astronaut.

Dish pig, porcelain technician, pot wash—Fruit machine Bob

Like me dragged up on a council estate within a dysfunctional family. Addicted to fruit machines and poor man's cocaine, speed. Doesn't say much, dresses like a football casual, 1980s sports gear and loves getting laid with middle aged single mothers with several kids.

Bar Manager—Bogdan the Muslim

Came across the channel on a very suspicious looking boat, claims he's a retired matador but also makes out he's a devote Muslim. Holds a Mexican passport, enjoys a bacon sandwich and a pint of Guinness for breakfast before hitting the Johnny Walker. Lifelong ambition, porn star.

Bar Replicas (babe runners)

Belinda: ran away from her family up north, parents, God squad lunatics. Not very well educated, white but thinks she is black, fit as a butcher's dog who could stop a man's heart just by looking at them. More baggage than Luton airport.

Mercedes: traveller form south Africa, thinks apartheid was a hoax and that Nelson Mandela was a long-distance runner. This one should be a supermodel earning big fromage in Paris.

Rosie pair: ex stripper, three mixed raced kids, Jamaican, Chinese and Russian. Loves ecstasy, pit bull dogs, designer clothes and climbing trees.

Owners

Jeff and George: Two extremely good-looking bastards.

Bruce: Private investor and music mogul to one incredibly famous 80s pop star, he also knocks out premier league Bolivian.

Lenny: Hardman, Pablo Escobar type, more handsome than Idris Elba, wicked sense of humour. I myself witnessed him almost pull the legs from a man, a piss head causing trouble in the bar.

Brunch

Beaujolais Nouveau day, the one day that stands out the most during my stint at the market bar and kitchen. It's marked in France on the third Thursday in November with fireworks, music and festivals. Under French law, the wine is released at 00.01 am, just weeks after the wine's grapes have been harvested. Parties are held throughout the country and further afield to celebrate the first wine of the season.

Many years ago, a race would be held to see which person or persons, team or establishment would be first to bring Beaujolais Nouveau back to British shores. Anyway, enough of the boring shit and back to the day in hand. The morning of the breakfast up super early. 5am, shit, showered, super large coffee out the door. Butchers, fish mongers, deli, bakers, fruit and vegetables. Quick trip to Sainsbury's and I'm in the kitchen at 7am.

I'm greeted by 30 cases of Beaujolais Nouveau plus Jeff and George well into their 3rd bottle of grapes. "Morning chef" morning chaps. "Chef, breakfast ready for 10am please", I'm all over it boss.

Thirty guests, plus staff, now it's none of my business what people get up to when they finish work, but most of the staff had been on it "the bugle" for two days straight. The bar staff had not even slept. Wayno-19 was on the fruit machine in the pig and trotter which opens at 7am speeding his chops off on yellow whizz. My assistant Butts had not been seen since the day before his day off which was the day before yesterday.

I crack on with prep, 9am Jeff pops in and gives me and FYI, "breakfast put back until mid-day chef", no worries boss. Miraculously at 10am on the nose the bar staff, Wayno-19 and my assistant Butts stumble through the bar door. I know this because I heard the bar door fall off its hinges from the kitchen.

Elsmasheo, according to local sources they had all been in the local casino polishing off copious amounts of quiver. Playing poker and talking several different languages starting the day before the day, which was the day before yesterday. I cannot complain about going missing during those crazy days. I would go missing for days, 3 to 4 days, disappeared somewhere over planet earth. Its wasn't for the fact I was missing I just didn't want to be found.

The day hadn't even started their shift, but it was a sign of how it was going to end. I sorted my assistant a cheeky little tickle to get him semi straight then cracked on with more prep. I wanted to be ready latest thirty minutes before service so I could mingle with the bandits. Mingle means lines of chop, "hey chef how's tricks, fancy a cheeky one, help yourself to some of that".

Within half an hour I would have scooped 3g's for the evenings shenanigans and made out I was pinged to the eyeballs. Cheeky I know, but that is how it was in the 90s. You gave someone a bag of chop, guaranteed they would scoop a nose for later.

Breakfast starter, Scottish oaked smoked maple cured salmon with free range poached eggs, sourdough bread and pea shoots. We had already started on our first bottle me and Mr Butts an hour before service. Starters served, five minutes later I head upstairs welcomed by a huge around of applause. "Fucking super stuff what's next cookie".

Next course, full English, livers, kidneys, flat mushrooms, shouting and screaming erupts in the small function space "fuck yeah, a fucking full English". Hands in the air I shout over the boisterous diners, you know the deal fellas. "Poor the man a drink"

Within 15 minutes myself and Butts had served sauteed calves' liver and kidneys, grilled portabella mushrooms, beef tomato with rock salt and fresh thyme. Baked goats cheese crostini just to mix it up, pork sausages from my local butcher and eggs benedict. Once we had sent the 2nd course, we popped out back for a well-deserved line of coke, a Marley red and a bottle of vino knocked back quick time.

We could hear the boys raving on upstairs, I look at Butts and say, one day sausage this morning will be talked about for years to come. It will go down in Ipswich town history. Back to the kitchen for a quick tidy down, then we join the mayhem upstairs.

"Hey cookie come and join us" shouts Roland from across the room, "where did you learn to cook like this", In the army, "what a fucking diamond, in the army aye, I thought they were all slop jockeys". "Everyone a toast please to our two diamond chefs, Auguste and Butts".

Butts gives me the node, "back downstairs chef", clean down, plate up the colossal cheese course with dried fruit, artisan breads, several chutneys and leave service to the girls. It was time to party, pigeon wash in the prep sink, lynx body spray, cool water perfume, its back upstairs for national lampoons vacation.

"Gentlemen, a huge thank you to Auguste and his partner in crime Butts for a wonderful morning. Thank you, girls, the same for a great service, we have shit loads of wine to consume so let's get fucked". Another round of applause then out comes the cocaine. Blocks, bags, wraps, sniffers, vials all out on the tables, "get stuck in" is the order of the day.

Like many functions this party did not end well. Well, it did, we all had an amazing day, but when you lock the doors to the swankiest brasserie in town. Fill it with the most hardcore personalities combined with staff members who have no filter. A kick ass DJ with more cocaine than a Columbian village, the brasserie did not stand a chance.

While all this carnage was going on inside, Saturday shoppers were walking past the huge steamed up windows. All they could hear from the street was the thud of bass from the music system and a small football crowd going off inside.

Double, triple carnage ensued, diners in the kitchen using my work top as a place of worship raking out fat juicy lines. An orgy was going off in the disabled toilet. Anarchists in the alley smoking mad crazy skunk and crack that had been washed in my kitchen. The bar had transformed into the opening scene of saving private Ryan carnival and it wasn't even 5pm in the afternoon.

All the grown-ups departed around 8pm leaving 15 boxes of Beaujolais Nouveau with the team and manager Bogdan the bonkers. Fear and loathing in Las Vegas, going into work the following morning was not pleasant. The bar had been flooded from a broken toilet. Apparently, it was I who had dropped a bottle of vino down the toilet. The toilet just erupted. My kitchen resembled a garden shed, the upstairs function space and the bar was a write off.

After a year of making a name for myself and the Bar I was let go the following morning with half the staff, after a failed attempt to clean the place up and botched repair of the toilet. Shortly thereafter the market bar and kitchen closed its doors. I moved on as best I could, working numerous dead-end jobs.

The café which is there today has been running successfully for the past fifteen years.

"Addiction: Being hooked or in love with a substance you know is harmful and can cause great grief Is like being on a merry go round until you fall off dead"

Football Hooligans

"Good afternoon, this is the Ipswich manor hotel, how can I be of assistance", can you put me through to the kitchen please, "certainly sir, may I ask who's calling"? Chef Auguste. "Hello chef, I didn't recognise your voice, how's things with you", good thanks. Can you put me through to the kitchen please, "certainly, here we go, putting you through now, have a pleasant evening".

"Hello, it's Donald the head chef speaking", Chef it's Auguste. I cannot come into work tonight. "Why an earth not, your shift starts in one hour", yeah, I know chef, I'm so sorry. "What's up", I've been arrested chef, "arrested, what an earth for"? It's Ipswich at home to Norwich, it's kicking off all over town. I got jumped by some away fans the next thing I know I'm in the police station with a bunch of hooligans. This is my only phone call, so I thought I would let you know chef.

"You stupid fucking bastard, I've got functions coming out my arsehole tonight, now I'm one chef down, stupid fucking twat". "Listen I'll sort the shift out; you just get yourself out of there quick sharpish and call me if anything changes". I'm sorry chef, speak soon.

The line of coke on the toilet seat in the glass house was as fat as a butcher's finger. My best mate Doug was stood next to me laughing his bollocks off. "You cocky fucking cunt, did he fall for it" Yeah, he did. "Chop, chop then, get down on that beast". Quiver at its best, Bolivian flake, with a new £20 note I get to work. The crystals hit my brain like a speeding car hitting a sorry ass hedgehog. There is no going back, it's going to be a two-day bender maybe three.

I have already explained, what happened to my head after my time in Bristol, it changed my mentality completely. During the 90s I did not care; I did not wish or want for anything. I didn't need anything, I was just living, living in my own complex world. Trapped in a descending spiral of anger and confusion. I didn't think about the future, I didn't have the brain capacity to think that far ahead back then.

The legend, Mr Conte

The bus journey from home to the restaurant was a good forty-five minutes if I caught the connecting bus from the depot. If I didn't, I was screwed, I had to walk for two hours. Believe me when I say, I missed that connecting bus more than once. The Jockey Club was a funky, renowned establishment that catered to the in-crowd on the outskirts of town. Winter of 1987, it was going to be my second and final work experience from college.

I had the basic skills in my locker: bread making, classic cuts of vegetables, butchery of all the basic meats and filleting fish. I knew the basic sauces and their derivatives, Françaises, cake making and pastry. It was time to jump back in and experience the world of hospitality again. I just hope broccoli isn't my first chore of the day.

Up, washed, porridge, college-issued chefs' whites, unlike the endless selection we have today, once you washed your whites, they would shrink. If they had creases, they were fucked; a steam roller couldn't get them out. They were like wearing Rhino skin, blood red nipples ouch.

I had my chefs' knives, again, college issued, wrapped in a tea towel-type binder made of the same material your jacket was made from. There were inserts for peelers, Parisienne cutters, a huge chef's knife, a filleting knife, and a boning knife.

I had a serrated knife for carving up work benches and bread, a carving knife and a steal which was as much use as a blunt spoon once you had chopped the tops of your fingers clean off. But they were free, and they were my tools.

I had the *Repertoire De Cuisine*, you had to buy it out your own pocket, it cost peanuts compared to what it is worth today; it's a collector's item. I still have mine, under lock and key mind you, stuck together with masking tape and covered in every sauce I made during my college years. Any chef worth their cheddar today must have one lying around somewhere.

I arrived twenty minutes early, hopefully a good sign for whoever was going to show me the ropes for the next two weeks. Good morning, my name is Augustus.

"Go fuck yourself, only joking, I know who you are", I'm here for my two weeks' placement.

"Not another one", the receptionist mutters under her breath. "Sit over there, I'll call the kitchen, let them know you're here". Another what, I pondered, a cheese grating wanker?

There was a certain smell about the place, like a damp storage cupboard. There was carpet everywhere, on the walls, ceilings, downstairs and up the stairs leading to what I guessed were guestrooms.

"Are you Auguste?" Yes, that is me.

"We've been expecting you. You're late". She must have heard my insides fall out my arse. First day at work and I'm late. "Jesus! Only messing with you, your early, silly twat, come on, I'll show you where to get changed".

I followed the female chef upstairs and through a maze of twisted low-ceiling corridors. "Here we go, a toilet". I could have gotten changed outside in the rain for what it was worth. "Get changed and come down to the kitchen". Yes chef, oui chef.

"Mr Conte is off this morning, he will be in this evening, so it's me and you, chicken, we have a party tonight for 120". Who's Mr Conte? "He's the head chef and co-owner, okay, hot section, larder which doubles up for desserts, cold room, and out back, across the car park, dry stores".

"Your first job is preparing chickens, follow me".

I grasped my blunt set of knives and follow the chef down a flight of stairs into a room that appeared to be a torture chamber. Hooks hung from the ceiling. There was one flickering light bulb minus the cover, a wooden butcher's block covered in salt, a leaking sink, and stacks of crates full of chickens.

It was fucking freezing, Baltic. Oh, I forgot the two kitchen porters locked in a bamboo cage in the corner. Talk about hell's kitchen, this was it.

"Here we go, butchery section". Butchery? What section? You kidding me. "You know how to prepare a chicken for sauté, don't you?" Yes chef. "Cool beans, give me a shout if you need anything, I'll be in a nice warm kitchen doing shit for tonight". A duffle coat and some gloves maybe.

"Ha, ha. Your funny, chop, chop".

I was down there for what seemed like eternity, hacking and chopping at these poor dead creatures. But it wasn't with the lack of knowing where to chop, where to slice, and what parts to hack off. I knew these fellas inside out—poultry half, breast quarter, leg quarter, leg, drumstick, thigh, wing, flat wing tip. The carcasses were used for stock.

Halfway through the stack of crates, I started playing around, cutting up chickens with my eyes closed, popping out the thigh bone from the under-carcasses with a snap of my wrist. It wasn't so bad after all.

All the time I was down there, my mind was free of all issues, childhood, girlfriends. I hadn't thought about anything, not a single thing but my sixty new friends who hadn't been slaughtered in vain. They were going to be something special, coq au vin, for tonight's function.

When I went to take a piss, I had to sit down because my dick had shrivelled inwards due to the extreme cold. My hands were blue, my feet, blocks of ice and my eyebrows iced over. "You all right down there, chicken, how are you doing for time"? I'm fine thanks, almost done, and it wasn't even lunchtime.

Split shifts were all the go back in those days. You were lucky if you got out. I spent my first split shift sitting in the toilet cubical, ironically eating chicken and chips cooked by my new nemesis. When I had finished, I just sat there wondering if I could get away with a quick wank.

4pm, its back in the kitchen. I wandered down to the slaughterhouse to check on my birds. The man himself, Mr Conte, head chef and owner of the Jockey Club was already there, inspecting my work. He was fucking huge. I mean Andre the Giant huge. He didn't don the classic checked trousers, the jacket made of rhino skin. Oh no. He wore Ron Hill joggers, Fruit of the Loom T-shirt, Hi Tec trainers, and a butcher's apron.

"Is this your work"? Yes chef.

"Did that bitchy lesbian lend you a hand"? No chef.

"Did you cut yourself"? No chef.

"Where are you from"? The other side of town, chef.

"Do you suck dick"? No chef, follow me, oui chef.

He leads me back into the kitchen, his stage so to speak. I got a funny feeling that he had taken a liking to me, probably because I didn't suck dick. What if I did suck dick, would that be a problem?

Maybe he liked my chicken chopping skills. Mr Conte was a people person who enjoyed working with young chefs delving into his world. He wasn't a chef like you heard about back then, pan-throwing lunatics. He was the coolest person I had ever meet.

He liked to show off his skills, he was a showman. That night he made me sit and watch him dance around the kitchen for the entire service. This huge Italian chef singing, cooking, joking with the waiting staff without a care in the world, apart from his cooking, he cooked well, really fucking well.

The following weeks we prepared game, offal, food I saw at the market in town many years back while shopping for the household, fodder for the weekend. The freshest of produce turned into beautiful, wholesome, delightful dishes. We cooked sole Colbert, sole Veronique, whitebait with lemon wedges, tournedos Rossini, steak Dian, steak tartar. T-bones and rib eyes, spatchcocked chicken. I lost count of the pasta dishes he cooked with what sauces and types of pasta.

I made potted shrimps, salmon roulade with the dodgy-looking female chef. I indulged in all aspects of the kitchen, dressing the dessert trolley for evening service. Scooping out pineapples, filling the shells with the pulp and Chantilly cream, making all sort of gateau's garnished with different types of fruit and berries.

There was papaya, physalis, star fruit, the most astrological fruit of them all, mint sprigs, berries, toasted coconut and almonds. Chocolate shavings, vermicelli, and glace cherries. There was nothing fancy about Mr Chef Conte, nothing complicated. Everything he did was done with simplicity, in fresh, cooked classic, garnished well, and served to the salivating customers.

He was the greatest chef I learnt from. My time spent with Mr Chef Conte for those two weeks was a time I will never forget. A huge gentleman of a chef who took me under his wing and made sure my journey through his kitchen was one of elation and delight.

Addict

When the mind has decided to pull down the shutter, we turn into clowns. We are beats without purpose or reason. We are addicts, we are nothing, we are not even classed as human. We are empty souls waiting for the bullet.

Why Do I Have a Head
Like a Smashed Vase?

Addiction is a biopsychosocial disorder characterised by repeated use of drugs, or repetitive engagement in a behaviour. According to the brain disease model of addiction while several psychosocial factors contribute to the development and maintenance of addiction, a biological process that is induced by repeated exposure to an addictive stimulus is the core pathology that drives the development and maintenance of an addiction.

Addiction, other names, severe substance use disorder. Brain positron emission tomography images that compare brain metabolism in a healthy individual and an individual with a cocaine addiction. Specialty Psychiatry Addiction and dependence addiction. A biopsychosocial disorder characterised by persistent use of drugs (including alcohol) despite substantial harm and adverse consequences addictive drug—psychoactive substances that with repeated use are associated with significantly higher rates of substance use disorders.

In part to the drug's effect on brain reward system dependence—an adaptive state associated with a withdrawal syndrome upon cessation of repeated exposure to a stimulus (e.g., drug intake). Drug sensitisation or reverse tolerance—the escalating effect of a drug resulting from repeated administration at a given dose drug withdrawal—symptoms that occur upon cessation of repeated drug use physical dependence.

Dependence that involves persistent physical-somatic withdrawal symptoms (e.g., fatigue and delirium tremens) psychological dependence—dependence that involves emotional-motivational withdrawal symptoms (e.g., dysphoria and anhedonia) reinforcing stimuli—stimuli that increase the probability of repeating behaviours paired with them rewarding stimuli—stimuli that the brain interprets as intrinsically positive and desirable or as something to approach sensitisation.

An amplified response to a stimulus resulting from repeated exposure to substance use disorder a condition in which the use of substances leads to clinically and functionally significant impairment or distress tolerance—the diminishing effect of a drug resulting from repeated administration at a given dose.

Addiction is a disorder of the brain's reward system which arises through transcriptional and epigenetic mechanisms and develops over time from chronically high levels of exposure to an addictive stimulus (e.g., eating food, the use of cocaine, engagement in sexual activity. All that in a snapshot and the fact my child like frame was battered as a child. I could go on and bore you with long words, medical terms but I'm no doctor so let's get back to carnage that has been my life. (Sourced Wikipedia) yes, Wikipedia, I'm a chef not a doctor.

Scar Tissue

Fell out of a tree as a child, a branch snapped and tore the back of my baby leg open, utter fucking bollocks A branch didn't do that, the scar is clean as a whistle. It's a slash across the back of my leg. If I had fallen out a tree and gashed my leg open, why wasn't I taken to A&E and had it stitched. There are no stitch marks, it was a gaping wound left to heal on its own. A wound inflicted on me so horrific as a fucking child. Fucking scumbags. No hospitals records, nothing for years. The years I was in the care of vermin. The fucking vermin you abandoned me too, you are a fucking bitch cunt. All of you, cunts.

Half A Yardie

For as long as I can remember I had always wanted to work on a cruise ship. It had nothing to do with the amount of cruise ship disaster movies I had watched back in the 80s and 90s, including under siege with Steven round house kick Seagal. I wanted to see the world, so what better way to see it by working on a cruise ship.

Straight to the waves, Interview London Regents Street 2pm, I sat in the waiting room filling out forms watching a video about life on board ship. It was like a soft porno movie. "Auguste Knuckles", yes that's me, "good morning, welcome, thank you for coming in today, so sous chef onboard ship"? yes that's correct.

"Listen Auguste I'm going to jump straight in with the truth", ok. "Look if you pass your medical you've got the job". So, you're not going to ask me how many ways you can defrost a frozen chicken? "No, how many ways can you defrost a chicken, joke". "I will leave you to fill out all these forms, I can see you've bought your passport with you this morning, which is good". Medical exam passed, which is a miracle, considering.

Fast forward to take off, second time across the pond heading for Miami, Toronto then Vancouver where I get put up in a 5* hotel for the night.

The next morning after a hearty breakfast I'm in a taxi to my new home for the next nine months. Arriving at the port there she was moored, Mercury. A Colossal, gargantuan ship, I had never seen anything so big, you could have put two football stadiums in her. Dwarfed by the sheer size I started to feel a little anxious. What the fuck have I done, what I have got myself into? Was I ready for this, or was I just along for the cruise and to pretend I was really into a career onboard?

All I wanted out of this was the experience, been there done that, exotic, yeah mate, lucky bastard. I board the ship where I'm escorted down what can only be described as the longest corridor I have ever been down in my entire life. 30 minutes in the mess hall with the HR manager.

"Welcome on board MV Mercury, your home for however long your contract runs, I believe we have our new sous chef joining us today"? yes that would be me mam. "Welcome chef", I detect a slight bow. After a quick pep talk, I am escorted to my cabin. One up one down, I unpack, square myself away and it's off to the kitchen to start my induction.

Destination deck 5 I've finally arrived, but it's not without the help of everyone I pass along the way, trying not to make out I'm a cruise ship virgin. They should have just told me to jump overboard for what it was worth. The ship must be moving because I'm walking sideways off balance. I push the doors open to the belly off the beast. This was total bonkers, how on earth can man create something so big, then stick a bigger kitchen inside it. This was not a place for a chef with weak knees suffering with IBS.

I have just stepped into something I had no fucking clue about. The ability to chop like the chainsaw massacre, the shear bullshit I was going to conjure up is what was going to keep me afloat. How many ways to defrost a chicken, what the fuck was that all about.

The SOP board the length of Tony Hearts weekday kids' gallery. Pictures of the man's work laid out before me, Roux Sr. From canapés to starters, mains, meat, fish and poultry vegetarian dishes, desserts, soups, garnishes, every single recipe for every dish served in the main restaurant.

"Good evening chef, bon jour Auguste, our new sous chef has finally arrived", yes chef. Bon jour chef, "marvellous, you speak French", Oui chef.

"We will start you with a little observation this evening then you can learn all the prep sections on deck three. Simon bubby him tonight please", "yes chef". I knew it from the minute he opened his gob, he was a sausage jockey, not that it bothered me. You could tell Simon had his nose so far up the Executive chefs back pussy, when the chef sneezed Simon farted.

"Well, it's you and me tonight sunshine, Port and starboard identical finishing kitchens slash passe on either side of the ship". "At the back, not my back, stocks and sauces plus roast section, are you with me treacle"? The fucking size of the stock pots took me back to my army days. Six huge boilers, you could literally have a party inside one of them with two gas cookers.

In the middle was the larder section, which feeds both port and starboard, these poor bastards got nailed. My time in the army was a day cruising around

Alton Towers compared to what these chefs went through every day, day in day out. At the front pastry which again feeds port and starboard.

"We have two services one in 15 minutes 7.30pm, then the second sitting at 8.45pm 1200 each sitting" excuse me? "1200 each sitting".

We walked over to the port side, "oh and this is special order", what's special order? "You get fucked in the ass basically, kosher this, Kosher that, vegan this vegan that, dietary requirements a list as long as my dick, etc, etc, etc. He must have one hell of a rabbit down his jockeys for a list to be that long. With the ship full of Americans, Canadian bacon lovers, European and Asian I didn't think the special-order section would be that busy".

I worked the section two months later with an Indian fella named Phil. If you can hold this section down without blowing your load all over the place, you deserve to be blessed with the ability to walk on water.

Take your busiest service within an enormous 5* deluxe kitchen. Multiply by twenty, add a dash of panic, a sprinkling of bedlam, one cube of debauchedness, eight handfuls of murder. A sprig of parsley, a gallon of sweat, then you will probably comprehend what I am trying to say. Rambo 1 2 3 4 5 6 7 8 and 9 all rolled into one with the hell raiser compilation for garnish.

I stood at the back off the passe on the portside almost 30meters in length, tall hat and not a mark on me. There were 30 odd chefs in teams of 3, one team per plate all wearing a dozen pair of plastic gloves, odd. Behind me eight huge Jamaican chefs on chargrills, eight south American chefs on the flattops and four chefs on special order. Also watching every move was hello boys Simon, who wants to break my cruise ship virginity in by smashing the living daylights out of my welfare canal.

The set up was mirrored on the other side of the ship. "Welcome to the real-world Neo, welcome to the Matrix", I'm so fucked, what the fuck do I know about ninjitsu. Can the ships mainframe plug me in, ten minutes I'm a cruise ship master? Everyone stood silent, waiting for the executive chef's call. Chef gives the nod to the FAB manager who then calls the waiters down. The noise is overwhelming, like an army marching into battle, I know what that feels like. eighty plus waiters some wearing red jackets, black jackets and white jackets all holding service trays the size of flying sources line up in front of the passé.

One chef in the line turns around to me and asks me if it's my first time on a cruise ship, not really on a ship, but I've done my bit I reply. Sweat running down my face, my heart pounding underneath my pristine chef's jacket. "Your first time right yeah, they're going to fuck you up man, proper fuck you up". That's reassuring, who is going to fuck me up? "don't listen to him, he probably wants you to be his wife", ok.

I have never to this day witnessed food go out so quick across a passé and I don't think I will ever see it again in my lifetime unless I decided to work on a cruise ship again. Michelin star food flying, the head chef shouting his head off. The Jamaicans look like the soggy bottom boys. The South Americans are head to toe in fish and I'm trying to fit in like black dude in a KKK souvenir shop.

The service ends making way for the second sitting, same set up as the first. Before I can say man overboard which would not be funny considering we have just sailed out of Vancouver I'm in the crew mess with my French cabin mate. Beer is flowing like Niagara Falls, every crew member getting smashed on cheap Corona. I'm being eyed up like fresh meat in a butcher's shop window by everyone. "He must be the new sous chef" I hear from the table behind us.

The next morning I'm with the French Executive chef. He's drumming it into me what is expected, does and don'ts so to speak. "As sous chef you will uphold and maintain the highest of company standards and enforce Mr Roux work", Yes Chef. He hands me my timetable and tells me to fuck off to the bottom of the world. First section butchery.

Seven ways to skin a cat, same applies to a leg of lamb, the butchery was small given the amount of meat that went in and out every day. Eight butchers who had lived and breathed butchery from the day they popped out mommas' hairy bush. Skilled beyond belief, I had done the odd bits at college, but this was one hell of a place to learn your way around a farm animal. "Welcome to butchery chef".

That night back to deck five for service, loads more shouting, tons more sweat, another night with Mr Roux. Crew bar, smashed. One thing there is to know about cruise ships every member of crew on board is a raving alcoholic, sex fiend or functioning junkie. The ship was in fact a floating Mansion playboy mansion. All you had to do to join the was pass your medical, and for chefs know how to defrost a chicken five ways.

There is a certain language you need to pick on board because you need to know when someone is calling you a sister, mother or father fucker behind your back when passing you on the M1 corridor. It's a mix of Portuguese, Indian and Australian. 1st stop Ketchikan Alaska. Try saying sister fucker in all three accents, yeah, I guessed, fucking mad yeah.

The Average Working Day Onboard

Wakey wakey 5:30am life on board begins, shower, cheeky wank, change into white's super large expresso. Report to deck five to supervise breakfast for circa 2000 passengers. Main duty to make sure the strictest of USPH is adhered to, (United states public health) and that there are no irregularities with HACCP, (hazard analysis of critical control points) with the cooking of eggs.

HACCP was in fact born out of NASA during the 1960s. The main reason for HACCP was and is to prevent an astronaut contracting a food born illness before or while in space. The science laboratories producing meals for astronauts are prepared in sterile conditions. You implement this level of hygiene onboard ship is another reason I can only surmise that most chefs onboard are alcoholics. I will go into sanitation further down the line.

The other thousand passengers onboard can either take breakfast in their fuck cabins or at leisure on the back deck. 9am super large expresso in the crew dining room then report to the lido kitchen. Duties oversee lunch for the back deck, 7-day Alaskan cruise, seven different themes prepared cooked and served each day. Monday, sushi, the biggest ball breaker of the week. This is also another reason why sous and head chefs are alcoholics and contemplate jumping overboard every working day. sushi Monday.

Sushi set for 500+ plus diners for lunch, eight sushi chefs working like twenty men smashing out sushi for every Yo-sushi restaurant across London in a confined space no bigger than bathroom was something I considered a miracle. Sashimi, maki, uramaki, temaki, tiger roll, California rolls, dragon roll, spicy tuna roll, shrimp killer roll. Salmon, octopus, scallop, bluefin, yellowfin tuna, squid legs sashimi. You name it when it came to sushi Monday the sushi chefs got battered, spit roasted, fucked in the ass, fucked in the mouth, screwed in the ears. A baby elephant thrown into the mix with his lipstick out mad for some elephant pussy, just to add a little more savagery.

My sole job for that service was to make sure the buffet never ran low of beautifully hand rolled, handmade bites of Japanese excellence. Alaskan cruise the toughest cruise there is. Catering for thousands of overweight, obese, zombie eating Canadians, Americans, Asians and Europeans. Prep time 5 hours, service 2 hours, super large expresso back to the cabin for a soapy shower and wank.

Thirty minutes break then it's off to deck three to supervise afternoon tea. Unlike fancy hotels across the globe offering afternoon tea, afternoon tea onboard ship is a mind fucker. A chef suffering with OCD who does not care much for sunlight is most likely on the job description when applying for a larder or cold kitchen chef position. Repetitive labour, intricate bite-sized sandwiches, canapes, nibbles, rolls, roulades, tarts, quiches, beignets and an array of miniature savoury snacks was the treat before consumption of an ocean of tiny, sweet fancies.

As many fancies as savoury options, as far as the eye could eat. 5:30pm starving like a lost lion cub on the African savannas I cram a few canapes into my chefs' trouser pocket and head to my cabin.

6:30pm report to deck five for evening service or back deck for alternative dining. I preferred alternative dining. A small kitchen serving 100+ guests a small grill menu. Steaks, chicken, pork chops or fish served with simple garnishes. Alternative dining was a breather compared to evening service on deck five hell.

As I've already indulged you with service on deck five previously, I shall skip to staff evening meal. Everything and anything left over from a dozen services during the day is transported across the ship to the holding kitchen for evening staff meal which I managed.

Evening meal for staff starts at 10pm, 650+ crew, service ends at 11:30pm with the sound of an army of kitchen porters. Night cleaners, porcelain technicians, swamp monsters, moon trolls, dick punchers and cabbage patch dolls making their way to any two dozen kitchens onboard to start the USPH, HACCP, slash hospital surgery deep clean.

My shift ends at 00:30am, cabin, shower, change, only to head to the crew bar to drink yourself stupid for an hour. Or get your end away with your cruise ship fuck buddy. 5:30am Tuesday repeat. The only difference back deck Tuesday Mexican theme. Not sure what those Mexican chefs had in their water bottles on Tuesdays. Same working space, 700+ Mexican foodies. A menu the size of a poncho. All I could do was watch on my knees and be grateful for their skills.

When you did manage to grab some R&R time when the ship was in port you would run like Forest. The one time I did manage to jump overboard and grab some much-needed supplies this happened.

How small is the earth? it is small I guess, the old cliche, "the world is so small". As chefs our industry is even smaller. In the United Kingdom it's impossible to escape the noxious cycle of the hospitality industry. You piss someone off, words out, you get sacked from a prestigious hotel in the UK every chef and his bitch ass general manager knows about it.

The hospitality industry in the UK is in fact no bigger than your average household kitchen. With the use of social media platforms, LinkedIn, caterer, Facebook and the outrageous amount of chef agencies the industry shrinks every day. You shred your hands on a mandolin someone across the country is going to find out. "Hey man did you hear that shit go down last week; some chef wrapped in cling film locked in a freezer froze to death"?

"Hey dude, did hear about that chef dude, who got sacked from that massive hotel yesterday, dude". "Dude that's old news, everyone who is anyone knows, fuck dude, do you live under a rock"?

Like clockwork come end of January, chefs move like it's the transfer window. They all put themselves out there looking for the next biscuit paycheck. The generation game conveyor belt of interviews. Dozens of chefs being lined up by dozens of chef agencies all being interviewed for the same job. It's true, executive chefs just apply for the next chef's job, like a merry go round. "Hey dude you applying for my job"? "Yeah dude I'm also applying for your job, dude put a good word in".

This tale is as true as the driven snow, the world in which we live in, my world appears to be tiny. That and maybe a splash of pure coincidence or fate is a short narrative I must share.

Circa 1996 I was working at a beautiful 5* hotel in Suffolk as a chef de partie, "football hooligans". During my anarchist time there we had a French chef with us for a six month internship, his name was Pierre. Funny super cool fella, we clicked during his first day. We became close friends, parting on our days off. I introduced him to the local faces around town. I do believe I have a few pictures of us smashed off our nut knocking around the house somewhere.

Pierre came and went like the seasons, we exchanged numbers, but we all know how life goes. We lost contact after a while and went on with our lives. I left the hotel abruptly as I was unstable, plus I could see the head chef was on his last legs. It doesn't go down to well when you're snorting lines of cocaine off a waitress's breasts in the dry store. Robbing anything and everything that was not bolted down, trying to nail every female that worked within the hotel's walls. A headache for a few, and a pleasure to work with for so many, time to travel.

I'm well into my 9-month contract onboard ship. I'm DJ'ing in the crew mess every Friday evening after service which was frowned upon by both head and executive chefs. They were pissed off because I didn't hang out with them or any other chefs after work, sucking dick taking it in the brown. Anyways if I did suck dick, it wouldn't be the dick of a blobby French chef with a Hitler moustache and ginger hair. It would be Stavros the restaurant supervisor, man fit.

Juneau, Alaska must be one of the most beautiful towns I have ever visited, stunning beyond measure, breath taking. I've got 2 hours to myself, so I head into town, for a cheeky beer and to purchase supplies from Walmart which is situated on the other side of town.

Cruise ship staff have their own transport ferrying crew between supermarkets, tourist attractions etc. On average you would have several ships docked at the same time. Juneau would be flooded with tens of thousands of tourists from across the globe, rich enough to afford such an elaborate 5* cruise.

Hundreds of crew members all wanting to get some free time, hundreds out and about being ferried all over town in staff vehicles. I've made my way across town to Walmart to perv over the endless selection of guns they have for sale.

Toiletries, CDs, decent filter coffee, vodka and socks, checkout. The first dozen staff taxis didn't even stop as they were all full. Bummer, I can't be late, or I'm stuck in Juneau for a week, your late your fucked.

I move away from the hustle and bustle of endless crew trying to flag a crew shuttle down and start to walk. One crew member on his own trying to get back across town to their ship has more chance than a load of pissed crew staggering around outside Walmart chatting Spanish.

Bingo I've managed to flag down a shuttle. It stops a few meters a head, I do legs and jump inside. Now before I continue, I'm in Alaska, Juneau on the other side of town. The other side of the world to be in fact, 4423 miles from Europe.

I thank the driver for stopping, the shuttle bus is empty all bar one person, one solitary human being. They are not Alaskan, neither are they related to the driver. What's the chances of me flagging down that crew shuttle in Juneau, on that given day, that given hour and minute? Hitching a ride back to port. Pierre, my old friend Pierre on the backseat.

That mad, crazy funny French chef I had the pleasure of working with years back. He was surprised more than I was, "bit far from home to be a stalker Auguste" Two old friends, chefs up to mischief traveling the world. What are the chances of that happening again? On the flipside, the world can't be that small because I haven't seen Pierre since.

It's Next to Godliness

The killer shift onboard ship, it's the 24hr sanitation shift, its brutal. You finish sanitation and walk half dead straight into a breakfast shift. We had three sanitation inspections per week. We would sail out of Vancouver which is situated in British Columbia. We would port at Juneau Ketchikan and Sitka some of the most beautiful towns in Alaska which is American territory once Russian.

Unlike the 5-star rating we have here in the United Kingdom, onboard health and safety, food hygiene is on an astronomical level. Our 5-star rating although much needed so that any outlet receiving, storing, preparing, cooking or serving food must comply with their local council legislations and legal requirements. Food hygiene within the workplace stops with the chef responsible for their respective establishment regardless of how prestigious the establishment is.

Or, if you manage a sweaty high street cafe serving breakfasts all day the manager, owner takes it in the ass if the EHO (environment health office) finds a dead rat in with the full English breakfast prep. You may be a poor bastard running a rotting kebab shop in a northern town somewhere for a rich businessman whose idea of food hygiene is a damp cloth, spit and elbow grease.

Before I continue let me explain the 5-star food hygiene rating system for food outlets serving food. One star rating, you have a serious health and safety food hygiene issue within the workplace which could cause harm or death to its customers. Your premises can be closed immediately by the EHO. Two-star rating, the same as one but you may be given a warning with an immediate action plan to improve the latter.

Three-star rating, you have not pissed off the EHO, but your kitchen smells funny and in need of blowing up and rebuilding. Four-star rating, obviously you have made an impression with your excellent due diligence record keeping. You also know and how to bullshit the EHO with long and important words. Five-star rating, most sweaty donkey meat kebab takeaways on council estates will have a five-star rating. Why, I will explain later.

During my career I have taken on deluxe hotels in the UK in serious need of immediate improvements regarding their food safety. The head or executive chef who was most likely removed due to a failed EHO visit has left the kitchen of a business corporate leisure hotel with a two-star rating. Footballers, pop and rock stars, movie stars, million and billionaires paying top dollar to stay in a hotel with its food production facilities no cleaner than a dog kennel.

The point I'm trying to make, some chefs working in such extravagant establishments today are unable to grasp the difference between chicken shit and chicken salad. So, should we employ Stavros me-no-speak-da-inglish from around the corner with a 5-star food hygiene rating. He serves 200 shawarmas per day, should he be employed to run a 5-star hotel whose chefs are preparing food by candlelight on the floor?

Back to the big boat, sanitation. As one of six sous' chefs on board, your sole purpose prior to a potential inspection from USPH (united states public health) Is to make sure we pass regardless. These three inspections would happen early in the morning soon as we came into port. So, when the cleaning god squad have finished their shift, they would all be on standby to return if needed.

One in three inspections they would all return, I was not the one who coined the phrase cleanliness is next to godliness. These inspections are also another reason why every chef and kitchen porter on board, 200+ are walking alcoholic zombies.

Take Tim Peak and the worlds most experienced naturally gifted Brian surgeon. Put them both in sterile hazmat suites with the skills they have, plus the knowledge and dedication of a master in the art of ancient samurai sword making. Ask them to make an omelette in a telephone box more hygienic than godliness without cracking an egg.

That was my job right there, to supervise cleaning on a level that even God has not witnessed. Mind bending apocalyptic, back breaking, Gestapo torture three times per week. If you cannot stand the heat, get the fuck out of the kitchen, I did. A half-pissed sous chef walking around neon lit kitchens at 5am wearing Michael Jackson gloves with a broken flashlight from a horror movie, that was me three times per week.

If I found a droplet of water anywhere and I mean anywhere crew would be hung. Bacteria needs moisture to multiple. If I found mixed herbs on the lid of its container people would be shot. Some mornings I wish I had a shotgun armed to the teeth like Rambo. It would have been easier to go on a kitchen porter cleaning god squad rampage.

Anyways next time your partner is out for the evening with friends. If they arrive home early in the morning with the shits, ask them if they have had a 5* dinner or a shawarma from Stavros.

You don't have to be an astronaut or a brain surgeon to figure out these apples. It comes down to turn over. Stavros who is smashing out shawarmas all day long is going to have very quick turn over. So, produce is flowing in through the delivery door and out across the counter to vodka fuelled cocaine snorting lunatics.

A deluxe establishment might struggle, because if they do not have a branded high street concept within their walls or a Michelin starred chef at the helm. Or the turnover of Mc Donald's, produce is going to sit longer in storage. Perishables, meat, fish, diary, fruit and vegetables. Shelf life on these items, two to three days tops. The reason being produce must be the best it can possibly be when preparation begins. Rotten, out of date produce isn't going to cut it for a passionate chef in today's culinary premier league.

A five-star rating could be the difference between one solitary mouldy tomato, a dickhead commis chef who hasn't filled out yesterday's fridge temperatures. That rating could even be the outcome of an irate EHO who has been cut up by a Russian twat in a G wagon on the way to your premises.

Now, don't get me wrong when it comes to a clean kitchen. I earnt my hygiene marigold stripes in the military. I sat inside stock pots for weeks on end cleaning them out with a toothbrush. I scrubbed floors with my fingernails. I cleaned cold storage units with rolls of toilet paper. But when it comes to the scores on the doors within the premier league of food safety, naming and shaming it's all about the money game.

Would I ever step foot back on a cruise ship as a chef, hell no. It takes a different bread of chef to crack the premier cruise ship league. I was out of my league; I had jumped into the deep end with no water in the fucking pool. I should have started at CDP level, but hey shit happens, I had a great time on the ocean waves. I visited parts of the world I may never have visited if I had ended up working in a shitty kebab sweat shop. Total respect to all you chefs onboard.

The Window

Ok chefs great service this evening, shower, change not all together by the way and let's head into town. Corsica 1999 hotel Roya saint Florent. I will meet you all at the back of the kitchen for a post service drink in 20 minutes before we set off, "Oui chef".

My room is practically in the kitchen, so I'm showered changed in no time. A cheeky line of cocaine to get me in the mood is first on the agenda before I hop in and out of the shower. It's a beautiful evening; the sunset yet again blows your mind away. Corsica happens to be one of my top five favourite Islands to this day. Ibiza, Sardinia, Koh Samui are also up there, magnificent islands.

I'm sat outside the kitchen in the staff smoking area tending to a frosty Corsican beer smoking a Marlborough light. A nice little fuzzy buzz inside, nothing too crazy. The rest of the team arrive all looking fresh, sharp and beautifully tanned. The beers and wine start to flow, and the evening slowly drifts into the late hours. "Chefs think we should stay local tonight maybe get smashed in the hotel bar", great idea Shaun I'm down with that. Let's get juiced before we enter as I cannot be in the guest bar sober.

I share my cocaine generously with the team, those that dabble and one or two that are curious. The conversation is what you would expect from summer seasonal workers. Sex, drugs, music and what we all want to be when we grow up. Well, I'm already doing what I love to do, so it's just sex, drugs and traveling.

To this day, for reasons unknown I have absolutely no idea why I did what I did next during that warm summer evening with my team. Buzzed, intoxicated, I say to my sous chef. What would you say if I told you I'm going to dive through the kitchen window? "I would say your fucking bonkers to even consider it let alone doing it". Yeah, I suppose that's a valid point, fuck it.

The kitchen window is huge, 3ft high brick wall then sliding kitchen windows with a fly screen. On the other side of the window in the kitchen is a chest freezer with empty wines bottles sat on top. Ok I suppose you are correct it's a stupid idea, I stand and walk to my chalet door, turn around and practice the stunt through my mind. I've a good 10 meter run up.

Guys can you move that table, that one there, cheers. The lights in the kitchen are switched off just the fly zapper on, the kitchen is illuminated. "Chef if you're considering what we've just discussed" before Shaun finished his sentence, I'm at full speed. Chefs, kitchen porters diving for cover. 6ft from the window I launch myself off the floor and make the shape of a clown being fired out of a human cannon.

Pause for a second, what sane, normal individual would contemplate such a death-defying stunt let alone follow it through? A chef with no fucking filter. I break through the fly screen first then shatter the glass. like a perfect strike down the bowling alley, I wipe out all the wine bottles which were sat minding their own business on the top of the chest freezer.

I land on the kitchen floor, several cuts to my arms and back, the scars on my back today resemble gunshot wounds. As I look up out through the once was window and fly screen several heads appear with their jaws on the floor. "What the fuck have you just done you crazy son of a bitch".

The hotel manager hears the shouts and screams and rushes to the kitchen. Kieran switches on the lights to find me bloody on the kitchen floor. "What the fuck chef, what's happened", "he dived through the window boss", "what the fuck do you mean he dived through the window".

Sorry boss I just had this overwhelming thought to dive through a window. "You mad cunt", I'm rushed to the local hospital to get patched up. The hotel manager who is still a good friend to this day was not impressed. But I still kicked his ass at table tennis every afternoon, best of three.

The Perfect Sprout

"Auguste is cooking are you serious, Brother please invite me", the more the merrier when I got the call from Smiles. Like a true chef working Christmas day the only way to start was with a cold beer and a shot of grey goose before and after I had devoured a humongous breakfast. I packed the car and headed over to Che's Smiles residence to begin my family and friends shift in full chefs' whites.

Team Smiles had a brand-new fitted kitchen installed, loads of space, shiny new work tops, bliss for a chef. "Beer or wine chef" I will have both please Smiles, "I like your style, excellent", let us crack on. Mrs Smiles had organised the starters, wine and cheese table, the menu was enormous.

Main course, pot au feu, beef chuck, great fat content, three ham hocks, 2kg gammon joint. Two organic free-range chickens all cooked in a 24hr veal stock I had prepared two days prior. Braised on the stove with bouquet garni, a hearty hand full of mire poix and a two-litre bottle of merlot. Cooking time 5 hours.

Garnish for the main course, braised red cabbage, braised with cinnamon bark, cloves, orange zest, bay leaf, brown sugar, blackcurrant jam, shiraz and seasoning. Potatoes gratin, self-explanatory, demi-glace, gravy, cooking liqueur reduced and thickened. It would not be Christmas without the humblest of vegetables. The baby cabbage, sprouts. I needed some how to get this flashback off my chest and out my system, for good. Let us give this little sprout bastard an Auguste makeover.

My road to recovery started back in 2013 to be exact just the start of what continues to this day. You don't just wake up one day whether that be at home or in A&E after an overdose. Take a pill and everything reverts to factory settings. No, we are not laptops or smart phones, I wish, but recovering from addiction isn't that easy. It's a long arduous road, filled with uncertainty and relapses along the way.

Sprouts prepared and blanched for two minutes in boiling salted water with bay leaf, butter and garlic. Refreshed in ice water, bake pancetta lardons until golden, do not overcook. Pointless trying to hide crispy lardons on Crimbo day, make extra as you are most likely going to eat half. Whole chestnuts, 250gms softened salted butter, sea salt, freshly ground black pepper, roughly chopped flat leaf parsley and lemon.

In a hot pan heat butter, toss sprouts for a few minutes, add pancetta, chestnuts, parsley and a squeeze of lemon juice, season and serve. That socially distanced Christmas, I had converted my entire family, Hindu and Catholic, including myself "a born again sprout lover". Sprouts truly did rock, that humble baby cabbage wasn't so bad after all. Lots of tiny steps is what healing looks like, small steps will finally get you a long way. Hopefully, the way to closure so that life one day may truly flourish.

Back to School

French Classical cookery for two full years in a snapshot. Lecturer, "The foundations, sauces, stocks and mis en place are of primary importance in cookery and their value cannot be overemphasised".

"It is important for the chef or cook to do excellent cooking. If the fonds de cuisine, fundamental elements of cookery are not made with the best ingredients obtainable and mis en place not up to scratch you will produce shit".

"The better the ingredients employed and your mis en place at the ready the better the result. It is therefore false economy to neglect these especially important parts of the culinary art".

"From grilling to baking, cuts of vegetables, stock making, you will be required to learn and understand all their key elements over the coming years and in due course implement your understanding into the workplace".

"Ok class we've made bread, extremely important with any meal, now the classic cuts of vegetables and methods of cooking".

"Brunoise: Vegetables cut into small dice, Julienne".

"Julienne: Vegetables cut into match shaped rods or match sticks".

"Macédoine: Vegetables cut into medium dice".

"Jardinière: Vegetables cut into small batons".

"Paysanne: Vegetables cut in equal sized shapes".

"A brief Explanation of some French Culinary Terms"

Abats heads, hearts, livers, Kidney's feet etc. **Aiguillette** any meats cut thin and long. **Animelles** delicate part of the lamb also known as criadillas. **Apparelli** mixture of different elements for preparation of a dish. **Aromats** all herbs and roots with a tasty flavour. **Barber** the wrapping of poultry, game or fish with thin slices of fat. **Beurre noisette** nut brown butter.

Beurre Manie equal quantities of butter and flour worked together to form a paste. **Blancher** Ingredients slowly bought to the boil in order to remove fat or scum. **Bouquet garni** a faggot made of parsley thyme bay leaf and celery.

Braiser cook slowly with little moisture under cover. **Bisque** Shellfish soup. **Chapelure** brown breadcrumbs. **Chaufroiter** coated with chaudfroid sauce.

Chiffonnade lettuce or sorrel chiseled cooked in butter for soup garnish. **Concasser** to cut roughly, **Contiser** to incise meat or fish and insert slices of truffle or other substance, **Consommé** clear soup. **Croutons** evenly cut pieces of fried bread used for garnishing soup. **Ebarber** to remove the border part of oysters, mussels or fish. **Emincer** to cut into thin slices.

Escalope to cut into thin slices sideways. **Farcir** to stuff the interior of poultry, fish etc with forcemeat or rice. **Fleuron's** lozenges crescents or other shapes made with puff pate. **Glacer** to colour a dish under the salamander. **Gratiner** to pass in oven or salamander a prepared dish sprinkled with breadcrumbs or cheese under the salamander.

This is just a few French terms from A to G that we had to learn from the repertoire consisting of several thousand dishes. Drop out of school with zero grades, get thrown under a French culinary food bus. Something upstairs clicked, it felt natural, it felt beautiful.

Spit Roasted

Suited and booted I depart fire town on the 5.45am to Euston, tailored black suit, Patrick Cox loafers, pink shirt, Ted Backer tie, funny bright socks and pockets full of bullshit. I hadn't felt so nervous since I walked through the gates of 28 Amphibious engineers in Germany back in 1988. This was it, the interview of all interviews, interviewed by men who had spent a lifetime perfecting their astronaut interview martial arts skills.

Now me being me I thought this was going to be straight up "can you cook"? yes, I cook, "excellent, you have the job". Twenty minutes into the journey, just out of Birmingham, sleep deprivation starts to kick in. I hadn't slept much that night, my body starts to drift off to random places.

Morning wood did not help either, that mixed with every conceivable question I think I'm going to be asked with every potential answer firing around inside my head. Answers bouncing off the insides of my eyeballs, pounding my thoughts sideways.

What happens if I don't get this job I thought? There is no back up plan, should there be a backup plan. Go strawberry picking, get a paper round, carry on doing seasonal work. Get it together Auguste I kept telling myself.

Can't stomach train food, overpriced and tasteless, go hungry stay on the edge. The train pulls into Euston station. I started sweating when I got on the train so the next hour getting to my destination it was inevitable, I was going to sweat more.

Destination interviews central, forty minutes early, hang back. Grab a coffee and a rubber croissant from once was a key cutting shop turned yuppie morning hang out best coffees in London mate, yeah wicked. "Nine slaps around the head please". A pound change thrown to guitar man on the corner. I dust myself down, sly sniff of my pits, button jacket up, button jacket down.

Hi, my name is Auguste Knuckles I'm here for an interview, the role in Dubai. Halfway up the stairs, I try and find the answer to the most obvious question. "How did you hear about the job in Dubai", what a twat. I'm meet by Ross the guy who has guided me for the past few weeks through the interview process.

"Coffee Auguste", yes please, now most people do not know this, but when I drank too much coffee in the morning on an empty stomach, I would go sideways strange. This is the reason why I haven't drunk coffee for the past 15 years. The office looked like the neberkanezzer flight deck and Ross was Morpheus. We have a quick chat about my journey down and I'm asked to wait with the other applicants.

All the applicants including myself are rounded up and detained in a small meeting room. A dozen chefs sat in a tiny cell at 9am in the morning with funny faces. This wasn't the time for party tricks and stupid seasonal banter about yellow snow.

Enters the Indian enigma by the name of Cumberland, he welcomes us all and explains the psycho symmetric test we are all about to sit. What the fuck is a psycho symmetric test? My head was in a pickle trying to compute what he has just been explained. I wasn't applying to be an astrophysicist, I just wanted to cook. Mad coffee sweats kick in.

The paper they laid in front of us was as thick as a phone book and dusty all over like some sort of Jumanji game. The questions inside were multiple choice, with questions upon questions in one question a labyrinth of mind-boggling questions. I looked up at my fellow competitors, one chef across from me looked like Frodo from Lord of the Rings.

My hands had pins and needles, my stomach started to knot itself inside out and around the houses. Post morning wood was as hard as a dining table leg pocking through my suit trousers like an alien chest buster. Lucky for me the table wasn't made of glass, a scene from aliens would not have gone down well.

I had visions of going to the toilet, having to walk on my hands through the office to take a piss. I opened the colossal paper, off to my happy place. Passing thoughts, random thoughts about my new life in the sand pit with camels. No booze, pork or pussy for three years. At least I would be sober, drug and snatch free, no dramas, head down switched on. How fucking wrong was I?

"You have 1 hour, please begin, and remember it's not a test". Yeah whatever, and Mussolini didn't eat spaghetti. This wasn't a test? this was who wants to be the next Neil Armstrong. What has this got to do with cooking frogs' legs and snails.

What felt like three days later, I was done in, sprawled out on the sofa bleeding from my ears and eyeballs being nursed back to life by Ross my fairy godmother with a long black from the office coffee machine. "On the house, here you go drink up". Ross, what the fuck was that all about? "Auguste it's only a test to test your IQ, gives them an insight into your managerial skills". Managerial skills, what has wheelbarrows and tractors got to do with kitchen managerial skills? Am I going to work on a farm, "you've got your interview next, ready steady cook"

Sid my interviewer came out to say hi. We exchanged a few words then he shot back into the MMA cage to start his interviews with Mr Cumberland Indian sausage enigma. The first of the potentials went in, good luck mate, thumbs up and all that. Another friendly face comes over to say hello. He used to work over on Oxford Street. I remember meeting him when I had my interview for the boat.

Good luck Auguste, "make sure you say bye before you leave". Thirty minutes had passed, out staggered the resemblance of what once was Frodo Bagging's. Bleeding brown from every orifice, shirt unbuttoned, tie on backwards and trembling like he had just seen his mother fucked by a rhino.

The interview room was small and stuffy, it felt like we were all sat in a Sainsburys shopping trolley and I had drawn the baby seat. "Ok Auguste tell us something we don't know about you"? I was born to cook; I was dragged out of my mother holding a cook's knife and a frying pan. The chef's whites and terminology I picked up years later at college. "Poor woman must have been painful giving birth to Ainsley Harriet and a cooker".

"So, you're in service and the fryer explodes", what? "The fryer explodes", call maintenance, "there is no maintenance", fifty fifty? Take all fried food of the menu after putting out the fire. If it exploded the pilot light would be fucked so no point checking that. "Ok, no fryer and the sauce chef has cut his finger off", intentionally? "Nice you're funny".

"Blood all over the workspace, all the fridges pack up and you lose all gas, what do you do"? Close the kitchen chef and take all the chefs to the boozer. While all this is going on Mr Cumberland is psychoanalysing my every move. He gives me the results to my Neil Armstrong test. On top of all that they ask me, "how would you find accommodation in Dubai and where did you hear about the job"?

"Ok interview over", no questions about cooking chef? "If Ross didn't think you could cook, you wouldn't be here". "Everything you have done, seasonal work in the mountains is more than any other applicant has done or will ever know about haute savoir cuisine". "So, am I correct in saying you have several years' experience working this style of cuisine"? yes chef. "Well alright then, because that's what Après is all about".

Quick goodbyes all around and its out the door heading straight to a pub I know on Piccadilly circus to get plastered on Jack Daniels and lemonade before my journey back to fire town.

Stolen Shoes

Finish college, no one will employ you, loaded with certificates no fucking experience and broke as a church mouse. I stumbled into the army careers office in Wolverhampton because of stupidity. It was the proverbial turning point in one's younger years, either this or back to Featherstone and I do not mean picking strawberries. Featherstone prison.

There was no room for error at college, your tutor showed you how to make a dish, you better make sure your dish is on point. For me there was nothing after college. This wasn't school; this was me being born again into the culinary world.

For me I had to shop lift my way through college, I don't remember receiving any of my government grant given to 90% of students in the 80s. I had just turned 15 so Doris held the strings to that purse. I robbed from book shops, catering outlets and clothing shops all over the black country. I worked at a DIY store Sunday morning to purchase clothes from the market, jumble sales and charity shops.

Nothing was given, everything was earnt or taken. It's a stroke of fortune how I ended up in the army careers office in 1988. I was in fact being chased by two shop security officers through Wolverhampton town centre that summer.

On my tail I had to lose them before the bus terminal. I had strolled into bacon's shoe store wearing a pair of shoes that were falling off my feet. Back then in town, shoes were displayed in pairs. It doesn't happen today because of criminals like me.

I'm at full speed running through town Saturday morning wearing a pair of brown brogues a half size too small. The only place where I could escape from these two fellas doing their jobs was hiding away in the army careers office pretending, I'm signing my life away. Well, the rest is history. I wonder if I had tried to hide in one of the many hair dressing saloons in town would I have become a hairdresser. No because that's just fucking stupid. Hair by Auguste

Knuckles doesn't sound to hair dressy. Sounds more like a curly perm with a sledgehammer, short back and sides with a pickaxe.

Well, I've said it before, and I will say it again my enigmatic journey through life was meant to be this way. Everything before me and my existence was all building up to one beautiful crescendo. The birth of my baby girl. If anything had been off by a second or a minute or I had walked down the other street or got on another bus my life may have been a different story.

My 2nd year, final project front of house I decided to write my project about the birth of coke cola. "Why not write your final project on any number of French regions that produce world leading wines Auguste"? because everyone's already done that.

My final project for the kitchen I decided after studying French classical cuisine for two years I was going to finish with planning, ordering, organising, preparing, cooking and serving a plated Chinese three course meal for forty diners.

My tutors thought I was mad "why Chinese Auguste"? Well, it's probably because of all those fucking nights I had to collect my neighbour's takeaway from Mr Wong's when I had just started masturbating. The French classical cuisine evening which everyone in my year was doing, I had to try something different. I was compelled, driven to do something that had not been done before at college. My special evening at college, my Chinese do or die dinner, we didn't just pull it off we nailed it.

A pair of stolen brogues a half size too small, stolen from a cheap shoe shop in Wolverhampton back in 1988 are the two worldly happenings that sent me to war. The fact I was a classically trained chef was just a coincidence to that day. The other circumstance, I was in fact just a petty thief looking for somewhere to evade those security guards.

Once Doris had got wind of my stupidity and heard that I had visited the army careers office, life moved at an alarming pace. "Army air corps, infantry or slop jockey"? excuse me, a what? "a slop jockey", what is a slope jockey? "Yes, I believe you've just finished catering college, it says here city and guilds 706 1 and 2, an excellent choice for a young man of your calibre and street knowledge". "I'm sure you've heard of the old saying, an army marches on its stomach", Trying to catch my breath from the fitness examination, I reply, army air corps. "What", starch pressed man senses sarcasm.

163

Army catering corps please, the following morning I was on the train to Birmingham not to shop life but to sign the oath of allegiance, property of her Majesties forces. The following week with £5 in my pocket a bag full of jumble sale classics and necessities I was out the door. 17 years of age stood outside Aldershot train station waiting with two dozen other recruits ready to embark on life in the military.

A Fractured Mind

Soon as we enter the playground our little ones are off playing with little friends in the park. Two dark figures come into focus wielding machetes. I'm lost, frozen in a huge ice cube. The dark figures have gone to town, mutilating little humas. The playground is a war zone. Baby body parts strewn across the playground. Screams echo through my paralysed corpse. I can't do anything to prevent the carnage. "Babe, babe, come on we need to leave the kids are hungry". I'm snapped out of another walking nightmare. Ok babe I'm coming.

Basic Training

Ironing, shagging, drinking, more drinking, more ironing, dismantle re-mantle an SLR "self-loading rifle" blindfolded. Illegal card games, camouflage, hiding in woods, German hardcore porn. 80s music, black box, right on time, voodoo ray, unique 3, SOS band, lose ends, more shagging and racism.

Three squares a day, WRACS, (weekly ration of army cunt), endless shagging on tap, join as a virgin sign out a porn star. 10km tabs carrying 45kgs of dirt and shit on your back. Run a mile and a half, run another mile and a half faster. Get on the bloody brass-line you horrible little black cock sucker. Being black wasn't enough, I had to be a black cock sucker.

NAFFI, pool, snooker, more drinking, fucking, fighting, smashed up bed spaces by training instructors with small dicks. Beatings in the gym until midnight, down give me 50, down give me another 50, tired give me another 100. Change parade, mess tins, number twos. Self-loading rifle, seven point six two millimetre, this is my rifle, this is my gun, this is for killing down there is for dancing.

More change parades, shagging, drinking, fucking, fighting, hot and cold showers, masturbation, shaving, swimming in canals. Crawling through shit, bested by women with dicks "arms stretched knees bent back against the wall pussy". "You want to fuck with me boy", no mam. Eighties racism, Koon jokes, nigger jokes, gollywog jokes, heads smashed against the wall.

Holding two 5kg floor buffers arms stretched for 15minutes must be 10kgs each, tears, smack, "ARMS OUT PUSSY", NBC, nuclear biological chemical warfare training, going to war, "BOLLOCKS". Aldershot town, crabs, STD's, army wife's praying on new intakes to fuck while their husbands are away on exercise. Top shelf mixers, alcohol poisoning, more eighties music. Chased by Para's and marines on the way home, kicked to fuck.

Bashed to fucking, high heaven, eating, sleeping disorders, up at 1am. Chin ups, star jumps, A4 t-shirts, squared away, ironed socks, more shit out of more windows by brown nosed intakes. "Get it out there boy that's the spirit", broken noses, laundry room scraps. Boxing matches, more 20–40km tabs with full webbing.

Night vision, tinned food, babies' heads, dehydrated ration packs, biscuits hard bastards, running around Salisbury plans cracking a rifle butt into some unlucky bastards' melon. Pumped to fuck, aggression, controlled madness. I'm getting paid a small fortune, C17's, Chippie, Fred Perry, Hugo Boss, Farah, Adidas, Lacoste fashion victim. Burton reward card, next vouchers, endless amount of pussy, Christmas parties, chocolate sponge and pink custard.

It got so messed up during training one night we weird a guy's bed to the mains, because he bought crabs into our living space. Spitfire you dirty bastard, the noise, the smell, fizz bang pop, highway to hell. Do the math, we proper fucked him up, boys to men, hoodlums to disciplined soldiers. Camaraderie, I got your back bubby, tattoos, drinking fighting fucking, pass out parade and all that before you even picked up a knife to become an Army chef.

For me I passed out winter of 1988 with an intake above me, I skipped the Army school of catering tower, due to my 706 1 and 2 status, Swiss role, sherry trifle, go fuck your mum.

Before you could say "there goes another nigger" I was flown out to Germany to join 28 amphibious engineers. I would become in the short space of time it took me to walk, a prodigy in the art of hardcore drinking, a drug trafficker, selling every drug known to man to soldiers on camp and a drug addict.

"Hey knuckles what do you call two niggers in a sleeping bag". I don't know sergeant what do you call two black men in a sleeping bag? "A Twix, LOL do you get it Knuckles, a fucking Twix".

Slop for Cunts

I arrived at my new home sharp as a boning knife with my trademark moustache, loud shirt, trousers and shoes purchased from top man. The entire camp had an eeriness about it. It was quiet, so quiet and really fucking cold, not like English winter cold shorts and flipflops, it was artic cold. I was meet at the guard room by an odd-looking fella who went by the name snakey. Snakey the chef, one of many chefs who was going to make sure I turned up for my first day on duty hanging out my eyeballs, arsehole and Japs eye. Orders from the top brass, "do not kill him, but make sure he cannot walk for a month".

"All right mate" yeah mate, "you're the new chef mate Pte Knuckles, nice to meet you mate, were you from mate"? Wolves "were", Wolves "yeah mate know Wolverhampton, it's a shit hole, full of cunts mate". "You're a darkie boy" mixed racemate, "half bread, yeah like the specials" yeah mate. "Not too many of your kind around here".

The place is quiet, "everyone is on crimbo leave", crimbo? "Leave, holidays, Christmas, Jesus and Mary, the three wise men, gold frankincense and more". "You're going to share a room with Darren, he's in Ireland and Steve" Steve, who's Steve? "Wot, Bob Marley" yeah, I like Bob Marley. "Drink Pte Knuckles" wot? "Drink do u drink", yes, I drink, we enter my new room, no one is home all bar 4 cans of hardcore 9% German treacle beer and my bed. "Right new boy drinks all that beer, shower change and knock on my door in 30 minutes" were? the door just there, Snakey points, cheers.

One room, 4 bed spaces and a dance floor, two huge windows, loads of locker space. All my new roommates have huge televisions and the craziest HI-FI equipment I've ever seen. Elephant beer, ring pull glug, chew, tastes like a monk's cod piece. I must stand tall and be a man in a man's world. 17 years old, stand tall in a man's world, it was either that or a gang fisting.

Shower, change, eat two more cans of treacle, five minutes to go Snakey kicks the door open and follows through, he almost flew out the window.

Staggering like the village idiot. He's got the shiniest red face I have ever seen on a human living being. His face was as red as a baboon's shit box, what comes out his mouth went something like this.

"Agh yak fucker Auguste get zemove on zebroys are in zecanteen waiting to meet zee new kreff". I take a quick look at my remaining can of treacle, cringe, glug, stagger two steps sideways and three staggers the other. I can only assume matey boy Sankey has drunk twenty cans of what I have been eating. "Right schnelmacken, out zee door", as we walk out into the fresh winter German air it does something to me which can only be described as witchcraft. I'm a new-born baby turtle on ketamine and I wasn't even 30 minutes into my 4-year contract.

Looking back at the journey from my dorm to the mess I was astonished we did not check in to a kebab shop, strip joint and a knocking shop. The night was Baltic, your breath froze as it departed you. Being chilled to the bone my bladder wanted to relive itself, So, we did. Snakey and I, the monster chef I had just meet, we unzipped and pissed all over the parade square.

I was no match for my new fellow chef as I only had a baby liver that hadn't had fifty odd years of pure utter slaughter liver damage. We arrived at the mess with piss marks down our trouser legs. We turned to look at our artistic pissing pictures which were frozen over, it looked like a huge bowl of spaghetti. "Better not say anything about pissing on the parade square boy, they'll hang us".

Entering the mess hall was something you don't see every day on civilian street. The final scene in the smash hit movie Gremlins two, a hundred squaddies all smashed on hardcore German booze. Their eyes balls shot to oblivion like the crossed eyed Mogwai chomping away on crimbo turkey singing crimbo songs at the top of their voices.

I was fucked, sentences that were once simple to pronounce like under the table, became, unzerzerrable, and the cat sat on the mat became the hat shit in the dog. We staggered over to the buffet; the food smelt amazing the buffet was plentiful with a varied choice of crimbo fare. Totally not what I was expecting as the chef's nick name in the army is slop jockey, so fucking wrong.

I peered into the partial open planned kitchen and noticed there wasn't a chef to be seen. I felt a tap on my shoulder it was Snakey, one eye on me the other looking at the roast potatoes. He tapped his nose winked his eye "the boys are all out zer black schmoking". Well, it was inevitable, I found out a year later what the chefs were up to. Shot gunning cans of elephant beer, puffing on Marley reds chatting about how fucked up they were going get after their day in the kitchen.

The following morning, I stood, well more like held up by both Steve and Snakey on parade with the chefs of 28 Amphibious engineers. The world outside my head did not exist, it was pounding from the inside. An army of bongo players beating my senses into submission telling me "Just lay down and die you stupid black cunt".

I stank of every spirit and German hardcore elephant killer beer known to German man. The thought of alcohol made my body shudder, it sat at the back of my throat and went all the way down to my toes. Verp, (vomit burp) which I swallowed repeatedly. "Pte Auguste Knuckles welcome to the army son, all that shit in basic training is behind you. This is a man's world boy you need to step up to the plate if you want to dance with these fuck wits" yes Sargent.

"Pte Auguste Knuckles if you ever show up for Monday parade in this state again, I will personally fuck you up so bad you will have wished you died as a baby" yes sergeant. My first day on the job I had been violated by every animal who marched onto the Ark including Noah himself. I don't remember German wrestles marching on to the Ark, my ass was full of Lego.

After dinner last night I was dragged around town, given the chefs tour of all the towns watering holes and whore houses. According to one chesty bar maid I had projectile vomited all over here fruit machine and bar top. I had fallen asleep on the dancefloor in the local disco, I had also been rummaged by a few local gas cookers and one dodgy looking door man.

I did in fact that day want to die, but that is how it was done back then. They got you so fucked up on alcohol you would never want to get that fucked up again. It took me a full two weeks to recover. Maybe there is the reason right there as to why I delved into drugs. Fucked if I was going down that road again on the grim reaper bus to fucked town. Laugh out louder, two kinds of chefs back then, junkies and alcoholics. Choose the Ecstasy or the alcohol? I choose both.

Squaddie Bath

Smelly bastard, there isn't much to tell you about this cunt all bar he smelt, and I don't mean just smelly feet, he reeked. He thought he was a Casanova around town and camp because he shagged loads of ugly birds. Ugly German birds, the kind that fell from the crow's nest. Penne decided to go on leave one hot summer for two weeks, pleasant holiday penne, say high to Blighty for me cunt.

Now all you chefs out there reading this will know, when you have just finished a 16hour shift, mostly spent on your hands and knees taking it in the ass. Chopping, pealing, baking, sautéing, serving, frying steaming and sweating like dyslexic on count down. You don't look anything like those chefs do on Saturday morning kitchen or ready steady "oh and its green peppers bullshit" cook.

No, you look like a swamp monster, a bush pig, a fucking moon troll, you stink, chefs' whites in the laundry basket. Shower changed and ready for some much-needed rehydration in the form of several frosty cold beers and hard drugs.

Oh no, penne pasta stowed a week's worth of chef's whites in his bedroom locker. Well after one week and a busted air con unit during the hottest summer in German history. We had direction from the man upstairs to smash the locker open and discard the maggot infested mouldy stinking whites. That is what we did, we took his bed space to the proverbial cleaners and hurled his life into the bins.

The shower room consisted of eight showers, four deep bathtubs and a dozen sinks, two days before penne arrived back to camp, we set about preparing penne's squaddie bath.

Ingredients

Two days of urine, invite your fellow squaddies to join in.

Two nights on the lash, vomit and left-over gyros from the Turkish kebab shop invite your fellow squaddies to join in.

Cheapest brand of German cereals, flour, eggs, soap powder, human shit optional, one portion will suffice, government stock otherwise known as water. If you are feeling fruity add gravy browning, lots of it.

Method

Upper cut on arrival, the perpetrators' dressed in full NBC uniform wearing gas masks, the victim out cold, Mr Penne. Once the victim regains ability to speak drag them to the shower room and submerge them in all the ingredients above, held down with deck scrubbers. The perpetrators then clean the victim with soap powder, deck scrubbers, squeegees, mops and a feather duster, "hello boys".

Wash setting, mixed fabrics for one insane minute, garnish with wire wool and used latex gloves.

Its without saying any squaddie back in the 80s who had experienced such beauty treatment by deranged rolling pin wielding chefs, know that gravy browning is a ball ache to remove from human flesh, that shit will stay with you for weeks. Why has no one ever thought about using it for a fake tan. Maybe Donald Trump has, I don't know.

Hitler Youth

The love-hate relationship between two old friends. The civilian butcher known as Bandsaw five foot no inches Bill. After 22 years' service within the army catering corps (ACC) Bill retired from the army and married a six-foot Bavarian goat herder by the name of Herman. A fine woman, the kind of woman who would most likely tear you a new arsehole if you stepped out of line. Bandsaw Bill always seemed happy, he stayed in the same job in the same barracks in the same town as a civilian chef.

Bandsaw Bill went through frozen carcasses like they were softened butter. Blade steak, rib chop, sirloin chop, centre lion ham slice, spareribs, chuck, shank. Brisket, round short plate, knee chop, karate chop, best end neck cutlets, chump chops, middle neck, belly, and bacon. After a morning on the saw Bills small butcher section resembled a dinosaur graveyard. Jurassic Park 12, mass slaughter, Texas chainsaw massacre five days a week, week in, week out long before I got there and probably long after I departed the army.

When Bill left in the evening his butchery section was always pristine like a surgery, immaculate. This old soldier had never heard of HACCP or COSHH, just old-fashioned elbow grease and a bucket of hot soapy water, "old school hygiene".

Johnny Bing Bong, the Pavarotti of the kitchen, throughout the day Johnny would always sing Hitler youth songs. By the way, Johnny was Hitler youth, still donning the blonde mop of hair and crystal blue eyes. He was a massive old dude, six-foot seven. His hands as big as shovels, his feet as long and wide as a roasting tray, a man version of Augustus Glupp His pastries, puddings, and desserts were incredible, out of this world incredible. During his weekends off he worked in the family bakery in town.

He always used to make this one dessert, simple beyond belief. He took bread dough rolled it out into a greased baking tray drenched with melted butter. He would then sprinkle it with loads of caster sugar, cinnamon powder and baked until golden. Soon as it had cooled Johnny turned it out, sliced it, and served with Chantilly cream. Double cream whipped with vanilla essence and icing sugar.

He also taught me every swear word in the German dictionary. Sclamper, arsechluck, and pimmel kuff were just a few of my favourites. Great if you are taunting the Nazi locals; bad if you were trying to pick up a six-foot hairy German girl with a Chris Waddle hairdo down the local disco.

Every now and then, to piss off Bill, Johnny Bing Bong would frog march up and down the workmen's entrance outside Bills butcher section yowling Hitler youth songs at the top of his voice. It drove Bill up the fucking wall, after twenty minutes of Johnny's Eurovision hooligan song contest effort, it was party time.

The most passive chef I have ever known turned into a psychotic, raving, five-foot, machete wielding lunatic, mumbling, "What about their legs, they don't need their legs" as if he was talking to a small army of Bandsaw militia.

More yowling. "Mein führer, it's mine, a yar, yar, yar, left right, left right".

Then from the butchery, Bill would respond at the top of his voice, "You fucking sauerkraut-eating, Jew-killing motherfucker, baby slayer, I'll slice your fucking face off if you don't stop that cock-sucking Nazi bullshit".

Once the rest of the chefs got wind of what was going on, they would all dash to the work man's entrance like trailer trash rednecks, shouting, "Black dude outside, let's roll". They would join ranks with Johnny like SS madmen. Johnny Bing Bong at the helm, frog marching up and down, chanting and singing.

Out from his butchery graveyard flew Bandsaw Bill, with carving knives for lung chukers, Mr Miyagi's roundhouse spinning-bird kick, tigers' claw drunken master, wax on, wax off. "What about their legs, they don't need their legs". Bills little legs working overtime like an Olympic sprinter chasing down starched pressed chefs.

"You fucking wankers, come on, I will fuck the lot of you up, come on, I will fuck your parents up too, dirty horrible bastards for having you horrible little cunts".

Everyone scampered, ducking and diving for cover in imaginary trenches and bunkers. "Come on, you felching faggot fuckers. I'll turn every one of you into mother-fucking spareribs if you think you can wind up Billy boy, now piss off, you bunch of Nazi loving twats". Knives slicing through the air, Bandsaw Bill gave the Ninja bow. My bottom lip was on the floor, catching flies.

"Welcome to the barmy army son", he said, and calmly returned to his colossal cutting machine.

No one got sliced up that day, but half of the chefs were in the medical centre with concussions, abrasions, sprained wrists and ankles caused by diving through doorways and out of windows. The master of butchery earned a black belt in pork chops, he is a living legend, Bandsaw Bill. As for Johnny, the master of chaos Bing Bong, you will always be my inspiration when it comes to the pastry section. Quite ironic when you think about it. Ex-Hitler youth inspiring a black lad from the Black Country. I suppose it was never meant to be.

Chocolate Sponge and Pink Custard

Where does one start when it comes to the main course. What must a chef take into consideration? Season, produce, location, team skill set, market trends, competition. Well thank fuck I'm not really trying to write a main course section for my menu. I am in fact trying to explain the time I almost cut my hand off while on active service with 32 armoured engineers during R&R making custard. Fucking custard of all things, unthinkable in today's high-tech kitchens were by a chef could almost cut their hand off making cream pâtissier, French for posh custard. Its unheard of.

So many SOPS's, health and safety manuals, risk assessments, the correct equipment and resources to carry such tasks during a busy shift. There must be a gargantuan fault or serious human error for a chef in today's culinary kingdom to sustain such a serious injury, self-inflicted amputation.

The definition of an accident, an unfortunate incident that happens unexpectedly and unintentionally, typically resulting in damage or injury. Or an event that happens by chance or that is without apparent or deliberate cause which may result in catastrophic injury or death. I suppose a half-pissed mate on R&R trying to improve.

the working conditions of another mate may also be considered unintentional or unexpected. Maybe even funny to the said individual.

As a student whilst at college during practical sessions you would often smell that milky poisonous cremated pan smell wafting through the kitchen. Custard burning morons everywhere. So many factors can result in a chef burning that much loved yellow sweet sauce we love with our chocolate sponge. Apple crumble, spotted dick, treacle sponge or just a mug of custard before bedtime, de-fucking-licious. I assumed my custard calamities where behind me when I finished college, wrong, so wrong on so many yellow sauce levels.

I was beyond exhausted during my six months active service during the first gulf war. But this is one of those stories, moments, happenings which stands out.

I suppose because of the scar the misfortune left. It's not so big now, after thirty-two years of healing itself. The week prior to the event I was out somewhere in the vast desert of Saudi Arabia. A chef on the front line assigned to 26 squadron, armoured engineers rehearsing battle scenarios.

Where 26 squadron went, I went, to feed and water them three squares per day, regardless, until the shit hit the fan and we liberated Kuwait. A1 echelon if the ground force ran into obstacles during the ground attack. They would fall back, myself and my squadron would move forward obliterating anything which stood in the way making safe passage for the infantry of achieving the obvious.

During these manoeuvres I wouldn't be in the back of my four-ton Bedford sat on dozens of boxed rations peeling potatoes. No sir, I would man a browning 55 calibre attached to the top of our Bedford truck. Whatever moved with a gun excluding camels, take it out before it takes out us. My browning could also take-out enemy aircraft and small reconnaissance vehicles. It was our final day in the desert before we relocated back to the military base near the port of al Jubail.

Al Jubail is a city in the Eastern province on the Persian Gulf coast of Saudi Arabia. Its home to the largest industrial city in the world. It is also home to the Middle East's largest and world's fourth largest petrochemical company SABIC. It was obvious Saddam Hussein wanted Kuwait's oil. Considering the oil wars in the middle east which have been going on for decades, this war was a lot more about liberating the Kuwaiti people. It was also stopping a potential Armageddon between the Arab worlds.

Being hypervigilant 24 hours of every day during those six months was beyond detrimental to one's physical and mental health. But we were soldiers who just drank that shit under the table or got bombed on weed and drugs. We were constantly jacked up, your dick rammed so far up a plug socket your balls are supernovas. Hurtling through the cosmos ready to explode on some poor virgins' forehead when you relocate back to the land that knows no difference.

I had managed to smash out my mise en place for breakfast before lights out. I sliced my tinned bacon loaf, halved my tomatoes. Opened my tins of bakes beans ready in a ban Marie. Cracked, whisked and seasoned my eggs ready for scrambled. Soaked a dozen packets of biscuits hard bastard ready for porridge. I was set, washed, ready to bed down for the night.

Confident there would be no stray camels or local smack heads roaming that night I left the flaps of my tent open. My bed that beautiful evening would be a camping sponge mattress laid out on the top of my number four cooks set. It's the equivalent of sleeping on shrapnel when I think about it today.

I cannot even remember how well I slept that night. No dreams, not twisting and tossing like I do today. Stone cold dead asleep soon as my head hit my sandbag pillow with my cold SLR rifle for company inside my doss bag between my legs, safety on. That beautiful Arabian night, the world could have exploded, and I would not have known.

Fast forward to 2021 my wife let's rip, farts in bed, I'm blown six feet out in the air. If my daughter falls out of bed, I'm awake. A solid night's sleep today with a wife who farts like a whale and children who rummage around their beds sleep talking all night is virtually impossible.

The following morning, I awake to a scene which I would witness a month later after the carpet bombings. My cooks' tent had been obliterated, fuck knows how I wasn't whisked from the top of my four-poster deluxe number four cooks set shrapnel bed and dropped on the magical land of Oz.

My once breakfast mise en place had been scattered across the harbour area. I had slept through a sandstorm. The kind of sandstorms you see in those Hollywood blockbuster movie sandstorms. The entire harbour area had been ravaged. Tents, camouflage netting strewn across the desert. Breakfast that morning consisted of an all you can eat buffet of tinned fruit salad, biscuits hard bastard and sweet tea. Knowing we were about to drive across country for R&R the cleaning up and repair of our equipment would wait until we had rested. Had a decent hot shower, which was as good as sex, a hot meal in the mess hall which was fine dining compared to tinned rations. Roast dinners, delicious wet dishes, fried fish, pasta dishes, fresh fruit and vegetables, an array of deserts, puddings accompanied with fizzy drinks. The best part of R&R, ice cold beers smuggled in by HMF and a cheeky few spliffs with friends.

During R&R chefs rotated through the humongous mess hall for all military personnel, the entire ground force. Considering the four-pronged assault to liberate Kuwait was the largest land move of military vehicles in the history of modern warfare the mess hall seated thousands. Fresh food shipped in, prepared, cooked by military chefs, served by local conscripts.

That given day, that given moment the bonzer can open had miraculously gone mixing. Most likely stolen by a "chef" fucked off with using a ration box tin opener in the field. A bonzer tin opener can open fifty tins of rations per minute. It is the Rolls Royce of can openers. Whichever cunt chef, kitchen porter stole it, it absolutely made their three squares per day in the field so much easier.

Custard powder added to boiling water and milk powder, add sugar to taste, easy as pissing on a half-eaten kebab in an alleyway. Well, not if you don't have a bonzer tin opener to open numerous tins of UHT milk and custard powder. Custard for hundreds of custard loving addicts who deserve custard after several weeks in the sand pit was down to me to deliver. It wasn't like I was trying to smuggle arms across borders to help hell bent Iraqis wanting to kill all infidels. If I didn't burn it, no one gave a fuck how I made it.

This over it, shattered, fatigued custard burning inexperienced doorknob decides to choose a 10inch cooks' knife over a ration box tin opener which opens fifty cans every twenty minutes. How difficult can it be to use the back angle of a cook's knife to puncture the corner of a tin and empty the contents. Easy as fuck until some half-drunk local slips behind you on split gravy while your arm is elevated ready to chop a car in half. Not good for moral, not good for me let alone a que of custard loving squaddies.

The sharpest edge of a chefs 10inch cooks knife misses the can and plunges itself deep into the side knuckle bone of my index finger. Fucked, the knife is lodged in my bone, blood spurts across the section, turning gallons of custard, pink. Hysteria, shock, I'm waving my arm, blood spouting out everywhere. The sound of a knife being pulled from human bone is ear crunching disgusting. Local kitchen porters just look on in amazement as do several chefs in white jackets now splayed with my blood. The custard loving que quickly disperses, knowing full well, its UHT cream on their chocolate sponge.

Morphine into my thigh, my hand is held down by two army medics. An injection straight into the gaping wound, no mercy. For what it was worth a camel could have done a better job in sewing me up. The next time out in the field would be the real deal. That whole cock in a plug socket thing, this time it was bare back, no WD40, life or death super hypervigilant eyes lids peeled back with a box cutter vigilant.

Due to field "war conditions" my gaping wound from R&R become infected, no medic, antibiotics, just field dressings, hot soapy water, Dettol and electrical tape. Every few days I would squeeze yellow puss from my wound. I would scrub an open wound free of puss, pour neat Dettol in hoping it would heal. Hands on, cooking on gas dressed in my nuclear biological chemical war outfit, those few weeks during the ground attack were excruciatingly painful.

Not just visually painful, everything I did, I would be on the verge of vomiting due to such pain. Wiping my ass was a no go for weeks. But fuck me sideways baby, if I had known my co-driver had stolen that bonzer can opener from the mess hall kitchen for me, I would have told that greasy local kitchen porter who fell on me like a girl that day to make the fucking custard.

Aaron

A life lived is the only measure that quantifies time.
Aaron's time quantifies the love within this space.
Our togetherness, our time today is the measure.
The measure that was and is the beauty that we all shall remember for our ever days.

The early days and years were spent cruising across town.
Easy riders, tip tops and plastic sliders.
Our youth was everlasting, smiles cries and not knowing the path that lay before us.
One sweet moment set aside for us and now we are here.
All of us beside you.
I think we can all agree it's been one beautiful ride.

Lost without a cousin, just hope he makes it home.
Emotional, caring, a smile being the tenderness.
Your memories will stand the echoes of time
lived through children left behind.
Traveling through the darkness of light you'll always hear our voice; we will guide them.

Our love will travel with you across an ocean of stars.
We will all ponder as we gaze upon the nights sky
Why, it would have made no difference said the eyes of truth as you drifted away.
Left with the undeniable fact you are that star that burnt twice as bright but half as long.

Aaron's memories are painted on all our hearts.

A legacy will be forged through the eyes of two boys, a family of few and friends of many.

Father, brother, friend a cousin I loved unconditionally

11TH February 1976 – 27th July 2022

Cooking on Gas

"When everything is going well and nothing is going wrong"

SLR, self-loading rifle, four-ton Bedford truck with enough rations to last six months. Rocket launcher. Dust-bin cook set; number 4 cooks set, twelve by twelve-foot cooks' tent. Four sets of nuclear biological chemical warfare (NBC) suits. Nerve gas epee pen, 55-millimetre Browning, (exceptionally large gun)

Before deployment, all soldiers, regardless of trade, had the chemical warfare menu. It was not a choice menu; you had all dishes, including the standard anthrax injection and the nerve agent pre-treatment set (NAPS).

Harbour area, a safe location for military personnel and vehicles, full camouflage, with heavy artillery guard posts. Trenches and makeshift bunkers in case we come under attack. Plus, the standard nuclear chemical weapon detectors located in several positions around the harbour area.

The number 4 cook set looked like a metal suitcase when closed. A little bit like a picnic table, you lowered the legs, then open out the table. There were four burners and a small metal oven which came separately. You sat it on top of the burners; it was useless for baking. It came with two temperatures, hot or fucking hotter so anything that went in had to be watched with a keen eye.

The cook set ran on petrol, so after popping my funny pills, I would fill the tank which was part of the contraption and pump air into the system with a bicycle pump. This would pressurise, then pass the gas through another pipe and out through the burners. So, you literally were cooking on gas.

A remarkable piece of equipment, it was a bastard to maintain and a fucker to clean. Rumours had it one blew up and robbed a chef of an arm. Mine leaked petrol all the time. I just filled the bottom with sand to soak it up. Fuck knows what would have happened if it went up. I would most likely be walking around today minus one arm and half my face.

The dust bin was an actual dust bin, you placed a metal piece shaped like a doughnut inside with a tube up the side and with a chimney. On the side of the bin, you attached a petrol tank with a tap which dripped droplets of petrol into the bottom of the doughnut. Once the petrol hit the bottom, it would ignite and heat the inside of the doughnut. When the bin was full of water and tins of food, it would come to the boil within fifteen minutes.

Army rations combined with a little imagination were not half bad. Each box had a different menu inside.

A: baby's heads, otherwise known to a squaddie as steak and kidney pudding. It apparently resembled a baby's head when pushed out of the tin. This came with mixed-fruit pudding (MFP), vegetables, dried potato powder, and oatmeal biscuits (which were magic for making porridge). You had to soak the bastards overnight as they were hard as nails. And forget about dunking them in your tea. One biscuit would soak up the entire cup.

B: Chicken curry, my favourite and so, too, the lads, although it did not come with endless amounts of poppadom, mango chutney, lime pickles, and naan bread, this recipe came with rice, tinned fruit salad and a few other bits.

C: Stewing steak which was great for making pies if you had a few fresh rations, which we did every second week—eggs, flour, pasta, herbs and spices, fresh fruit, and meat. Also, in the ration boxes came tinned luncheon meat, beans, donkey meat sausages, powdered milk, tea, coffee, and sugar.

D: Dead man's fingers (hot dogs), hot dogs made with all the crap from an abattoir floor. Seasoned and pipped into edible scoff. Same bits and bobs as box A.

There are a few stories which stand out from the chaos of war. One of them involves a frying pan. We had just set up camp. It was early afternoon, and I was stretching my legs around the harbour area when I came up on a battered old frying pan.

I mean this thing was fucked. It looked like it had been run over by an entire army. The handle was hanging off, and the sides were bent back. But when I rubbed the sand from the inside, it had a non-stick base, something rare in army-issue pots and pans.

I took the pan back to my kind of kitchen and gave it a good seeing to. I smashed the sides back as best I could with a spanner. Then I screwed the handle back and taped it with duct tape. Gave the fella a good wash and proved it with salt on my petrol burner. Then I gave it a good wipe with grease.

A few days prior we had picked up fresh rations of flour, eggs, fruit, and vegetables. So, after reincarnating my frying pan, the only thing I could think of which was fitting for supper was Spanish omelettes. A dish I hadn't made since college and one the lads would not be expecting that night. More like a wholesome all-in-one stew with mash and MFP for dessert.

I prepared all the veggies, taking into consideration I had to knock the omelettes out quickly, I precooked the vegetables. I cracked, whisked, and seasoned the eggs with pepper. Ready for service for thirty to forty lads using one non-stick pan. I also prepared jacket potatoes with beans.

The sun was setting and what a sight it was, a huge red ball of fire disappearing beyond the sand dunes. One of the sergeants strolled over to my cooks' tent to see how I was faring. "Evening, Private" evening, Sarge.

"What's on the menu tonight then" Spanish omelettes, jacket spuds, and beans.

"Bollocks", replied the sarge" honestly, Sarge, no fucking around. I opened the flaps to my tent and there to his surprise was my mise en place, ready for service.

Within ten minutes, all the boys had turned up and formed an orderly queue outside, ready for a feed. "What's for tea, sloppo"? Spanish omelettes you silly cunt. "Yeah, get fucked".

I strolled behind my number 4, cranked up the heat, popped on my apron, uncovered my mise en place, and started the show. Omelette, "Yes please, sloppo" he answered with a startled look. He turned and shouted down the queue, "Chef's really cooking fucking omelettes".

Four omelettes later, the pan was well seasoned and in full swing. The first two had stuck a little, but I wasn't going to give in. Ten omelettes down the line I was on fire. The burners were pumping out maximum pressure, the oven was acting as a plate warmer for the spuds and the beans were bubbling away nicely.

"You're a madman", shouted one squaddie. "This omelette is fucking to die for". It would have been quite ironic if a Scud had fallen short of its target and blown us all to kingdom come. You're welcome. Enjoy. The sergeants stood back and watched as I fried, scrambled, tossed, and served piping hot tasty omelettes to my fellow men.

The sweat was pouring off me. My tent did not have the luxury of extraction or AC, just a cool breeze wafting through my tent, 140 degrees tops. After twenty minutes, I had fed all the lads, including the top brass.

I was so pumped and buzzed out I wasn't hungry. I just skulled a bottle of water. That night I didn't wash a thing, neither did I prep anything for breakfast the following morning. The old boys knew they had seen something never seen before on exercise, let alone during active service.

I received a standing ovation and a pat on the back. One of the sergeants came over and asked where I purchased the frying pan. I found it, Sarge, over there.

"You're a legend, the boys are well impressed with their omelettes. They were expecting the usual".

Not tonight Sarge, a few eggs, a chef and his pan it's all gravy, baby. "Less of the gravy baby private, I'm old enough to be your dad", Yes Sarge.

After the carpet bombing, we were well on our way to Kuwait. There was no hanging around. Sleep deprivation and being in an NBC suit twenty-four hours a day was tough to say the least. My driver taught me how to drive the Bedford, hour on, hour off. This was hardcore trucking, cannonball run with bombs overhead.

We stopped for an hour, time to unpack the dust bin, spark it up, and feed the lads. It must have been midnight. The bin was full of tins bubbling away, A, B, and C, which would be mixed to make an all-in stew for supper.

I set up a table with tea and coffee, milk and biscuits. I must have been two to three metres from the Bedford. I stared to open the tins to empty the contents into serving containers when the Sarge came running over. "Auguste, you fucking lunatic. We need to move this shit to the back of the truck now, quick fucking sharpish".

Chop, fucking chop. I could sense the Sarge was in a panic. Three others came to help, it was all hands-on desert, moving my little canteen set. What's going on Sarge what's the panic? "Just move, boy".

We dragged the bin full of tins and the tables to the back of the truck. What happened next brought me to my knees. In the distance I heard a rumbling sound, the earth beneath my feet stared to shake. All around me sand was being whisked up by the howling wind. The air was hot, it was difficult to breathe, the rumbling noise got closer.

It was impossible to see more than thirty metres ahead of you in the sand-filled darkness. Then headlights came out of nowhere. Moving at full speed, a whole squadron of Chieftain tanks sped past right where I had my little canteen ready to serve supper to the lads.

I was on my knees, watching in bewilderment. I was taken to the back of the Bedford and given a sweet cup of tea. If the Sarge had come over five minutes later, I would have been splattered all over the dessert.

Being on the move every day and night was really taking its toll. You don't really understand true willpower and determination until you're involved in a real-life war. Having to unpack and repack two or three times a day, off load and on load all your cooking equipment fuel, weapons, and rations. In the wind, rain, pitch-black after driving hundreds of miles through the desert with multi-launch rockets (MLRS) flying over your head.

In full webbing with a tin hat that weighed the same as a five-kilogram bag of sand got on your nerves, but you couldn't give up. You just absolutely couldn't. I remember one night like it was yesterday. We had just moved into our harbour area. The boys had dug in, I was still setting up my cook's tent. The wind was howling, it was pissing down with rain.

Trying to do this singlehandedly was mind-bending exhausting. After an hour or so, I had my tent up, but I was soaking, shattered, and starving. But there was no time for rest, I had to get food on for the lads.

Tins in the bin, I am good to set my sleeping quarters up, two dozen boxes of rations with a dos bag on top. Five-star luxury considering the circumstance. Out of fucking nowhere I hear a high-pitch siren.

Military procedure states you have nine seconds to get your gas mask on, a fine piece of kit compared to what the Yanks had at the time. Nine fucking seconds. It's nine seconds whether you live or perish. Many of you might have watched The Rock, an epic movie in which bad guys rob a chemical weapons post and move into Alcatraz. One bad guy drops the nerve gas, his skin bubbles, eyes pop out, tongue turns into a three-piece sofa, then dies a slow and horrible death.

Well, I didn't get my gas mask on in nine seconds due to exhaustion. Overcome with some sort of outer-body experience, my brain fooled me into thinking I had just received an uppercut of nerve agent.

Gas mask finally on, I'm crippled, I have another handful of seconds to get into full NBC kit; it's not happening. I give in to fate and except the fact that I'm about to rock up at the Pearly Gates with two wraps of cocaine, a few crushed ecstasy pills, two acid tabs, and 40 boxes of army rations.

When I came to, I'm propped up against several boxes of rations with an epee pen hanging out of my thigh and my gas mask off. The Sarge was standing over me. "Private, are you okay, Son, Son, do you hear me, if you hear me, nod your head"? I nod my head.

The objective of the carpet bombing was to annihilate the main highway to Basra and basically everything in Iraq. The main command from Schwarzkopf, destroy everything. We had to cross the highway on our way to Kuwait, where we would be stationed just outside the city for a few days before Saddam Hussain admitted defeat and surrendered.

The stench, nothing compared to it. The place itself cannot be compared to any blockbuster movie. What we witnessed me and my fellow men those few days was something else. The sky was scorched black with smoke from burning oil wells. Cars, trucks, lorries were still smouldering, the stench of burnt flesh and hair made vomit. Snap, crackle, and pop from fires still burning.

Camels splattered all over what was once the highway. Bomb craters the size of Olympic swimming pools. When you have truly witnessed what another man can do to another man, your outlook on life becomes vastly different. What gets me to this day, almost thirty years after the first Gulf War, is the smell, the burning rotten smell of flesh.

We set up camp a few miles from the highway. My tent was up, my kitchen set, and my bed made. So, I decided to take a stroll around with my driver, helmets, body armour, SLR, and our wits.

We must have been gone ten minutes when out of the blue, out from a trench came a conscript, one solitary man who had been hiding for God knows how long. Soon as he noticed us, his hands went in the air. He shouted the only words he probably knew in English, "I Surrender".

No messing around safety off and a bullet cocked in the barrel, aiming straight at the enemy. Was I really going to kill a man, could I kill a man if I had to? Yes, I would have put one in his head without even thinking about it if he had flinched or made any random gestures. As he got closer, I could see he was wearing pink flip flops, pink flip flops, utilities and an army jacket two sizes too small.

"On your fucking knees, get on your fucking knees, hands behind your head" screams my co-driver. I might have forgotten to mention in the army you are a soldier first before anything. That is what they teach you in basic training. I noticed how skinny this guy was, this man who probably had a family and children somewhere looked like shit, battered shit. Apparently, he had been hiding in that trench for weeks.

We bound his hands and took him back to the harbour area. We informed our sarge, who came over to my tent, where my driver was guarding our prisoner. "Fucking conscripts, harmless bastards, feed him, water him, and then he's off to one of the POW camps". Yes sergeant.

I sparked up my cooks set and got a tin of stewing steak and beans on the go. I gave the POW a bowl of water, soap, and a towel and kept a close eye on him, I could not keep my eyes off him to be honest. He must have been three times my age, what was he doing wearing a pair of pink fucking flip-flops. The way he washed it seemed liked he hadn't washed for months. He was so meticulous; I had never witnessed anyone appreciate something so basic.

When he finished, I gave him a set of combats fresh socks, sat him down and gave him a hot bowl of stew and beans I had prepared. If I only knew then what I know now, a piece of Arabic bread would have been a treat. He ate all the beans and left the stew. "No like meat only beans, boss". Sorry it's not halal, mate, fussy bastard.

When we departed, I could see the anxiety in his eyes. I could see the fear, I could only say, everything would be okay. What could he be so scared of? I was to find out years later after leaving the army, most conscripts were shot dead by the thousands for surrendering.

The power, the force, and strength of the ground attack would have been too much for a well-equipped military force. But thousands of conscripts were dragged from their homes to fight for a dictator. Not a chance in hell my man, not a chance in hell against the biggest ground offensive in history.

When I returned to Germany, I received a commendation by the commanding chief of the allied forces for outstanding services during the Gulf Conflict. Many soldiers receive this award for bravery, aptitude, professionalism, and upholding military values. I believe I received mine for those omelettes.

The Gulf War

Its mind blowing to think that it's 30 years to the date that I started preparing for war with 32 armoured engineers in Germany. Bizarre to think that I'm sat here writing my 3rd book. Little did I know even as a chef on the front line with my squadron. What we all experienced during those months of the 1st Gulf war would change our lives forever. It would change how we look at life even to this day. Fucked for life.

That boy who flew out from Germany to the middle east 30 years ago never returned, along with his frying pan he also got lost in the dessert. I lost count of the times I got stoned in those magnificent sand dunes. The night sky bursting with a trillion stars, super nova's traveling at light speed from horizon to horizon gone in the blink of an eye. Insects, snakes, desserts rats, sand sharks and camels wondering free throughout the cool peaceful night.

Did I pull the trigger that afternoon, did I leave my body in my cook's tent, brains splattered across thirty boxes of rations? Is this heaven, is heaven here on earth or am I still lost in the desert searching for peace wanting to rest.

"We were soldiers, desert rats, operation desert storm 1990–91".

Married to Cocaine

How much cocaine do you think you have snorted, an ounce, half kg, a whole kg or more, it's not a competition by the way? When we are in denial time seems to pass us by extremely quick. I suppose we are in the moment, living that moment like there is no tomorrow no future let alone are we even considering the sun rise the following morning.

2002 I had just finished a nine-month contract with celebrity cruises as a sous, a seven-day Alaskan cruise, cruising out of Vancouver stopping off at Juneau, Ketchikan, Sitka and a stop at the Hubbard glacier which was very picturesque.

The entire F&B offering was designed by Albert Roux, so being a sous chef on board ship was a big deal, you were treated like an officer and had privileges. I had to oversee all preparation and that dishes were served to specification during service. 3200 passengers, 150 chefs and food available for 20 hours per cruising day, output was insane, 17hr shifts 7 days per week nine-month contract.

Its without saying I had a good time onboard, I DJ'd once a week in the crew mess and organised parties and was sort after by both Male and female staff if you know what I mean. Once my contract had run its course I flee back from Vancouver into Heathrow and attended my brother's wedding.

It was the wedding of son number 2 with Boris, Soon as I land, I'm on the gin and tonics on the train to middle England. I arrive at the Doris residence put my brave face on and go with the flow.

A few hours' sleep I pick my partner up at the time from the airport, we drive back into town where I get fitted with my tuxedo and shop for a stunning outfit for my partner. Doris was divorced from Boris so things at home were bearable apart from her excessive drinking which she didn't hide and her wicked tongue.

The trick was not to get on the same level as it would only end up in an argument and you would only be exposed to the same slur and verbal abuse I witnessed most days growing up.

Son number 2 with Boris married into money at a young age, he had literally freed himself from mother's apron strings. Son number 1 was serving in the Air force at the time and Boris was living in Liverpool. Wedding, piss up, 3 courses, more booze, silly dancing, crap speeches, more silly dancing, fall over, Egyptian gymnastics, off to bed.

I had already secured a job that coming winter, I was going to work as a freelance chef working in the finest chalets in the French Alps. Snowboard all day cook during the evening and DJ and consume drugs through the night. We had two months before the start of the season, so we decided to fly out to Italy and harvest grapes for a month. Best decision we ever made, total bonkers. Up at 6am, local breakfast half a litre of wine and out to the vineyards.

Back at mid-day another awesome local lunch, menu cooked by a demon old lady on the pans, more vino and back out until early evening. Shower change, another awesome meal followed by stunning wine and a few spliffs, we had more shenanigans than you could shake a stick during that month.

We drive to the alps, set ourselves up in our tiny, shared apartment and it's on with the season "24hr party people". I'd been working at a very beautiful chalet for a wealthy executive, 70€ per hour plus tips and booze, one evening I was asked by this certain fella who was well impressed with my culinary experience if I would like to fly out to the costa del sol and look at a restaurant, he and another partner were looking at to procure, all expenses paid, why not.

The following week I fly out to Spain from Geneva, hope skip and a jump and a short transfer I'm set up in a beautiful apartment overlooking the coast. That evening we ate the finest of meals drank the best wine and it's off to the local disco "skull fucked". Now this is where it gets surreal the following morning I'm stood in a massive tropical style German restaurant, palm trees, camels, flamingos' "all plastic", the place resembled a plastic rain forest come dessert very strange restaurant.

It was obvious the restaurant made a killing in the 80s and 90s and early 20s but now suffering, the kitchen was a shit hole, God knows how they did what they did, but obviously they did what needed to be done. The location was bang on the beach, after an hour of over the head chit chat in English Spanish German and Geordie I was asked what I would do if the restaurant was mine, knock it down and start again. Awesome lunch, tapas with local wine and it's back to the mountains.

Before we knew it, I was back out in Spain looking at a shell, the restaurant had been procured and we built our dream restaurant, it had a huge terrace, with an awesome bar. The kitchen was open planned with a huge 2-meter grill with all the mod cons, changing rooms and office at the rear.

My two partners were also friends with the financial backer who had hired a bar team from England. A week before opening we all ended up at a beautiful nightclub situated close to the beach, a local club for the locals.

A very drug free evening loads of bubbles banging tunes and more Spanish snatch than locals at a bull fight. We staggered out of the club hoped in a taxi and back to the villa, as soon as we are out of the resort the cab driver turns to us and says "coke, cocaine", "you lika da cocaine".

This dude had been scoping the new restaurant, he recognised us, new venture, new money, new prospects new clients. Before, he said "aine" it was an instant yes, small detour to the gypsy camp and this wasn't no ordinary gypsy camp out of snatch. It was huge, caravans everywhere it was like the stage crew for cirque de Soleil.

Everyone male or anyone who looked like a male was armed to the teeth, ak47s everywhere. Fires burning in oil drums, meat being barbecued it was like Afghanistan, but the driver insured our safety and that it wouldn't be like deliverance.

He pops out pops back in, we have cocaine, a lump the size of a match box car, solid of the rock 90% pure. "No cash pay tomorrow I come restaurant", fairfuckingdincum, we've just invited Pablo to the party. Talk about living in the moment, I'd just spent a 3rd of a million on a brand-new swanky restaurant and bar, what's there not to love about life, how does the saying go, Live well so we can die well.

The opening party turned a few heads within the local community, restaurateurs, local businesses, clubs and our new friend Pablo the taxi driver were all there. A wise man would have known getting in that taxi the restaurant was flat on its face before we opened. You give the keys of your Aston Martin to a Welsh boy racer from the valley and tell him not to go racing, what's he going to do? Go racing.

Everything we had in Spain was at the expense of someone else, for me it was the party, I was so naïve, I lacked so much in life, irresponsible, immature and I was totally inappropriate at times, young dumb and full of cum.

Growing up without a care in the world just pushing it to the limit every day, some might say that's rock and roll but the amount of cocaine we started to consume, consumed us. It consumed us all to the point we didn't know what the fuck we were doing, morning lunch dinner throughout service days off, no fucking clue, apart from we had wasted a golden ticket opportunity, "twat".

I was long boarding "skateboard" to work half naked in just my board shorts barefoot, coked to my eyeballs. Smoking it, snorting it, washing it, snorting the stuff off gas cookers tits, spanking a grand a night I didn't have in strip clubs, wolf of wall street in the Balearics.

I started DJing in a local club around the corner from the restaurant, the owner of the club frequented our place a lot, as we didn't close until the last customer left and most evenings we were serving until the early hours. We started chatting one evening, few glasses of vino that lead to a few lines, yeah, I can DJ blah blah blah DJs, nightclubs, drugs I had it all, life was utterly bonkers, life was triple bonkers.

I knew there was a problem when I started swerving my business partners and work mates staying home alone sniffing coke getting off my box on my own. I had everything at my fingertips to educate and gain experience, grow up become mature and responsible but I just couldn't grasp the concept. No matter how hard I tried something was missing, something didn't connect, it was the live fast die young mentality.

The restaurant didn't last more than a year from opening, we snorted everything, one year of cannibalism, parties' clubs, coke, parties club coke hookers. I had lost the plot again; I had lost it in the military, and I had lost it and everything in Spain including my partner Grace.

Everything positive that had and was coming into my life I had no clue how to handle it, let alone control it, but when you put the bigger picture into perspective cocaine had its day.

I decided not to go to the festival because I know me, you may think you know me, but I know me more. Three days of beautiful house music, smiley people and drugs. I can't do it anymore. So, one shall not play Russian roulette with an aging heart. My children need a father, not a corpse on the wrong side of the grass they deliver flowers too once a year on its birthday.

Blessed

August 2007, I set off from switch down the A12 heading for London. I'd just been appointed the new executive head chef of one of the largest hotels in Europe. 900 bedrooms, 2 conference centres, 3 kitchens and 160 staff who require breakfast lunch and dinner.

I was responsible for the entire culinary department, 25 chefs 12 kitchen porters and a multimillion-pound revenue stream and all the whistles and stress that goes with such a huge operation. I nailed the interview while I was working in Dubai as a head chef of the most famous Après restaurant and pizzeria.

The restaurant Après overlooked the in the indoor ski slope located at the Mall of The Emirates. Beautiful shopping mall with the world's largest indoor ski slope, bonus considering I was made for snowboarding. As a chef I didn't mind split shifts at the restaurant as I could get a slide in before evening service.

120-seater all day dining restaurant, I designed all menus, trained staff on the style of cuisine, implemented all H&S policies and managed the kitchen from the front on the passé. I spent 3 years out in Dubai I travelled well lived the high life as well as any other expat. I made some awesome friends survived 2 car crashes, sustained a broken collar bone on the indoor ski slope, partied with celebrities and dated a few models.

Soon as Après opened we had the media all over us Justin Bishop the GM who sadly passed away years later was a fantastic PR man, he put Après on the Dubai dining scene. That year of opening 2006 we received runner up for best brasserie in Dubai in Time Out What's on awards.

Into the 2rd year in the sand pit I realised Dubai wasn't doing it for me, I just wasn't thinking straight. I started acting erratically, my mind was bouncing off walls, I just wasn't me. I was ripping into chefs, couldn't concentrate during service let alone life outside the kitchen, I was severely losing the plot, my mind was shot to pieces, once again.

I Must Be Fucked

"You fucking stupid homosexual, dick eating kiddy fiddling bastard, felching mother fucker", swearing makes you nervous, holy mother of god, "do you fuck your mother, or eat your sister's pussy" I don't fucking believe it, "you're a fucking CHEF" and you're telling me, that when I swear in the fucking kitchen it makes you fucking nervous.

"FUCK OFF OUT OF MY SIGHT, FUCKING PRICK", no better still eat shit and die cause "I'M GUNNA FUCK YOU UP TONIGHT BITCH, BARE BACK". "You ever made love to a man", no chef, "well tonight is your lucky night baby me and you in the dry stores over the tinned tomatoes..." YEAH BABY.

Hey fellas who wants to join in and make it a spit roast, Mumbles, you fancy getting your load off tonight son, absolutely chef, "put some music on, let's boogie".

"Hey guys", one of my devoted badgers, "Bruce don't fuck with me I'll stab you in the eyeball mate Bollos Lee", "THAT COCK EATING SAUSAGE JOCKEY HAS JUST TOLD ME I MAKE HIM NERVOUS WHEN I SWEAR IN THE KITCHEN".

Silence...hell breaks loose sounds of laughter and chanting in several different languages rain threw the restaurant from the kitchen, PUTANGINA ANONG NANGYARI, OGAG, PUTA, MABABA ANG LIPAD, can't believe it chef, lame ass bastard, what a pussy dhal eating prick.

Then the inevitable happens, rug munching bongo head, been there done that I've been in this industry years and I'm only 23 new girl "I'm a proper foodie", calls herself the restaurant manager sticks her head threw the passé, and like some ponced up Nazi dinner lady, "What's going on", "what's this commotion", has someone been burnt, cut themselves, "NO" I've just chopped matey girl's leg off, 'matey girl, whose matey girl? Oh, and for the record I'm about to deep fry Bruce Lee's head in the fryer, and when I'm done, how about you step into my office and rim me for a minute or two before service, I'd like that a lot.

A typical and immature way of responding to a manager but that's me, losing the plot was an understatement. Now I don't claim to be any kind of psychologist but the look on her face tells me two things, one either she is going to make the 1st biggest mistake in her new found job and stamp her authority down, Or two, Pretend to join in and have a giggle about something she has no idea or clue about, the childish mentality of a chef who had forgotten his past, forgotten how he was introduced to the industry.

Guns at the ready backed by a small army of knife wielding auks braced for battle and a young sous chef eager to make his mark on his chicklings, we are ready to go over the top.

Deep breath, I brace myself, bongo head replies, "WHAT THE HELL IS GOING ON IN HERE CHEF, TELL YOUR CHEFS TO PIPE DOWN and CARRY ON WITH THERE CHORES".

Like a lunatic on speed, I unleash what only can be described as madness to the outside world, normality in an everyday working kitchen, or was it, no I don't think it was, the next day bongo head resigned.

2007 was the year I realised I had a problem a serious problem, that childhood ticking time bomb had gone off, exploded when I least expected it. I had moved out to Dubai in 2005 wanting to start a fresh, make a new start, be my own man, live a good decent life and make some good money. I'm not surprised she didn't friend me on FB when I sent her a friend request years later.

My life changing plan didn't work out "Dubai" as I knew I needed help, so I packed up my life and headed back to the UK and walked straight into a job that almost killed me. The first year into the job I was trying to hold a long-distance relationship down, I travelled out to Thailand and Australia weekends away in stunning hotels around the UK, but it just wasn't working.

The relationship I was trying to hold down literally blinded me to the issues I needed to sort out in my head. As us chefs would sometimes say, my mental health was put on the back burner simmering nicely and the physical and mental carnage that I was about to endure had well and truly been put in the rational.

George Foreman

2006 Après was well on the Dubai dining scene map, all thanks to Justin Bishop a food and beverage icon. This guy knew people, people in big places with big titles in front and at the end of their names. Mall of the emirates had fully open with an indoor amusement park on the top floor, just one of its attractions. Après also overlooked the indoor ski slope. The largest indoor ski slope on the planet, also the world's biggest freezer.

This is the role I got spit roasted royally in London for, this is the role I started to suffer with mental health issues. All day dining, French haute savoir Alpine slash brasserie slash modern European cuisine. I was the chef behind the food and the chef on the passé 6 days per week. Unless I was holiday which wasn't often, but when I was, I went bonkers in Thailand or Australia.

Word on the beach in Dubai George Foreman was coming to town. It wouldn't be the first or the last boxing icon I would meet if we did end up meeting. I had a brief conversation with Chris Eubank Sr outside the Kempinski hotel on the sheik said road when I had finished a session on the ski slope. Thursday was freestyle night, so you had to be intermediate level or above to get involved. It would also be the session where I would snap my collar in two and spend 2 hours in taxi with an unfortunate soul who had broken her neck laid out on the back seat.

Justin Bishop approached me a month prior to the event and asked if I had heard of the George Foreman G range. Yeah, I've heard of them boss. "Ok, well Mr George Foreman is coming to town and his PR company want to use Après for the launch of his G5". Boss, I'm all over it, you know I am.

Après had hosted the Emirates flare competition a few months prior, so big events we had them dialled in. The night before the event, we closed the restaurant early so the crew could set the stage. Lighting, seating and sound gear, it was a huge set up. The world's top sporting journalist would be in attendance, plus boxing fanatics from across the globe. I was into my boxing at the time but after my afternoon with George foreman I was hooked, not on George but boxing, well maybe a little bit into of George.

The brief from the PR team, "super-fresh raw ingredients, all the vegetables that work well on a grill or BBQ". Meat had to be free-range organic, the best fish I could hook. line caught seabass fillets and half a dozen fat juicy tiger prawns, olive oil, rock salt and cracked pepper, mise en place ready.

George Foreman will arrive with his son and entourage at 1pm. The buzz that morning was off the scales. Press and journalists had all arrived early. His PR team had set the stage and interview corner. They also had fifty G5's delivered plus all the G's. I would be showcasing my non-existent George Foreman grill cooking skills in front of the entire sporting world, journalists and press.

There is no way I could fuck this up, my custard burning moron days were long gone. I had to be in shape, on top form or the big man would most likely might spark me out cold. We had a large African crew mix within Après, chefs and front of house. So, they had all heard of Big George from the most famous fight humanity has ever staged. Yes, the rumble in the Jungle with no other than Muhammed Ali, "If there's a heaven, I want to see it" me to Ali, fingers crossed.

1pm, Après staff have been informed George will enter Après via the work man's entrance, the back doors. Sneak through my kitchen, out through the staff entrance and pop out on stage. Back drop huge freezer, big ski slope, me and George on stage.

His PR team appear first, instructing us to stand by our beds and not to lose the plot when he walks through the kitchen. The atmosphere in the kitchen is on fire better get the extinguishers ready. George Foreman appears, a colossal man strides through the door touching all sides of the door frame. Huge, the size of a telephone box. "Afternoon ladies and gentlemen where is the chef", that would be Mr Foreman, "please call me George", yes Mr George.

"Short and sweet, I will cue you in as the new heavy weight champion of the world, got it"? Yes, Mr George I've got it. "Just relax and we'll flow on stage". No makeup no messing about, we don our G aprons ready to get it on.

George enters the media frenzy restaurant, journalist, fans the press, screaming and shouting his name "there's only one George Foreman, one George Foreman". The restaurant has erupted, camera flashes blinding the big man. Anyone skiing on the slop that afternoon, apologies if you crashed into the que of people waiting to get on the chairlift. "There's only one George Foreman, one George Foreman".

2 hours back and forth from journalists, the questions are all about boxing and the Rumble in the Jungle. The fight was a massive historic boxing event in Kinshasa, Zaire, on October 30, 1974. It pitted the undefeated world heavyweight champion George Foreman against challenger Muhammad Ali, the former heavyweight champion. The event had an attendance of 60,000 people. Ali won by knockout, putting Foreman down just before the end of the eighth round.

Ok enough of the gable, George then shouts, "who wants to see the grill in action". "Ok folks I would like to introduce the next heavy weight champion of the world, chef Auguste Knuckles, give the man a round of applause".

I float like a butterfly and cook like bee, whatever. I enter to the screaming hoard; George and I are both wearing boxing gloves. We spare for a few 2nds, a jab here a jab there a sweet upper cut which knocks me 6ft off the ground onto the stage. That part is fiction by the way.

From left to right I've got the G1 all the way to the G5 with my pression cut mise en place ready to dazzle with my non-existent George Foreman grill cooking skills. First round G1, I have presented grilled vegetables and a toasted sandwich. 2nd round G2, grilled burger, chicken inner fillets with grilled Vegetable to garnish. 3rd round G3, grilled fish, chicken breast, vegetables. G4 the same as G3 but with BBQ grill marks after 15 minutes I'm cracking on with the G5, all of what was before but with omelettes and fried eggs.

George Foreman, "Ladies and gents can we have a huge applause for the new king of the grill and the new heavyweight champion Auguste Knuckles". Sweat pouring from me I'm pumped to the max buzzing; I jump of stage hi five George and make my way to freshen up after a cold beer. Come 6pm the show was packed up and the screaming hoard had departed. George Foreman and his son stayed for an extra two hours to chat with the staff of Après.

An afternoon spent with one of the biggest Icons of boxing history will stay with me for all my days. George Foreman if you are reading this, you are a true gentleman, it was an honour to have spared with you. Next time we spar, I will spark you flat out, one love. **For Justin Bishop RIP boss.**

Reflection

Just a mid-read FYI, I don't want my narrative to be 2000 pages of wasted words trying to explain in a hundred chapters that I drank a few beers, snorted a few lines of cocaine, drank a few cases of wine and partied with celebrities. No, that's not me, John Wick none stop in your face, lemon juice in the eyeballs, candle wax on your nipples a feather duster up your welfare canal.

I'm only going to write about the prime cuts, the offal and not keep you zoned out with, "once upon a time I shagged a tin of sausage". That would have been my co-driver on exercise Bavaria 1989. Neither is it going to end, "we all lived happily ever after". It all ended in a fucking mess, bruised, battered, broken, totally and utterly plastered being hunted by the Mafia.

The Mafia Wants Our Blood

What I said on page 81 about shit getting fucking real, it gets fucking worse Guest list, Mindy, Bruce, Jockey, Tickle and not forgetting me. Itinerary fly to the moon again and none the fucking wiser.

Specials du jour
>   Vodka breakfast and ecstasy (standard)
>   A day in Santa maria (tourists)
>   Mud bath cocktails and a leisurely lunch (savage)

The shit highlighted below wasn't meant to happen, but when you have smashed half a dozen mud bath cocktails and ecstasy before lunch shit went fucking sideways.

> **Naked pool and spiderman**
> **Five-man twister in the back of a van**
> **The mafia on our heels**
> **Escaped on a boat like Jason Bourne**
> **Going in circles**
> **Cocaine surfing**

How I ended up in Calabria in southern Italy is absolutely and totally mental, it's just another chapter in my career whereby I just must shake my head and ponder the fact I might not even be of this world?

We were brand spanking new into the millennium and thank god for all of humanity the world kept on spinning. Well according to Nostradamus the world was going to end. I guess a lot of people held their breath with eyes shut for a minute on the 31st of December 1999 at 11:59pm. I wasn't, I was walking through two foot of snow in the ski resort of Courmayeur smoking a Cuban making love to a bottle of champagne in my pants. If Nostradamus had been on the money, go out in style.

I returned to the UK, hoping to settle down and get a proper job, what a load of bollocks that thought was. Anyone doing seasonal work whether be summer or winter knows a few things, fun, sex and lash. I was no amateur when it came to this kind of lifestyle. I was seasoned and at the time able to inflict catastrophic abuse to my body, drugs, alcohol and a stuntman mentality in how I walked through life.

These years of my life were carnage, every birthday I had before my 30th I would need to outdo the ones before them. I would celebrate for an entire month in the summer. Anyone who knew me must have thought I was a spoilt son of a millionaire living of my handouts with a fuck life mentality. Doing seasonal work just to give some sort of reason to my debauched madness and to fuck the parents off. Wrong, I was a broke as a Mexican bandit on a broke ass donkey with a broken head.

Arriving back home I joined an agency, nothing special, working low level jobs across the region. Bored shitless with what I did not want to do or thought I would become. So just out of curiosity I applied for a few summer jobs with decent agencies who specialised in exclusive beach resort hotels across the Mediterranean. Within a few days I had a couple of decent interviews in London for two roles. Head or sous chef in southern Italy.

Bingo six-month contract, bags packed I'm off to Calabria. The kitchen in Calabria was poorly set up. Full of kitchen porters who had yearned for their first experience in the kitchen, wannabe commis chefs basically. A kitchen full of kitchen porters, half a dozen locals with a splash of my kitchen lingo I had no concerns that I couldn't make this work. Trick is, to spend the first month working like a donkey, establish yourself as a god like leader. Enforce kitchen protocol, get management on my side and have respect for everyone.

In a short space of time, I had become very friendly with four members of the team, two windsurfing instructors from Australia who liked lose woman and cocaine. Two bar boys from Ireland who also loved cocaine plus anything lose, including hello boys and not forgetting the local nannies. Nannies worked in the hotel creche, they would suck your dick for a vodka lemonade or a mars bar.

July 26th, I had turned the big three zero, I had to go large, I had to super large. 9am my hotel door gets kicked off its hinges from the outside inwards. My four hoodlums who have obviously had a fat line of something and most likely a quadruple shot of sambuca fall helplessly onto my bedroom floor.

"Right chef, chop chop, wakey wakey no eggs but vodka shakey shakey". Mindy crawls back into the corridor to retrieve the 5kg tub of mayonnaise, only this tub isn't filled with mayonnaise. It's a mash up of what they robbed from the hotel bar with lots of ice.

Before I've even scratched my balls and risen from the dead, we have smashed the entire 5kg content of the tub. Better get a wiggle on before the liquor starts to take effect. Up, showered, changed and out the door. Taxi for five hooligans please.

10am, we arrive in the small sleepy village of Santa Maria a few miles from the hotel. We head to the only place we think will be open, a small bar for locals with a pool table at the rear. The bucket of mayonnaise cocktail is working a treat, not to slurry or docile.

As we enter the drinking establishment for locals, we are respectful well-mannered holding down a buzz that was posted back in my hotel room. Ecstasy, several tabs crushed up and sprinkled like chopped parsley on to a beautiful sole Veronique. I do not mind being spiked by friends when they have also spiked themselves.

We seemed in control, a bit like going for a piss before bed while brushing your teeth in control. We are greeted and asked if we would like an espresso, no thankyou straight to the fizzy Italian pop please five large Peroni with vodka chaser. With a strange double take sort of look on his face and muttered words under his breath we are served our breakfast beverage, "crazy fucking English". Well, if the truth be told I am the only English man for quite a few miles me old fruit, "eh, menospeakadainglish".

Last man buys the next round, we are out the blocks like Ben Johnson plus growth hormone injections. Tickle is the first to slam his pint on the bar top, same again please. We ask for change and head to the pool table at the rear of the pub, which is situated in its own pool room. I could have just written pool room. Beers flowing, we are ripped, buzzing and it's not even midday. It's not even 10:30am

Jockey the Ozzy windsurfing instructor decides it's time to do a mud bath, 2nd breakfast. A mud bath, top shelf bar man's choice, lime juice and cream. For the record, these drinks are not shots. Once they have settled you eat them with a spoon. Well, the trick is to down them before they settle. The big boys will do two tops, we did a round each. Savages soon to be on the rampage in a small sleepy Italian village while the locals are still fast asleep.

When things cannot get any more savage, we decided to play pool for items of clothing, strip pool. "Guys were the fuck had Mindy gone, he's been missing for 10 minutes". "Hey guys I'm out here, over here, look out the window". What the fuck, Mindy is on the wrong side of the window, outside of the pool room. We all stagger to the window half naked. Mindy is naked on the other side of the window standing on a ledge no bigger than 10inches.

Not only is he smashed peeled ripped he's two stories up, what a fucking fruit cake. The result of hard liquor and ecstasy for breakfast had done its jobs and turned us into beasts. Not only is Mindy hanging out the window he has managed to shuffle around the tiny ledge to the next window. Well, that just started a chain reaction of madness. "Right, next man to lose at pool strips naked and climbs out the window, along the ledge and in through the other window". Game on, five grown men, acting like Eaton frat boy's half naked doing the spiderman thing in the middle of a sleepy residential retired mafia dwelling.

Southern Italy, retired gangsters, wannabe mafia, two smashed Ozzy boys, two peeled Irish fellas and a six-foot black man from the black country. What's the worst that could happen? Five naked men standing on a ledge two stories up singing rock songs. Not good for morale if your retired and wanting peace.

The barman enters the pool room, no one to be seen all bar our clothes smashed glasses and vomit. like Russian dolls we all appear naked jumping through the window one by one. My Italian isn't bad, but I sense the bar man has fucking lost it. Staggering all over the place we grab our clothes and do legs dressing ourselves on the run, being chased by a lunatic with a pool cue. Was there really any need for violence during that time of the day? Fucking savage barman with a pool cue, ridiculous.

Having evaded the cue wielding barman, we park ourselves at a beautiful pizzeria on the beach. Four litres of vino, four half-eaten pizzas later we must move. I've received a phone call from our hotel manager asking if we are in Santa maria boss. Why I reply, "several old age pensioners dressed in black have been severely traumatised by five grown men with swords out naked trying to burgle a bar in town".

Well, we've got our clothes on now, "what do you mean now, you crazy bastards, you've got trouble coming your way, grandsons of the family want blood". "I'm sending the hotel van to pick you up, be at the fountain near the carpark by the square in 10 minutes". Yes boss, grazie boss.

Ok boys, we need to get out of the village quick sharpish. Italian Kozaks with guns and machetes are looking for us, they mean business. Time to make like Jason Bourne and get the fuck out of dodge to our pickup point. The floor is lava, we grab a bottle of vodka from the souvenir shop then make the mad dash through the village. We are meet by the hotel engineer, "get the fuck in the back you crazy fucking bastards" five grown men in the back of a white van wasted beyond measure playing twister is a sight for sure trying to down vodka from side to side.

The engineer wheel spins off, several black Audis zoom past on the other side of the road, "you lucky fucking cunts, do you know the shit you have caused". No, we don't think we do. The carnage was not over yet, we are dropped off at the beach bar 100 meters up from the hotel, bad move. "Stay here act like tourists, don't make a fucking sound, I will be back later".

It's in the 90s, blistering day, the beach is packed with hotel guests and locals with the addition of five epileptic zombies. The carnage which ensues is madder than the naked spider man thing. Fuck knows whose idea it was, but we back stroke out to the hotel rib, which has a small 75cc motor. We all clamber onboard, unhook the mooring, start the motor and head out to sea.

Five lunatics, pirates of the Mediterranean have escaped nurse ratchets mad house. The sea air sobers us all, or so we thought, it just intensifies the mood. Realising what we are doing it's too late to head back to shore as we are fucked anyways. There isn't a more serious version of proper fucked, maybe death. We head for the next village along the coast. Thirty minutes of Titanic banter we arrive at our destination. We secure the boat to the jetty and make our way to the village bar.

We chat, we drink, we are alive and enjoying the birthday festivities. "Ok boys let's head back and face the music", not having any ocean knowledge of the sea around us, we set off in the wrong direction. Bad move as we shank the prop on a concrete mooring in the shallows, bad move, unbelievably bad move. "Stop saying bad fucking move", screams tickle.

Now that version of proper fucked has just taken on a new meaning. Not only are we to far from shore but we are miles from home. All is not lost handsome Bruce has the get out of jail card. The prop is fucked but if we drive the boat in circles we will sooner or later arrive home. Fucking genius, we arrive back to base 3 hours later dizzy as kids jumping off a roundabout. Beach deserted, all bar flashing blue lights.

The hotel manager and local authorities greet us on the beach. Handcuffed we are taken to the local sweat shop in the village and grilled for an hour. The local police make it clear that we are banned from entering the village or local restaurants in the area. If we are caught in Santa maria form this day forward, they will let the dogs lose on us. We are told to fuck off in Italian. We walk back to the hotel; shower change and continue the carnage in the hotel beach bar.

We end the night surfing naked, pinged off our eyeballs on the finest Italian cocaine, its without saying my shift the following morning on the pans was a right off. My body resembled that of a shark attack. I had cut myself to smithereens on the coral trying to hang 10 on a wake board. I didn't mind the grilling down at the sweat shop by super by Mario and his gorillas. We were out of pocket and in the bad books with the waterfront manager for fucking his boat up.

Four-Legged Octopus' Shuffle

When the final check has been sent, the scrub down finished, sections sanitised and the last chef out the door, life can only go two ways. A group of you head straight to the pub, find a nice corner and start what was only meant to be a few beers and to discuss the evenings service.

Two, maybe a few members of the team will most likely jump on public transport and head off home to lick the wounds of a 17hr shift and a savage hammering up Bourneville boulevard from the head chef. The group that heads to the pub are shortly joined by a handful from front of house. It's a Wednesday so everyone's intention is a quick whistle wetter then home. The chit chat is flowing, the clock strikes 1am, you find yourself sat in a disco pub surrounded my hundreds of students on the lash.

"Fuck it, let's get a ticket, it's a great atmosphere in here tonight, just one then we'll be on our way". Excitement sets in because scoring 1st grade A1 cocaine In Bristol is as easy as popping to Starbucks for a pumpkin soy latte. Another round of shots and the instigator pops around the corner to meet his dealer at the Argos collection point. Business must be good, there's a few bodies all looking shifty rubbing their chins waiting for the sound of the moped engine.

The moped has landed, please make your way to baggage lounge, "Listen bruv, I'm doing deals, fat packs all night, three for a hundred two for 50". Bruv I'm working in 7 hours, fuck it, give me two for 50. The crew inside the disco are giddy chatting knocking back shots of Tequila. "Yes bruv, you sweet", believe me we are good to go. Its nose tag for the next fifteen minutes.

The kiddy with the quiver decides to occupy the disabled toilet, nice and clean. Enough space for three, plus the folding baby changer against the wall makes a superb table to rack crystal fat lines.

You can cut the atmosphere in the disabled toilet with a credit card, whispers, "let me rack them bruv", "it's cool I'm all over this". It's a ceremony, crushing the shiny rockets with a crisp bank note, then cutting through to make three beautiful identical lines.

You lick your top teeth with your tongue and swallow any spit within your mouth. A length of toilet paper is pulled from the toilet paper holder. A hearty blow to clear the passage for the cocaine to travel well. A £50 bank note is rolled perfectly, not to thick or thin, it's a perfect vehicle.

A deep breath and exhale, you bend your hips, elbows out, holding the note gently to your nose, there is no going back, work in 7 hours. A clean swift movement left to right not over snorting just enough for the quiver to vanish. The cocaine hits the back of your throat, head flung back eyes as wide as frying pans looking at the ceiling, "oh my days, oh my days, that is the fucking bomb".

Knees bent, arms stretched, elbows out, left to right three amigos make their way back to the party. The cocaine is quick, the conversation is a mashup of movies, politics, religion, sex and cooking. The clock strikes two, it's back to the watering closet to finish the tickle, only this time you are wired, senses in 13th gear with a sprinkling of paranoia.

There's no ceremony this visit, it's in and out like Bonnie and Clyde, the clock strikes 3am, your off to a house party. The brain has switched from I need to be up at 6am to, let's get bang on it. The house party is across town, two Johnny cabs we are off, dealer dialled in to drop three for 100 on arrival. The party is mad bonkers, a seductive vibe, intelligent drum and bass echoes through the house. Skunk weed stings your eyes, a smoky haze fills the dim lit rooms.

The bass line pounds your heart, beautiful people from all walks of life, bouncing on the balls of their feet. Dealer on a moped drops three magnificent wraps of Columbian quiver. The clock strikes four, no sign of the sun for a few hours. We crack on with a fat one followed by a blaze in the middle of the room surrounded, encased by a beautiful buzz of bodies on the same level.

Smiley shinny mellow people buzzing, the music so sweet, head drops back, eyes closed rushing, bottom jam trembling. The crew have dispersed into the misty morning dew. Check, three wraps, a cheeky one from the corner of my bank card, sharing generously with new friends, the clock strikes five.

Time to make a move, eye lids so heavy, stoned, buzzing, ripped you taxi a lift across town to Barton Hill. Before you exit the car, you share a joint with two beautiful Rastafarian's, no chit chat just appreciation for a wicked morning. Stoned nods, merci my friends. I hand half a wrap to the driver for fare, "sweet", yes, it sure is.

A journey of twenty steps takes a lifetime, you make it inside, upstairs to the bathroom. Bloodshot eyes, tiny rocks lodged in your nose, heavy cheeks, aching legs, sleep is a Christmas present. The cocaine is busy at work, it's time to make the call.

"Good morning this is the exit me gently hotel, there's no one around to take your call. For meetings and events press 1, for concierge press 2, for HR press 3, better not. Sales and marketing press 4, for leisure and gym press 5, for restaurant bookings please press 6. For housekeeping, please press 7, for engineering please press 8, for the kitchen please press 9, for anything please stay on the line".

Chef its Auguste, I can't make it in today, I'm suffering with stomach cramps and vomiting, I will call tomorrow to update, regards Auguste. I hang up the phone, close my curtains, put blue lines on by massive attack and rack out the fattest line.

The day is spent in and out my scratcher knocking back shots of vodka, doing little hits, listening to Bristol's finest. Was it worth it? fuck yeah, I'm alive, I'm young with no responsibilities all bar to show up for work and cook. Well, show up when I'm not alone and lost in my own world. When I did show, I was lost, alone in my own world.

You Cunt

Mr Jeffries was his name, St Andrew's junior school, Coleman Street Whitmore Reans. I have tried so hard to remember how and what caused this teacher's outrage towards me. I didn't say boo to a goose at school in the 70s because I knew the repercussions at home would be on another level.

A memory so clear it hurts; I felt everyone was out to get me in some shape or form, even at Infant school at the back of that crumbling house. I remember I was told I had to do PE with only my vest and shoes on because I had forgotten my shorts. No underwear, no fucking pants, a child no older than six told they had to perform PE half naked.

But who cared, those two humans battering themselves stupid? No, I don't think so. A kid who wore shoes hanging from his feet to school held together with plastic cored. I remember as clear as the driven snow being pushed and pulled aggressively by my arm, being slapped on the bum, repeatedly. Mr Jefferies shouting and screaming to the class "look at him, look what we have here, a snivelling horrible creature" pulling, shoving, slapping, pushing me for almost ten minutes.

I wish my arm had dislocated or broke, he would have been proper fucked, but it didn't. Tears streaming down my face, half the class just stared at me, mouths open, unable to explain what was going on. Unless like me they had come from a battered home.

The rest of the class laughed, laughed as he continued his rage. I have never been able to figure out what started the assault on me. Maybe one day while doing something random it will dawn on me. But until that day he will always be that bully.

Evil, demented, toxic abusers, they prey on the weak, the vulnerable, the disadvantaged. Vermin hiding in the shadows waiting silently for their next victim to pass. There is no wit or punch line to this chapter, no smiles or fond memories for those schools, just hatred and disgust.

209

Head Hunted: Head Severed

The worst move of my career and the joke of all hotels. There is one thing being head hunted, but it's another to have it severed. Being sacked as a chef de partie today is not a big thing. You dust yourself off and move on to one of a thousand jobs being posted across two dozen job sites. Being removed from office as an executive head chef for "bullying and harassment" is not good. It's going to have a detrimental and lasting impact on your career.

Sitting here almost a decade later, having told a few lies at a couple of huge interviews I'm somewhat ashamed. Not because of the lies I told to get my foot in the door when applying for two prestigious hotels. I'm ashamed that after all my worldly experience, I didn't see the red flags during my first contact from the agency who head hunted me.

Head in the wrong place working away from home, I should have done my homework. But I didn't, I was desperate to be home with my wife and kids during the week. Sleeping in my own bed, present seven days per week was my objective.

Today I cannot even comprehend the amount of chef agencies out there. Chefs get pissed off with the industry, they leave and start up an agency with a few other reprobates. Their goal to make as much money as humanly possible in the shortest space of time. Now these so-called, pop-up agencies, they have no regard whatsoever for loyalty or trust.

The reason why they lack these qualities is because they have zero HR skills and are truly unable to empathise with the frustrations of the average working chef as it's highly likely they've only spent several months in a working kitchen. "This industry is struggling, let's make it struggle some more", combined with a 20-year-old general manager these two bodies are toxic to the industry.

The reason why chefs choose to work away from home during the week can be down to a multitude of reasons. Jobs in their local area, unless they work in any major city, salaries for such experience have not been reviewed for decades.

Another reason, their local area is awash with budget hotels, branded menus, shocking working conditions. Dilapidated kitchens, unrealistic targets to achieve or robotic programmed managers. Or some establishments are in the middle of now where, no public transport let alone staff accommodation.

Now considering the size of this certain establishment in question, the grounds it sat on with the sheer amount of revenue that it was turning over, with an 18-hole PGA golf course. It still mystifies me to this day why it had so many flaws and why I didn't sniff them out when I got the call. I was head hunted for a few specific reasons. Regardless of my current state I was still able to sort out kitchens that were in dire need of restructuring.

We are not talking about kitchens that churn out one maybe two-million-pound food and beverage revenue. I was a chef at the time who managed huge teams, 40+ chefs, 20+ kitchen porters, multiple restaurants and outlets. Large conference and banqueting, meetings and events, leisure facilities, branded coffee shops and fine dining. Considering the start of my career, my career in general and how challenging it was, decades later I had become a wanted chef.

The property was generating £500,000 food and beverage revenue per calendar month across the estate. It was a monster with plans to increase revenue by ten million within three years on completion of the 2nd conference centre. This was going to be the biggest establishment I would manage for a brief moment.

Several phone calls after the initial "hello we have a job you might be interested in" I was invited to the property to dine in one of the many outlets. Our party was greeted by the food and beverage manager. I must say, first impressions were spot on.

Buffet or ala carte was the order of the evening, steaks from the back and buffet from the front. Drinks ordered; we are invited to the buffet. First impressions of the buffet, shocking, a poor attempt at a Mediterranean buffet. Over cooked, unappealing, not well thought out, let alone presented well, lukewarm dog vomit. The two chefs who stood behind the buffet leaning against the wall looked like kitchen porters. They dressed like kitchen porters but in fact were both chefs.

I asked about the buffet in a polite manner and what was being served not making out I was a chef of cause. Both chefs left the buffet to fetch another strange looking fella who came around from the back to explain what was on display. "Sorry boss, chef who cook, make buffet, he goes home, nobody here

211

boss", so what is on the buffet? "We have roast vegetables boss, with lamb boss, some salads over there, cheese and desserts boss".

The food and beverage manager hurried over and kindly asked for my feedback when I and my party had finished. The only thing we enjoyed was the ice cream and free wine. As we departed, I asked for the manager, I was informed he had left for the evening.

The following week I was interviewed by the resort general manager. First impressions, this GM was in a state, their physical appearance was that of a retired overweight middle-aged man who had been blown up and put back together by kids. I was given a thorough interview and shown the entire estate, 3 hours, exhausting. The two main kitchens needed some serious investment which I was informed the budget had been signed for a refurbishment. It was also mentioned that a new build for a fine dining brasserie had also been signed off.

We discussed my management experience in detail, I was asked whether I would have any challenges managing two head chefs. The two head chefs managed their teams accordingly within the two main buildings, my response, no. I politely asked if any of the head chefs had applied for the executive head chef role, "yes both have applied". It's obvious both wanted the job.

We shock hands and I departed, that same evening my agent called me, we discussed the package which I was happy with. What I should have discussed was the executive management team and their agenda. I should have done my homework regarding the company I was about to work for. Sleeping in my own bed, being home with the family the huge salary and bonus had blinded me to the chaos I was about inherit.

This company had bitten off more than it could chew, they had hotels everywhere, managed under several different brands and managed by several equity companies. In a nutshell a fucking mess, a dozen different brand standards for each property. Different employment policies all with different contractual responsibilities.

I was appointed a week later as the new executive head chef and greeted like an African king on my first day at work. Headfirst into the dog shit, fire alarm full evacuation soon as the morning meeting had ended, strange. I meet with my two heads chefs and given the grand tour, again.

It was evident from the get-go there was serious issues with how front and back of house worked, communication between the two departments was non-existent. The kitchen teams hated the sales department and sales team hated the wo head chefs. The F&B director was the nephew of the general manager which nade the whole process of moving forward virtually impossible. Any form of onfrontation the F&B director, they would run to their "uncle" and kick off lating everyone who wore an apron.

My first day, 1pm 2nd fire alarm, 4pm 3rd fire alarm. 80% of produce served vas bought in readymade convenience garbage. The food cost was tracking the vrong side of 50%. Food waste was on a level I have never witnessed. 12 food vaste bins on each loading bay for the two kitchens 24 in total. At the end of the nonth all bins would be full of food waste.

Both kitchens flooded with agency chefs, 6pm another fire alarm. It wasn't ong before it clicked, the general manager wanted a yes man chef. Yes boss, no oss, I'll sort it boss with as little confrontation as possible. Turn a blind eye and et every manager working in food and beverage who had been there for the past ecade do what they had done ever since they signed their contract, fuck all.

I was a get the job done kind of chef, I didn't give a fuck who I pissed off to et what needed to be done and fixed. I've been employed to turn this estate round and give the culinary department a face lift, so be it. It was me against he world, sales, HR department, front of house they could not deal with the pace was working at. I was in everyone's face day in day out. A yes man, brown osed whip, a chef on all fours with a sign on my ass saying, "all inclusive".

The ops meetings were a joke, it was just an opportunity for departments to lag each other off, civil war within the hotel and they all seemed to get a kick rom it. The GM was not any easier to communicate with, he had a chronic illness anged up on pharmaceuticals day in day out. It didn't help when trying to hold conversation with them once they had taken their medication. They would just it there and drool. During the interview process they came across as a healthy ndividual.

Fresh produce, freshly prepared food wasn't on there to do list. As this would equire skilled chefs, no wonder I was always getting knocked back by HR. Sorry chef we don't have the budget for chefs", WTF, tens and thousands of ounds on agency fees each month and I'm being told we don't have a budget.

Then the proverbial shit hit the fan. I had left work one evening, arrived home hanged and set off for the gym. Thirty minutes into my workout I have several issed calls and a dozen voicemails. "Chef the hotel is on fire; we need you back t work". What the fuck, this must be a joke. I call Phil the head chef who managed the Victorian building. "Chef the entire conference building is on fire, its madness, you better get back here".

1hr later at the entrance to the grounds. Good evening my name is Auguste I'm the executive chef, I need to get onsite and assist the management team. It was madness, security and emergency flooded the grounds. The entire block of 400 hotel rooms was a blaze. Scary fucking shit, guests and staff in a state of shock at the sheer size of the fire.

I head to the Victorian building, the kitchen is packed with 40+ chefs and kitchen porters, rush hour Oxford circus. The brief, to make grab and go snack bags for all 400+ guests and staff. I instructed all personal that are not needed to leave and go home once the grab and go bags were ready. The grounds of the estate resembled an apocalyptic movie set. Switched on, tuned in with everything going on around me and the implications of my actions I make from this moment moving forward.

It was obvious, last man in first to go when the flames are under control. My head chef in the driving seat of the Victorian building Phil had only been in the role for a month. He had been with the company for several years, not very vocal in the kitchen. To laid back and never challenged a chef regarding any kitchen issues. He thought I would do his dirty work when issues or confrontation occurred.

Phil was also the chef on the buffet that night when I came with friends to test the waters. He had been given the thumbs up by head office that his years with the company he was able to manage the Victorian building as head chef.

My brief to my two head chefs was to batten down the hatches. Make sure HACCP, COSHH, health and safety food hygiene was a 100%, no gaps in our due diligence recording. Reports came in that no one had perished during the blaze, all guests and staff had been accounted for. The GM was off the hook but had a lot of explaining to do.

The following morning an investigation into what or who caused the fire was underway. Considering the amount of fire evacuations that were conducted prior to the fire, I knew something was south of the boarder. Something was off, out of date, past its best with management.

The week of the fire Phil my head chef had turned into a liability, he was letting chefs run wild, he had no control over his team let alone was on top of health and safety, like I asked. Food hygiene was a mess, several inspections of the kitchen and storage areas it was time to pull this chef into the office and see what was going on.

I informed HR that I would be issuing a verbal warning once I had addressed the issues in question. Cross contamination, meat and fish out of date by days, rotten food in the vegetable fridge, the kitchen a bombsite. If the EHO had visited us that week to carry out an inspection "no star", closed. Considering the shit that was going on around us, I also had to micromanage an able chef who had been given the thumbs up by head office.

Knowing what I know today I should have let HR deal with it from the get-go. Totally oblivious to my temper with everything I was discussing regarding the state of the kitchen. Phil, span the argument 360 and started to blame me for his failings, the fucking cheek of this chef was on another level.

I flipped, full blown in this Individuals face, curse words pouring out my mouth. The meeting ended with me screaming at Phil telling him to fuck off out my office. I gave him 24 hours to get the kitchen in good shape.

Back in the office the following morning, I changed and started my inspection of the Victorian kitchen. The place was a fucking war zone, raw chicken left uncovered on the top shelf, blood dripping freely onto prepared salads. Green lamb chops, dairy produce out of date, food debris all over the floor. This wasn't neglect or incompetence; this was a set up. Why didn't I sniff it out?

As soon as Phil came on shift, I summoned him to the office and went to town, I lost the plot. little did I know on the other side of the office door some sly little cunt was recording my verbal rampage. Like the first meeting we had 24 hours prior, it ended with shouting, get the fuck out my face and sort that fucking kitchen out.

I'm summoned to the GM's office a week later, for what I thought would be a weekly catch up, human resources are in attendance. "Chef we've come across a recording of you verbally abusing another chef, which is classed as harassment, which is gross misconduct". The recording starts to play. I can see where this is going, several minutes of me kicking off. I'm asked can I explain the incident? Yes. The fucking idiot is a liability who has no regard whatsoever for food hygiene let alone health and safety of his kitchen.

"Chef off the back of this recording I'm in no other position to suspend you pending an investigation which will most likely lead to dismissal". Talk about a fucking stitch up, I didn't have a leg to stand on. I had been at the establishment for a few months, so taking these fuckers to court wasn't going to happen. The whole charade was a fucking set up. Fuck the kitchen hygiene, turn a blind eye to a potential legal battle if we give a guest food poisoning or better still kill them.

Let's fuck chef over, we can save a large amount of money "my salary". I was out the door. If they had said "look chef, the fire has caused considerable damage we need to let you go". I would have taken that on the chin.

I was informed years later while being interviewed for another job, I was set up. The kitchen was set up to fail that morning. Not going to go into it as I still feel embarrassed for taking on the role. The recording was staged, why? Why employee an experienced executive head chef to be a yes man. Nine out of ten managers within this industry do not like being told how to do their jobs. When they are, they get their backs up, the inevitable plan to oust is set in motion.

I was informed through the toxic grapevine Phil was sacked and fined by the EHO for being an incompetent twat. After an investigation, it was declared that his incompetence had caused an outbreak of food poisoning which left several guests seriously ill within the kitchen he went on to manage after being sacked from the Victorian building.

Fast Forward Backwards

It was my first Christmas party at the hotel the woman I would marry 12 years later was also in attendance. One of the most amazing chefs I've had the pleasure of ever working with was also in attendance with a ticket.

My journey with this chef will be kept private, sadly he was taken from this world way to early leaving a beautiful partner and children behind may you find eternal peace with the angles my brother, there isn't a day goes by where you are not in my thoughts.

It's not going to be easy telling you this fractured part of my journey It would require me to write another book. So, we'll dive right in. One ticket you'd want another ticket and another ticket, cocaine is like pringles once you've popped that's it, you're on the pringle rollercoaster.

The issues with my mental health are still simmering on the back burner, to be honest I've totally given up on that subject and now in fifth gear managing this beast of a kitchen.

January 2008, I move into a lovely 2 bed flat and need to sort out a local deal as I'm new to the area and the quiver I've been getting isn't cutting it anymore, nose garbage. Who's the man that knows a man, anyone for a nose in any London hotel knows it's the concierge team. A few phone calls and a text message I'm hooked up.

I'm in and this is where and this is when the whole fucking party went south. Work five days get bang on all weekend back to work Monday morning feeling wavy. Work five days get bang on all weekend end back to work wavy repeat. I'm single so no dramas, so it becomes routine and that's the killer there, routine, work, cocaine, alcohol, work repeat, repeat, repeat.

Before I know it's the norm, this is who I am, a functioning junkie, but did I know it, no I didn't. I'm still procuring my gear from the same dealer when one evening he says, listen fella, you've been getting the £45.7 cocaine, try this it's the £60.5 Bolivian, yep why not I'll take three. By the way I'm earning good money, no kids' casual lady friends which means I'm snorting thousands of pounds every month.

My routine takes a turn, I'm now knocking off early on Fridays just after lunch, meet my guy, bang boom cocaine sorted, Friday Saturday Sunday bang on it. Wavy Monday, Tuesday I'm feeling ok'ish, 2008 has gone, still nothing sorted regarding my simmering pan of dynamite. My simmering pan is now beginning to mutate into other forms of mental health and illnesses, do I have a clue? No, I do not.

With cocaine as we know comes an avalanche of other goodies, extreme alcohol abuse, extreme addiction to porn and sleeping with a multitude of casual fuck buddies, with a huge risk of contracting all sorts of nasties and believe me when you're out there and I mean orbiting Saturn the last thing on your mind is protection.

I'm holding down the job but now taking risks, Mondays is a no go and Fridays is a blur. I'm now having major come downs on Monday after a crazy weekend, sick as a pig Tuesday wavy Wednesday back on top Thursday only to think about scoring my gear on Friday.

I forgotten to mention unless I was out on a Friday or Saturday night which was very rare, I'd be home doing all this coke alone it was very rare I'd do it with anyone else, cocaine was my mistress. I've now lost it full blown junkie, calling the ambulance was now a regular thing, A&E was a regular thing but guess what I'm fine as far as I was concerned, I'm in tip top shape on top of the world enjoying life.

The years start to pass me by, the weight is falling off me and I'm literally snorting half a gram per line, nosebleed I'd smoke it, then snort more. Paranoid in my flat curtains closed with my boxers on at 2pm in the afternoon covered in cream, porn playing on every device looking through the keyhole thinking I'm going to be busted by a huge fairy bunny rabbit smacked off his bunny ears.

Finally hope my future wife moves in, but I'm living in denial, I'm living with the most amazing human, but cocaine is still the lady running things in the yard. So, I conjure up the most stupid idea in my condition during these crazy years I decided I wanted to connect with my biological father. With all this shit going on I decide its time, time to inflict the most stupid irrational thing I've ever thought of, reconnect with him.

I'm an emotional wreck and I've made a conscious decision to let him in with all his baggage. I'm sniffing coke of the toilet floor I've lost all sense of decency I've lost all sense of identity I cannot relate to love; I cannot relate to reason I can't even relate to reality. I've OD'd several times I'm 6,3 65kg I'm a dead man walking, I'm still ashamed to this day of that person "me" and the things I did to my wife.

Do I Moan when she kicks off during the special period in the month? No, I don't, I don't have the right to kick off, do I moan when we go shopping and she wants to spend two weeks in the same shop? No, I don't. Holidays, she books we go. I don't have a right to moan, I'm humbled by her for her forgiveness, has she forgotten, no she hasn't, I'm in no position to rock her world, all I give is love and I fucking listen with an open mind when she speaks, I'm present today more than I can imagine, why, because I need to be.

There are things I did that I can't discuss but any junkie alcoholic will know the depths we slump to, some junkies come back, some are still out there just waiting for death to come to them. I had lost the will to live I had lost the will to be part of anything, without my wife being there, adios for me, adios in the ground with worms.

Why did I want to die so much, was suicide the only way out, out of what, what was it that I couldn't grasp? What was I ignoring, the pot simmering on the back burner had well and truly exploded? In 2013 I walked into my GP's office and asked for help.

What has happened between 2013 and 2020 has been the hardest journey I've ever taken, a journey back to life. A journey which literally killed me, "Lazarus", I had to stare death in the face and only when I knew the meaning of life, the true meaning life and all its wonder, death might look me in the eye, and say "not to today" only then would hopefully live.

January 2020 the memories flashbacks the trauma the mental scars almost and I mean almost had the better hand. I experienced what can only be described as a psychotic lightspeed earthquake of a meltdown driving home from work.

Between 2013 and 2020 I had slipped in and out of a few jobs, big jobs across the country and the journey back to life was taking its toll. I had been in and out through the NHS system numerous times prescribed all kinds of medicines, more assessments than I can remember, referred to various clinics across the county but nothing was working.

My OCD irrational thoughts were getting stronger, I was having frequent anxiety attacks, I was super hyper vigilant every day, the nightmares off the charts, on top of all that I had started to hallucinate without the acid, hallucinating walk down street, in bed, in the shower, nuts, I was tripping, and I didn't want to.

While all this was going on I decided to apply for master chef professionals 2020 and this is when everything above intensified 10-fold my mental health went haywire. I had two very successful telephone interviews with MCP (master chef professionals), I decided to start practicing my signature dish. I'm sure you are familiar with MCP and the competition format.

Skills test, signature dish, knockout stage, invention test another knockout stage, cook for the critics then you're in serious contention to be scouted by any number of 4* deluxe 5* hotels, fine dining restaurants development chef positions across the globe, its life changing.

I was then invited for the audition stage in Camden London, very confident and positive audition. I'm now geared up and in what I thought a "good head space". All my senses and my thought process were super intensified I'm practicing every evening after work.

I'm also in talks with a friend of mine and in the process of setting up a pop-up food stall, Biriyani Bobs, work is busy my food is getting mad crazy positive feedback. We are taking more private functions and bookings for weddings, birthday parties and bar Mitzvah's than ever before and moreover I'm hosting a monthly chefs table.

On top of all that I'm at the gym every other evening, I'm taking a test booster, BCA, creatine and protein shakes. January 6th, 2020, I leave work, I've already practiced my signature dish a dozen times in my head that day but need to finalise garnish.

By the time I've pulled on to the M25 at jt19 my thoughts are travelling at lighting speed, and I have no control of my thought process whatsoever. My thinking becomes dark I'm wrapped in a cold grey blanket, and I can hear my own thoughts speaking to me as clear as day. My breathing becomes erratic I'm hyperventilating and there's a weight on my chest I cannot shift.

Out of the blue, I'm telling myself end it now, just pull the car over and end it, pull over and walk into traffic these are the thoughts I can hear in my head as clear as day. It will be quick, painless I promise you, just pull over and walk head on into rush hour traffic, scared is an understatement I'm past scared I'm trapped within a cloaking force around me, I've been possessed, I need more than a priest, my days have finally come, it's here, is this how I'm going out, suicide.

This is it; this is the day I leave behind two amazing children and a loving wife, I'm indicating to pull over onto the hard shoulder. Full beam in my rear and the horn from an artic lorry snaps me out of hypnotised state which is right up my arse.

Decades of denial, ignorance, stupidity, drug and alcohol addiction decades of CPTSD (complex post-traumatic stress disorder) anxiety, years of being super hyper vigilant. Years of carnage and damage I had done to others in my head mainly loved ones. The destruction I had caused upon myself finally caught up with me driving home from work and to this day the lorry might have been there at that given moment for a reason "driving somewhere right", it was an act of a greater being or something that got me home that day.

I've been asked a dozen times what was the driving force that evening, well it might have been my car, but something else was at play that evening. If I hadn't had been full beamed by that lorry, then I honestly believe I wouldn't be sat in my garden continuing this project. Was it the end of the line, was my journey on the biscuit train finally over? was I was kissed by God, I cannot help but look up at the heavens and ponder is there a greater being out there?

I arrive home in an absolute pickle, erratic vision, my head traveling at light speed mully mushed. I look at the knife in the kitchen sink contemplating shall I drive it through my neck. My wife knew something was seriously wrong, I blurted out my mental health quivering uncontrollably, straight away she's on the phone to the crisis team. Within minutes I'm speaking with a crisis team member I was on the phone for what seemed eternity before I came back down to earth, bruised, battered, somewhat lifeless and mentally broken, my mind in a million pieces and a donkey is trying to put it back together.

The following morning 9am I had my first assessment with a crisis team psychologist and psychiatric nurse. This was going to be first time my wife would truly hear the extent of the abuse inflicted on me as a child and the horrors I experienced during my deployment as a dessert rat during the 1st gulf war.

This was the beginning of the end, this was the start of enhanced trauma pathway treatment and CBT, cognitive behavioural therapy for adults suffering with extreme CPTSD. The non-existent relationship with my biological parents which I tried so hard to reconnect with finally burnt out. For me it never felt natural anyways, every phone call or face time was an effort, I felt they were clinging onto me for their own self-pity or some sort of closure to the past.

It wasn't me who needed them, it was them who needed me, those few minutes with me every other week over the phone, so that they might feel in some sort of weird twisted toxic way that I might have forgiven them both. In April 2020 I decided after lengthy consideration I had to let them go, for me to get my head straight and live life without distraction I needed to do this, I finally plucked up the courage to walk away, my terms my decision.

Scorched Cash

What has it really cost you, have you ever sat down and really thought about the cost of what you have sacrificed to the hospitality industry? Your trade, your craft, your passion, cooking, that's what it all comes down to at the end of the day. It's just cooking at the end of the day. But, somehow, somewhere it has turned into an industry which is killing people. Driving chefs to breaking point or has the industry always been like this, long before I signed up?

So, I'll ask the question again apart from the cost of whites, knives, crocs, fuel, childcare, drugs, alcohol, medication, therapy, marriage counselling, divorce, poor mental health and addiction. What has it really cost you to be who and where you are today in the hospitality industry as, the average working chef in todays and yesterday's culinary world?

I attended a very prestigious food and beverage conference back in 2017 in Paris for several days. Out of the box brain storming, with a multitude of chefs, F&B directors and general managers. During this wonderful event and it was wonderful. We discussed how to drive more revenue through our relevant hotel outlets. We also discussed being in a position whereby we could compete with standalone restaurants, "our new competitor". E majority

The new competitor for majority (90%) who work within hotels within the hospitality industry. It's not the other hotels within our vicinity. Not anymore, it's now the magnitude of high street branded, privately owned, rosette, Michelin starred outlets, brasseries, swanky cafes and pop ups. The age of being Insta famous, Instagram intellectual and posting every dish you eat online is the world we live in today. But you knew this already.

Its bonkers how a 4* establishment can compete with the Adam Handlings of this new world unless you invest, and invest I mean big time. But I've asked myself which hotels sincerely want to invest in the future? It just means pay rises, promotions, development, refurbishments, recruitment. By the way and for the

223

record, this narrative was in the post long before COVID-19 bought the entire hospitality sector to its knees.

This event was so lavish they had Michelin starred chefs flown into Paris from all over the globe to design, oversee, prepare and serve the gala black-tie dinner event. The gift bags alone were Russian oligarch exquisite, no expense spared. They even had a DJ playing funky lounge music during breakfast, lunch and dinners.

Anyway, getting back to the point, during the final day that morning after a night at the Rex club a little worse for wear we all took part in a mindfulness exercise. We were asked to turn and face the person next to us, take a deep breath, close our eyes and relax. During this what seemed odd exercise to me as I have been practicing mindfulness for years, the mindful coach starts speaking. "I'm just like you and you are just like me, we are like each other". One eye popped open to see what was going on, everyone hypnotised and hung over from the night before.

"I'm just like you blah blah blah", then it clicked, how the fuck can anyone within touchy feely distance be like me. I'm a chef how is finally at the end of a long and painful journey battling drug and alcohol addiction. My mental health is blown to smithereens, my kitchen cabinet is like nurse ratchets pharmaceutical locker. No, this guy is wrong, I do not get this whole group mindfulness bollocks. I can do the mindfulness thing on the toilet at home, driving to work even brushing my teeth. A group mindfulness orgy, it just isn't working for me. Mindfulness is individual, it is for me, we all have different personal issues to deal with. Sorry but I can't do the tree hugging thing.

So, I guess there is a little clue, what has it cost you right there in the last paragraph. And no, it's got nothing to do with an orgy. Well, I will tell you what its cost me but before I start, I am like you and you are like me, "chefs". If you have read my first outing as an author, beaten black and blue, born into racism you will have gained an insight into my struggles with addiction.

Physically, mentally, emotionally its cost me everything being a chef for the past 30 years. Day one my marbles were taken out the bag, thrown across the playground, trampled on by every kid playing British bulldog. Thrown against the wall, scraped on the ground and inserted into places I care not to think. Only then my marbles were returned. My head blown out from the insides then patched back together with blue plasters with every delicious side dish known to mental health dropped at the door.

So, let us start with cocaine, between the years 2007–16 and just these years alone I was spending roughly £1500 each calendar month on the devil's dandruff. That is without the alcohol. The years leading up to 2007 from 1989 I'm ashamed to even go there with the amount of money invested unwisely.

The cost to my health was rock and roll, it was carnage. A&E, emergency call outs, some paramedics even had my mobile number. In and out of crisis centres and rehab more times than I've had big macs. I even turned to God and the church. I had passed out smashed beyond recognition more times than I can remember. Woke up naked in a pool of blood and vomit half a dozen times.

A lost, broken, run down chef holding on with chewed fingernails for what, ask yourself for what? So, you can stay in the fight, get through endless 17hr shifts, for who, for what, the fucking team, the fucking establishment, the fucking restaurant. Killing yourself for someone else who doesn't give a fuck. A company who would replace you within the blink of an eye and doesn't care if you see the sunlight, your wife and children. Working away from home for years, then boom, your wife says, "I want a divorce".

Now these are the grown-up years of your career. The amount of cash I had spent on drugs, alcohol and stupidity "addicted" I could have bought a yacht. A family home, a home which some chefs have lost, why? Only they will have the answer. Some chefs could just be horrible wankers and I've meet a few, and there is a few.

The majority are just trying to make it, stay in the fight, keep it together. If covid-19 has taught us a few things, the one thing it has taught me, fuck it all, family first, fuck the corporate wankers and their values. The only value which some of us have ignored is standing in front of us every day, our families.

If it were not for a few sick and twisted wankers who tried to micromanage my operation in London back in the days, a beautiful friend would still be with us today. He would be raising his children. He would still be the amazing father and the exceptional friend to dozens of lucky people who knew him. Those fuckers changed the course of history for that soul and its why he's on the wrong side of the green grass in Africa.

There's also the endless amount of chef's trying to gain a rosette within a hotel. But the hidden agenda from the general manager, "yeah fuck it, he can work like a donkey producing great food, but who said anything about gaining a rosette in the first place". "Stay in their chef, the kitchens having a full refurb in a few months, pay rises and promotions all round".

Back-to-back 18hr shifts, its 1am in the morning, I'm summoned to my office with nuclear energy group exec chef sat in my chair. "Close ze door, I vant you, all ze chefs in at 4:30am, yes correct in three and a half hours". Qui chef. We have all been there, fucked over, that's why so many have left the industry, because they realise after years of sacrifice, they can't sacrifice no more. Make muffins, sell them at the village fete, invest in a food truck, pops ups. Make a chutney, sell it online, do anything that generates a steady income without killing yourself for a few Instagram likes.

That work life balance yarn so many general and HR managers throw about at interviews, it's a yarn so far from the truth. "Join us, have a great work life balance" Work life balance my ass. I had to go to hell and back before I realised I was on the verge of suicide. I wasn't even sure I was going to make it that given day, but it was the place I was at, when I decided enough was enough.

I have found peace with the industry, some regrets but asked if I would do it all again? You can go fuck yourself in the belly button or eat your own head. Being at the end of the road about to end it all, really? The cost of a life is not worth the carnage endured my thousands of chefs today.

Work life balance = wife, kids, family, friends, subtract work and balance what do you get? life, a life worth living for. By the way I'm not an individual, a chef pissed off with the industry. Blinded by the haziness of reality, my reality. I was a junkie for the entire duration of my career. I joined the army to better myself when that random opportunity was handed to me.

For many soldiers they eat the dog shit in reverse. Serve their county, they are exemplary individuals throughout their service. Where did it get them, on the streets of every major city within the United Kingdom, homeless fucked on smack. So, the next time you are offered the dream job, weather be in the military or civvy street. Ask yourself, what is it really going to cost you?

My Darling Wife

I hear laughter
I hear giggles
It's not me playing
It's the beauty of my childhood
My children laugh out loud
I laugh out louder

Imagine me mother
Smiling towards the sun
Am I worthy of love
Am I worthy of this life

More cuddles than a parent could give
Kids playing loving the moment
It's the moment that makes them
It's the choices we make that bonds memory
Memory, memories are beyond reason or doubt

I love you
You love me
I love you more
I love you more're
Is that a word
Who cares my love

Love is blinding
I love you daddy
Innocence personified
You were loved before our worlds collided
You're my son you're my daughter
before you it was all a test

There is no more darkness
It's just us my love
A test of endurance
A test that would bend and break me
A test only fools would take

I'm no fool but I sat the test
Did I pass
My children will decide
My smile is yours for eternity
My match was a one-sided affair

Me in goal
Defence
Attack, defence, attack
I attacked me
I attacked a greater good
I broke me

Only I can rise
Did I rise mother
Do you see me
Not black not white
I sit in the sun to be more black
I'd rather be more black than white

My history is rich
My history is survival
I am courage
Who cares if I'm a love child
Back to the top

Laughter giggles
Remember the past is done
The future is in the noise of giggles
The noise of grace
The noise of beauty
The voices of our children echoing long after we are no more

There is no person within me
There is no person that can do what is being done
I can hear your screams of bondage
I feel you I breathe you
why me

A life once lived is a life today
It's gone tomorrow my love
Remember this day

The day of all days I looked upon you
Humbled by love
Humbled by you
Humbled by the love of our children

Pathetic Sports

The role which finally broke the sledgehammer across the camel's back. The finale nail into one's coffin so to speak. The past 15 years I had blinded myself to the sheer dedication I inflicted upon myself as a chef to achieve something I could be proud of when I retired. To be appointed executive head chef within a five-star hotel in London. It was my dream, my goal since college.

I thought that my career would be a lifelong fervent affair up until the day I would retire. This backstabbing course of events, sly, conniving, spiteful, disgusting behaviour by administrators. My terms, I decided to walk away from corporate hospitality.

Executive head chef no more, I had lost the energy. My devotion and passion for the kitchen was coming to its natural end. I had trained, developed, mentored and inspired hundreds of chefs throughout the years I had managed at top. I still have many close friends who I speak with often, they always answer the phone "hello chef". Even on social media I feel truly blessed by their respect when exchanging messages or posts. They know who they are, its why we still talk.

I had learnt earlier on in my career in Bristol, that all management are all looking out for number one. All those company values which global corporate hotel brands preach today during interviews through to orientation are futile. Empathy, creativity, loyalty, fun, humility. When push comes to shove, these values go out the window with some general managers.

Whether you are a passionate, eloquent, confident, experienced out outspoken individual your expendable, regardless. When the shit hits the fan, and someone's head has to role you better make sure your head is buried deep up someone ass.

The sheep in wolves clothing within most hotels is the general manager and his side kick, the operations manager. When these individuals are appointed to a new hotel, their objectives, to fuck everything up. Regardless of who's life they fuck over during the process of change.

Towards the end of my corporate, business hospitality executive chef days, I was appointed executive head chef within a stunning hotel on the outskirts of London. During my short stint, I witnessed three Gm's come and go. "Huge change is happening within the company, investment, opportunities, prosperous times ahead for all who are willing to work hard and embrace our company values". Bullshit, 90% of the time it's the only lame ass line they can muster during, get to know me, get to know you drinks and canapes, bollocks.

The carnage and unrest which ensued during each appointed of a new general manager was on a level which drove HOD's (heads of departments) to breaking point and general staff to move on. In the early 90s I remember only a handful of agencies for chefs, most were mixed, chefs, labourers, plumbers, builders, etc. Into the 20s, chef agencies had multiplied at lighting speed, it did not take a monkey with a wrench to figure out why. Over worked under paid chefs working in miserable trench conditions day in day out month after month year after year.

Chefs leaving the industry on mass because of those fake promises, fake promotions, pathetic meetings about organising a meeting. kitchen and front of house rebuilds it was all bullshit. Promises of pay increases and a better work life balance, it just doesn't cut the mustard any more in any interview process.

So, ask yourself, why would a solid chef de partie working 75hr weeks in an understaffed kitchen, earning minimum wage working all sections with a cunt of a head chef, with a bigger cunt of a GM want to stay. They don't, because they've been systematically broken by a flawed system that believe values are going to pay the bills and put clothes on their children's back. So, what do they do? they join several "decent" agencies and earn £13.50 per hour and that's just for making sandwiches.

"Work life balance" was a buzz word for managers wanting to recruit chefs because they have no tricks left up their sleeves. Fuck time wasting development modules, fuck being a supervisor basically fuck it all because the times are a changing. Chefs are getting wiser to the ways of failing establishments and management.

Objectives from the top and regional directors was to increase revenue through the outlets. Create a new concept for the main restaurant using the freshest of locally sourced ingredients. Restructure the entire culinary department, create a pizza brand and capture footfall from the thousands of potential customers that passed the establishment daily.

The hotel restaurant was not of concern to me, it was well furnished, slick design. The restaurant was used for breakfast, conference and events, M&E (meetings and events) lunches during the day. During the evening, the main restaurant for several hundred guests we had in house on any given weekday. Leisure guests, celebrities, actors or premier league football teams in house on the weekends.

The culinary department was achieving and exceeding revenue every month. Food cost, payroll on point, budgets achieved, money in the bank, bonuses achieved. Now this is when shit gets proper fucked up. As opposed to being happy with achieving KPI's staff morale in the 80s, lets spin the whole fucking hotel on its head.

"Head office" have now decided they want us to compete with the endless number of standalone restaurants on the hotel's doorstep. The Adam Handlings and Tom Aitkens of the culinary world. Several meetings over the course of a month begin, 4, 5, 6hr meetings in how we are going to compete with celebrity fine dining, branded, individual concepts and Michelin starred chefs. "If it isn't broken, why the fuck take it apart and put it back together with cow shit", yes that's exactly what I said my friend.

Food and beverage team including myself are tasked with ripping up the already successful outlet, rebranding it with a new ethos, concept which hopefully will put us on the same playing field with everyone else who isn't on any playing field.

Consultations begin with all staff, including the staff members who have been there since the place first opened. Unrest and panic ensue, the dole office and UB40 is the next stop for a few unlucky staff members who have poured their hearts and soul, "life" into the establishment. "Fuck pensions let's get them out of here", savage.

Highly skilled concept designers are bought onboard to rebuild the restaurant and kitchen. Suppliers are contacted from all four corners of the globe to supply their niche brands to us. More meetings regarding, "have we got the go ahead from our global head office". Meetings about, "do we have the funds to achieve such a mammoth task", no. Meetings about redundancies and recruitment. Meetings about dining out at several of our new competitors "stand alone restaurants". Meetings about fucking uniforms, meetings about time frames and goal setting. More time was wasted sitting in function suites discussing the colour monkey cum.

Months seemed to disappear like passing cyclists on the high street, then shit gets super fucking frustrating. Let me rephrase that, this is where it gets boarder line illegal. This plus the personal issues I was dealing with at the time was the sledgehammer. Management playing very emotional and sensitive games with staff members wellbeing. Poor morale and uncertain times turned a lot of people within my team to drink.

Over worked, the project was nowhere near going to be completed on time. Several designers had submitted blueprints for the new restaurant but frustration, tension was setting in with the management team. Arguments occurring daily between strong minded individuals. Then out of the abyss came the single most calculated shock to the system.

Summoned to the discovery conference suite with human resources and the operational director. "Chef we want to bring a celebrity chef onboard to oversee the new restaurant". The audacity, the fucking cheek knocked me off my seat. So where do I sit at this table? I didn't. Meetings months before had been going on behind my back, these individuals had concocted the most outlandish somewhat illegal plan which would in fact have serious repercussions. Considering human resources were involved I was gob smacked that they even had the balls to run this not well thoughtless plan by me.

Overthrow the current executive chef, who had the food and beverage team in his pocket. A chef who bought harmony to all departments, stabilised the entire culinary department and gained confidence with returning guests, for what? more money. If that wasn't enough, they had a recruited a burnt-out restaurant manager who had never worked within a hotel environment. Their goal, sack the current team and bring in their own, which was done within weeks. I had been informed the new front of house team coming onboard had all been sacked from their previous place of employment, a casino.

The idea of having another executive chef in the kitchen wasn't going to sit well with me and the team I had built from scratch. A team one can be proud of, a beautiful mix of down to earth open-minded chefs from all walks of life. Talented, educated, respectful and eager to learn. A team which the establishment hadn't seen for decades, my team.

"So, chef, what do you think of our plan our proposal"? No disrespect but it sucks and its border line illegal without the proper consultation procedures. Why go to all this length to fix something that isn't broken or didn't need fixing in the first place? Maybe a few tweaks and investment in new tables and chairs but this is bonkers. Well, my reply didn't go down to well, considering these individuals had an agenda they assumed was fool proof.

Designers started dropping out due to lack of commitment and funds. Engineers, construction teams started withdrawing their proposals as weeks had turned into months. A lot of influential people within the industry had been pissed off. Closer to home general staff from the F&B team had resigned and handed in grievances for constructive dismissal. Which is fair enough considering their contribution and sacrifices they had made.

During these months I had documented every meeting, as I knew something was riding out of Denmark. My personal life had taken a turn for the worse having been told information about my early years which only added to my gaping wounds. Panic and anxiety attacks were frequent, everything was spiralling out of control.

When I thought things at work couldn't get any worse after wasting weeks drafting a contract and job description. Negotiating a salary for this celebrity chef. She decided during the final handshake, here is your contract meeting, they were not interested.

On top of my daily workload, I was being lined up, or so I thought, for the dream posting in town. A brand-new build, a stunning 5* hotel overlooking the river Thames. Multiple food and beverage outlets, super hi tec with a team recruited from across the globe. I had even reached out to catering colleges across London to host an opening day. I had my head and sous chefs ready to chop onions.

Several positive meetings with the regional and financial directors plus the CEO of the company, I was about to achieve my career goal. Everything was brushed aside, my health, my personal life, wife, kids' and friends. I had tunnel vision. I had gone after something with so much conviction and undying passion, it almost killed me. "Be careful, for what you wish for".

Then the ultimate head fuck from the top. Global head office had heard of the shenanigans going on and the proposed rebuild we had wasted so many months on. Final meeting, "ladies and gents we have decided to pull the plug on this project. The man in the chair has overruled that this isn't an investment worth doing. As of now please reach out to all suppliers and share the news".

Just like that, people's lives ruined, staff thrown to the gutter, plus the new food and beverage management team bought onboard by a manager who lasted no more than a month turned out to be gremlins.

The dream job in central London fell through due to dishonesty and bullshit. So, I decided I had to walk away from such mental and physical exhaustion. I had to rest a battered body, I had indeed come to the end of the line of an agonising, painful, emotional, stressful but beautiful career. A career cut short.

Having finished this chapter, I've felt an overwhelming sense of satisfaction, a beautiful natural buzz, a natural high. The kind of high I used to get during my early days as a chef. Those natural highs, the buzz, the pressure the excitement. Chefs smiling, loving the vibe of the kitchen. It feels like smoking a crack pipe for the first time, such a buzz, such a high. We purchase a 2nd hit hoping the 2nd will emulate the first. Silly me, I spent a lifetime chasing that high.

"We may encounter many defeats, but we must not be defeated but then in fact it may be necessary to encounter defeat, to know who we are, what makes us stumble and fall, what we can overcome, miraculously we rise and go on"

Maya Angelou.

Spain the Uncut Truth

When I initially wrote about my experience in Spain, I was an author virgin. A huge part of the process for authors is the content evaluation process. So, after some serious thought I felt compelled to write the uncut version. Why? Because regardless of how it ended, a nuclear fallout with everyone and the bank. It started off as that amazing opportunity, an opportunity that does not come around every day and probably never will again, a natural high.

During the first few months living on my own making friends with many locals before the French holocaust and my girlfriend joined me after the winter season it was sheer bliss. It was super unreal bliss. I had not procured any cocaine as I was the face behind the restaurant. I hadn't even thought about getting wasted on chemicals. I was in fact clean; I just drank like a local Majorcan.

Considering checkers has long closed its doors, every member of the team moved on. I'm going to write the honest version with no filter. My time on the Island of Mallorca. Opening my dream restaurant with a bunch of French cocaine snorting maniacs and a crazy Spanish pot wash salad assistant thrown into the mix. It was going to be a fifty-fifty chance of checkers surviving.

Every word I wrote in beaten black and blue born into racism regarding working for a wealthy businessman in the alps was true. So, I will pick up from when I flew out to Majorca and not to the mainland of Spain to start the build of checkers restaurant. During the flight to Palma, I had a raging harden on, not only was I opening a restaurant, but I had also designed it with a wealthy friend of the financier. I was also going to help build it and source all the equipment a super modern open planned kitchen would need.

A restaurant which would sit practically on the beach in the bustling residential town of ca'n pastilla. During the summer ca'n pastilla would be mobbed by tourists. The restaurant which was torn down to make way for checkers was a cash cow in the 70s 80s 90s. With a different type of tourist and holiday makers into the millennium business started to drop off. I remember visiting the existing restaurant on a quick visit to Majorca. What was surprising was the size of the kitchen these owners or chefs were working from. It was no bigger than a small storage room.

No extraction hood, no pot wash let alone a modern combi oven. They had been working from a char-grill that had seen better days and a household gas cooker with a ban Marie. The four walls were dripping with grease and there was a clear sign of rodents. The restaurant resembled a tropical island. Plastic palm trees and plastic exotic animals. I could only imagine back in the 70s it would have been the modern day tropical fun pub for hordes of Germanys.

The next seaside village down was Arenal. Magaluf for Scandinavians, the beach stretched from the front of checkers restaurant all along the coastline miles past Arenal. Sensational, one thing the financial backers did have was local summer knowledge. They did their market research, research during the summer months.

They both believed we would make a killing during summer, the winter months a casual style cafe set up for locals and ex-pats. I joined the local builders once I had constructed, costed the menu and finalised the menu shoot and design. Hard hat, steal toe caps it was time to get my hands dirty, build my restaurant and learn some Spanish street lingo. Learn how to eat tapas and drink like a proper Majorcan local builder. Auf weidersehen pet in the Balearic Islands. This version of that 80s sitcom only had a mixed raced chef from the black country minus the Geordie contingent plus a dozen Spanish Barcelona fans.

My day on the bricks would start 7am in the local cafe with the builders. The local cafes in ca'n pastilla opened their taps when they opened the doors. Beers for breakfast enjoyed with the finest of Majorcan savoury pastries, tortilla, fried local chorizo with potatoes and fried egg, tostada and churros dipped in think hot chocolate. forty winks before we even started work. No wonder everything was always manana during the spring through to autumn.

The builders were in no rush to finish the restaurant, while they were working, they were earning pesos. More money to put paella and local vino on the table at home. If I weren't on the bricks I would either be in Palma attending meetings with the bank. Followed by a lengthy Spanish lunch until 4pm. 4pm in Spain is the end of the working day, it's time for delectable tapas at one of a dozen local bars either in Palma on the maritimo or drinking hierbas back in the quaint village ca'n pastilla were I lived.

Twice per week I would be over in Andrax with the big boys discussing the restaurant and when the team from the Alps would be joining me. Being with my financiers during the week, evening dinner started early. Bottles of quality scotch accompanied with delightful local nibbles. I was a sucker for Hamon iberico sliced fresh from the pig's legs.

Once our drinks consumed and mouths lined with the taste of walnut black pig fat, we would stroll into the tiny fishing village of Andrax. Living the dream, we would eat out on the waterfront. You could not compare a dozen restaurants. During the short few months, I dined out at restaurants savouring the finest Majorcan food and local wines. Forget Michelin stars and rosettes those local chefs had the quality produce. Minimal fucking about with maximum flavour impact.

Spoilt rotten, life was utterly amazing, I had become close friends with bobby who was the head chef of the Thai restaurant next to checkers. Bobby had spent several years at the notorious Bangkok Hilton for drug trafficking offences. We clicked from the first handshake. The hardest man I have ever had the privilege of knowing. He fought within the prison Muay Thai league throughout Thailand. It was money that got him out. Once free from the clutches of the Thai prison system he fled to Spain and never returned.

There was also Carlos the bartender with the giant dog. He would walk past the site most mornings with his monster pet dog. He would always stop and have a nose about like a typical local in the mornings with not much to do. He would ask the same question every morning. "Que es esto, es un restaurante no"? Yes, we are building a new restaurant. "Muy bien". Unless I wasn't paralysed after a day with the Spanish brickies, I would be at Carlos bar. No cocaine, no heroin, no hashish, no vitamin. Sloshed on local wine, or down in Arenal getting blasted with mad Scandinavians in many strip joints.

I partied hard as the next man, woke up in random beds with one or two Spanish local beauties. What is there not to love about life. Sundays on the dance floor of Tito's, a Spanish club for locals on the maritimo just down from the club Pacha. I quickly picked up the lingo and fitted in with the locals like a flip-flop on the beach.

There was going to be a long delay for restaurant and bar completion. It didn't bother me one tiny little bit. Out of work being paid in the Balearic Islands beats being broke, out of work in middle England. I was doing well; I didn't need or yearn for drugs living the Mediterranean mental and physical diet was good enough for me.

Shortly after the winter season in the mountains, I was joined by my girlfriend Melanie, the French connection and my two business partners. Gwen and the Irish equivalent of Matthew McConaughey, Evan. I gave them all the village 360 orientation and a tour of our new place of work. The villa on the beach I had occupied for those few months alone, well, with one or two Spanish beauties had now become Disneyland.

I knew the entire crew as we had got to know each other in the mountains, I was "resident" DJ at the black diamond pub a few times per week where they all worked. The financier owned the bar so finding a team for Majorca was easy as purchasing cocaine from a Majorcan taxi driver.

I had departed the local bricky team and was collaborating closely with Scot on procuring all the equipment for the kitchen. Evan was working on the bar with his head bar man Jan. With several of the team working on their tan day in day out including Melanie due to the push back of completion, team focus started to slide sideways. As soon as Yan and Mika introduced themselves to that local taxi driver who bought them back from Andrax one evening, it would never be the same. The course of our journey had shifted from businesspeople to party monsters.

We could not have partied any harder those coming months. I alone partied like a dozen men. Two meetings per week to be in contact with the money men which could not have been anymore lavish. We were being paid, accommodation sorted, the start of summer, we lost it, we became beasts. One end of the maritimo a short drive away we had Magaluf. A short stroll down the beach from checkers we had Arenal and everything in between, 24hr clubs, strip joints, knocking shops was up for grabs and in play including ourselves.

We dined in some of the finest restaurants across the island. Pit restaurants barbecuing local meats. Hidden little gems, tapas bars off the beaten track, fish restaurants for locals hidden away on secluded beaches with the most amazing scenery. We partied in every club across Majorca consuming cocaine at frightening pace.

When Yan and Mika returned that evening, they departed the taxi with a bag of cocaine, pure uncut cocaine, straight of the block. That was how the devil entered the building. "Chef sad news I'm afraid, the opening has been pushed back again, all being well we should be open August". "Planning permission for the plumbing was an issue, we needed to run pipes under the building which will be exposed in the car park roof below checkers".

Melanie and Gwen decided they would fly back to France for a month leaving us boys to it. Cocaine, hookers, 24hr parties proceeded while we waited to start making some pesos. My birthday that year I spanked £2500 in one night partying with half a dozen Japanese businesspeople and Evan in the finest strip club on the Island. These strip clubs everything goes, everything. A jacuzzi full of ripped Japanese tourists, two locals from the UK, half a dozen gas cookers, cocaine on tap was the perfect set for a porn movie. I was mandingo compared to these little fellas.

Straight out the Japanese porno the following morning we drove we to the centre of the island a village named Sineu to watch a bull fight. The only cure for such a barbaric hangover was more beer and wine. There is nothing crueller or savage than a bull fight. Nothing graceful or enigmatic. Once the matador had killed the said bull who fought for the best part of an hour. The entire stand of peasants including my party threw missiles into the ring. Empty cans, bottles, food, bricks in sheer disgust. We did it for the bull who had his ears and tail cut from him and dragged out of the arena by the assassins.

Opening night "checkers restaurant", the menu was everything Spanish and Majorcan. The guest list was family and friends, local businesses, most of the builders and a taxi driver. I had employed one local kitchen porter slash assistant chef. It was just me and Tod a French chef running the kitchen.

Out front we had a rotisserie with a dozen local free-range chickens roasting. Iberico ham on the bar top carved by the bar team. We had a two-meter Parrilla, grilling sea bass, sea bream, whole squid, gambas and lobsters, courgettes, peppers, aubergines and whole Spanish garlic. Seafood paella. Slow roast leg of lamb stuffed with rosemary garlic and thyme served with all roasting vegetables and liquor. Simple Salads using only the freshest of local produce. We served one cut of steak that evening a 12oz rib-eye cut from the finest organic free-range Castile-la Mancha Spanish cows.

On the office table that night we had a pile of cocaine the size of a jacket potato. On the pans, grill, rotisserie smashed immaculate. Scarface in the kitchen, there was no after party that night it just continued that is how it was for several months, we did not stop. After closing the restaurant one night, I arrive back at the villa having walked back with just beach shorts on.

I'm greeted by the craziest BBQ, house music pumping with the largest of characters no other than the 80s glam rocker who I cannot mention for legal reasons with his chaperone. He was touring the island, Evan spotted him next door eating at Bobby's Thai restaurant and invited him back for a Brock out roll party.

We ended up devouring so much cocaine and that was before we even hit the clubs that night. I passed the fuck out on the beach opposite our villa. The average night after service, we would change and snort cocaine until we had to be back at work the following morning. Sleep was something we did if we could, we didn't let our wild ways be hindered by sleep.

I don't even no were to start when it comes to my mate Kiwi. The cockney gangster who ran a small English cafe around the bay. I would skate on my longboard half naked around the bay every morning during that summer on the way to checkers. I would stop at Kiwi's for a few beers, then on the pans for my breakfast. The few times Kiwi did join us for a nose tug of war, I would leave him by a telephone box in the village just in case he wanted to ring an ambulance because we got so smashed and paranoid.

The locals soon got wind of our escapades, the parties, the drugs, the fuck life mentality. It would be our demise it would be our downfall. Nothing that good lasts forever. You just need look at how many icons of music, actors' celebrities, chefs who have died living that lifestyle. Considering, we ate like lords drank like kings and partied like gods not one of us overdosed. Our cocaine was pure, cocaine chess, cocaine scrabble, cocaine connect four, cocaine charades, cocaine drinking games. Cocaine sunbathing, cocaine sex games, cocaine picnics. We ended up cliff jumping after a hit. Cocaine was the air we breathed.

Checkers didn't even make it past the year of opening. Spanish pastries and coffee alone would not have sustained our overheads during the winter months. Shit endings are shit, "how did it end"? It ended shit, a huge shit sandwich with a side of pubic hair what else can I say. I had no intention in checkers up, if I had said no to the cocaine, it was fucked anyway. The golden ticket handed to you on a golden platter. Broke, busted minus a French film star girlfriend, I flew back to England broke as a tramp on meth.

I had learnt a valuable lesson in Majorca, do not trust anyone, especially those with too much money, a nose for the devil's dandruff and bored. It might all be sunny horizons in Hollywood movies, but the real-life deal is an emotional breaker.

The last correspondence I had with my financial backer was also a rugby tackle to the shit box. Even if we had our shit together and straight as a bent politician checkers would have failed either way. Clarence my financier was being robbed by his close friend and business partner Tom. Clarences health deteriorated dramatically within a short space of time.

Tom had stacked up £200,000 in fake invoices from checkers and several other projects he had going on in Majorca. The investment in checkers alone and those dodgy invoices Clarence sold off all his assets and closed the doors to his investment company. A company which I would have become CEO of if checkers had worked. Life has not always been about the party, but when certain circumstances are out of your control shit can go either way. The cost of checkers almost topped £500,000 and that is without the dodgy invoices.

A decent resume, having travelled and collaborated with decent companies, cooking would be my saviour. After sobering, up getting myself clean after two weeks on vitamin c and vodka I jumped straight back into the kitchen. Executive chef in Austria, the final winter season which ended up with me in crutches and in intensive care.

"During those darkest days of addiction there are no more lines to cross, there are no boundaries. We are beats with no filter, there is no horizon, days come and go with no recollection. That goldfish bowl we were once in has become a cement mixer, trapped, soon to become stone. A hand from the heavens appears, no face, just a voice on the other end of the line. A voice so soothing and honest is a voice I shall follow. I shall journey with you if you keep me from harm, I shall journey with you until you are free from addiction".

Mumbo Jumbo

We can't choose the time we are born into neither can we pretend our past didn't happen.

"Who the fuck is that dish rag whore", it's my girlfriend Doris, "don't you ever bring that fucking bitch to this house again, do you hear me". That is how it went down when I bought my first girlfriend home.

You cannot tame a wild animal, a crocodile, Hitler, a lion, a shark' it just doesn't happen. Anyone who says they can, have either been eaten for supper, lost a limb or butchered in the process of trying such madness. Doris looks at me, she sees one person, the man who she still blames today for fucking her life up.

If Adolf Hitler hadn't taken his own life in that dreaded bunker when he realised, he had lost the 2nd world war what would have been the consequences for him. Most likely put-on trial for crimes against humanity. Now if during this supposed trial if he had found God Jesus some greater being, would he have been forgiven? Absolutely fucking not, "we find the defendant guilty", hanged' job done.

Soon as Boris and Doris are divorced, she turns to the church, becomes a born-again Christian, forgiven, I do not think so. She goes bible bashing God squad over the top full-on sandals and socks. Antiques, valuables, family butter dishes, lock stock, fuck the kids let's give it all to the church. I'm not sure what Doris was trying to prove if anything, but a kick in the teeth the same.

If the truth be told that "dish rag whore" got me through the gulf war. Fond memories that sort of define us. There are too may snippets in time during my life on which I can reflect. Tap of my heels and I'm home, not literally in Kansas but the past. There are too many experiences, words which transport me back to a moment in time. My own virtual memory time machine which we all have.

Relapse is a word I remember the most, it's not a dirty word, we shouldn't be ashamed of the word relapse. Relapse, dealer, cocaine, drugs, alcohol, ambulance just some of the words that were used most back when I didn't care about the consequences.

We should in fact embrace the word relapse, because soon as we start talking about it and using the word more often for me it was the start of the long road to recovery. The first time I started using the word relapse was 1996. Yes, it was indeed a long road to recovery, almost as long, as the great walk to freedom by Mandela.

I had headed into London with a group of friends for a mad night and crazy morning at club UK in Wandsworth East London. It was when smack started to make its way onto the scene. Ecstasy started to be cut with heroin, nasty vibes on the dancefloors across the country.

We headed back home in the late hours of the morning. Back to one of many after hours' parties across town. The mood in the house was very subdued, not much movement, most bodies were mangled on the sofas and floor.

Half a dozen nut jobs sat around the breakfast table smoking bongs. I head to the kitchen to rack out a line of cocaine and ecstasy. Bang up both nostrils, I lace a joint with cocaine and head back to the living room.

Gable is the conversation as everyone's minds have been bombed, I pass the zoot around the table, puff puff pass. I assumed the joint coming in from the left was my joint coming back to me, wrong. Little did I know it had been laced with a sprinkle of heroin. A huge pull followed by another. I hold the smoke down for as long as possible can then exhale. "Yes bruv, sweet", mumbles a random.

Cocaine, **heroin**, weed, ecstasy is in the post. I had done mad crazy combos back then but never anything with heroin. The room starts to shrink, voices become distant, and I slowly start to disappear into a world of agonising paranoia.

I salute the table and slowly slide of my chair onto the floor. My body feels like it's encased in concrete. Every move is agonisingly painful. I look around the living room, faces are miles away in the death zone. I grab the door handle, make my way out onto the street. It is quiet, drizzle splatters the back of my head, the chill stabs at me with piercing columns.

I make my way between to parked cars outside the house. like an axe to the back of the head I belch, followed by blood and vomit. The convulsions start, it's obvious with the amount of dope in me I'm going to lose this fight. Within minutes a taxi pulls up, time relapse. I had been between those two parked cars curled into a ball for what seemed hours. My body in and out of shock, shaking uncontrollably. Someone inside had called an A&E lift, who? I have no clue.

"Get in, get in now, where too, A&E"? No, Christchurch Street. I am holding my jumper to my mouth blood splattered and covered with human gunk. The rain batters the taxi as if bombs are being dropped from B52s.

Swaying from side to side, 100% focused on getting to safety, the fear is overwhelming. Black shadows circle me, coming out from everywhere. It is like the movie ghost when the demons come for the wicked. I am beyond scared, stop, stop here.

I throw the driver a handful of crumpled notes and exit the taxi on my knees, guided by shadows I make it into the hallway of my rented house. I strip naked grad a girlie magazine, a bottle of coke and crawl out into the back garden.

The rain is cats and dogs pelting the patio, African drums pound my ears, deathly visions surround me. I slowly curl up into a tiny ball holding my possessions. I am in a bad place, the clouds above are grey and black. fluffy animals winking and talking to me. My eyes roll to the back of my head lights out.

"You mad crazy bastard, do you know where you've been, where you went"? What, what the fuck, "you mad fucker, that's it it's over between us". "Why did you leave and go with those fucking smack heads". Slow down, what the fuck, how the fuck did I get here. "You live here you stupid fuck".

"We picked you up outside that fucking smack den, fucked, covered in vomit and blood, it looked like someone, or some people had fucked you up". Why am I in bed, "we've just got back from A&E you dick". What is with the hostility, slow the fuck down and why do I have a hospital tag on my wrist. "Toxicology reports say you had heroin and ketamine in your system, beside the usual cocaine, ecstasy, weed and over the limit blind sozzled".

Heroin, what the fuck, "I love you Auguste, but I draw the line at smack". Fuck me, my head feels like someone dropped a taxi on it. "We picked you up, drove straight to A&E, your stomach was pumped". "Your lucky brother, we thought you were done". So, what about the taxi, me naked in the garden, "what fucking taxi, which fucking garden".

It was not for the fact I had been spiked; I was not, I had ended up on the wrong side of town with the wrong fucking crew, doing the wrong fucking drugs. That is it I'm off the gear, I'm going straight, the famous words said by Renton in Trainspotting.

The first of many times, I was in no state mentally to kick the party drugs, I relapsed a week later. Headed back into London for a mash up at Bagley's. Today I've been clean for several years. I am not counting the weeks months or years, it's not my thing because I'm fully aware of the brains power in convincing you that a cheeky tickle, line of cocaine will not hurt. "Go on just a cheeky one". Healing for me was the distance in between the sessions or usage.

The distance, the time in between was my way of trying to break the routine I had fallen deep into. Somehow, I had started to use cocaine as my reward. Relapse, get smashed, it was no longer becoming a cocaine hammering to the system. It was me relapsing' that unproved method of recovery worked for me.

It took me the same amount of time to kick drugs than the same amount of time I was smashed on them, years. I had in fact used the thing that was killing me to in fact free myself from her grip. Cocaine is not discriminatory, cocaine loves everyone who dare to tempt fate that they can somehow control what cannot be controlled.

I had spent six months thinking about that "dish rag whore bitch", my first girlfriend while serving on active service during the gulf war. Assuming we would pick up where we left off was a slap in the face. A slap back to the top of those stairs living with Boris and Doris. The relationship ended when I returned from war. Regardless there was no chance in me dating let alone marrying a posh girl with racist parents' no chance at all.

After a brief visit to her house which ended in a very confusing upsetting conversation on her doorstep I about faced and walked away. I could not bear to think of the abuse her parents might be giving her. The same abuse I had witnessed first-hand. The damage, hate, racism families would go to' to protect themselves from shame.

My past was in fact playing out in adult life. Drugs was not just about losing myself I hated myself for being me. The world can be so hateful, full of vermin, venomous families. I suppose today, I suppose, no, I do suppose and have done subconsciously since the day the abuse started in that crumbling house and before then as a baby. The world is a hateful place, families can be unbearable, some families are so contaminated, its best just to walk away.

I have somehow disconnected myself from such hatred and transcended all who have finally come out from under their lumps of cheese to orate displeasure at my achievements. They squabble amongst themselves that the kid who would achieve nothing, be nothing had in fact become something. I do not sit her today giving it, I'm Freddy four dicks, I'm amazing, been there done that, I'm a super star King fucking Kong author number one, NO. I am the total opposite, I shy away from compliments, I keep myself to myself, I have a handful of close friends and every day I feel blessed that I'm here.

The Haziness of Reality

I remember popping my cherry, I was 12 it happened near the sports field by the bushes near the little park, lasted all but a minute. I remember my first spliff I had just joined my regiment in Germany "bonkers". I also remember my first line of coke and my first ecstasy pill.

A good friend I was serving with popped one on my tongue, gave me a French kiss, patted me on my cheek and said, "have a mad one". We arrived at the rave in Hanover an hour later, its without saying I was flying, absolutely flying. The feeling was unbelievable, I was rushing from my toes to the tips of my fingers down the back of my neck the feeling at the time that was better than sex.

The first time I really popped my cheery "virginity" would have also been In Germany, I remember it like it was yesterday, such a cheesy cliché. My cheery was popped for me by the most beautiful German woman. She must have been twice my age at the time, she totally blew me away.

In fact, there was a lot of first-time things I did in Germany during my posting with the army, so many good memories, so many good times with some beautiful people. The first time I did a prison escort, I had to transfer a soldier back to the UK to the military prison in Essex.

Strange experience being handcuffed to someone on a military flight, if he jumps, I'm going with him. First time I kissed a fella was another strange experience, buzzing my chops off in the most famous club in Bristol called Lakota. The 2nd was in a nightclub in Austria "bizarre", also the first girl who broke my heart, not going to go there but her racist parents didn't approve of me and there was a lot of that going on the 80s.

Cocaine, my first line of cocaine was at the container cafe In Hameln with the bar's owner a beautiful Turkish fella he reminded me of Claude Van Dam, always dressed elegantly, smart, decadent, and classy. I would hang out at the cafe to get away from army life, mix it up with the locals, when in Rome and all that.

He introduced me to so many influential people within the cocaine scene, he took me to some impressive clubs and introduced me to some very elegant women. Could have been hookers but who cares they had their wicked way, and I was loving it, all on the house.

The first time I met my BF is the first-time thing which stands out the most. It was my birthday 1994, I didn't have a clue what was going on behind the scenes, totally oblivious to what my auntie was cooking up. Summer 1994 the scene was going off all over the UK, house music, fashion, clubbing, so many good clubs and good drugs.

The day prior I was out with friends, we had been out all day, drinking getting high, then hit the clubs around town. Push your luck at the Caribbean club was on the menu that night, it's a shame what happened to that venue a decade later the council knocked down and turned into a car park, a fucking car park.

Throughout the 90s after parties where a big thing, we got smashed at push your luck and once kicked out on to half a dozen parties across town. 24 I would be up for 2 or 3 days with ease, well not naturally awake for that long, wired, plugged in, tuned in, bugged out fully charged on all sorts of pickles and olives "drugs".

Saturday night turns into Sunday morning, now most Sundays I would visit my auntie take my washing round, get cleaned up and have lunch with her, social visit. She knew full well I liked the party life. I used to get juiced up on acid and speed during my time in the army when I was on leave before hitting the town in the switch. I would smuggle back all unusual types of weed and get everyone in the household stoned immaculate, proper nice warm fuzzy stoned.

I leave the after party late morning, taxi to pickles road, pick up a change of clothes and my bag washing, then a short stroll to olive street. The day was amazing sunny skies a warm breeze, beautiful, I was still buzzing from the night and had been buzzing all morning.

I arrive at my aunties house greeted with a warm hug and a kiss on the cheek, she knew I was flying but I was never on the smack, so we were cool. Lunch smells nice, roast chicken with all the trimmings "umm" might not get much down my mush today apart from liquid in the form of alcohol, cold beers are calling me.

My auntie treated me like her own son, and I treated her with the upmost respect like a mother until she passed away of cancer in 2004, one cannot describe the loss to our family, we were truly heart broken. So, let's get showered and changed, I pop upstairs to the bathroom, before I jump in the shower, I pop half an ecstasy tab "green apples".

I am just topping myself up ready for an afternoon on the beers at the pub with my party people. Feeling fresh with a nice little buzz going on I make my way downstairs, I told auntie I was flying so could she skip the main course and go straight to the dessert.

Apple crumble with custard, I pass on the crumble and swallow the soft stuff, ding dong the doorbell rings. My auntie is all jittery and excited, I've got a surprise for you a surprise. Hey, a surprise rumbling my hands together a surprise "happy days" the gang have come over for a Sunday afternoon mash up, nope.

My auntie answers the door, hi, come on in he's through there, she walks this fella straight into the breakfast room where I'm sat swallowing my dessert.

Fubar

Hello son, I'm your father, the first fucking time I had heard such a phrase, "hello son". It echoed throughout the entire house, through my flesh, my bones, I was utterly and astronomically shocked. Where had this come from, I'm buzzing, there's another buzz in the post, the one I popped before my shower. All my senses had just been mined fucked, utterly mind fucked, jacked up, FUBAR.

We hug, more him than me, mines more of an air hug, hugging a total stranger more like, well he is a stranger, I didn't know this fella, it was like I had just meet father Christmas, black father Christmas. I'm now in a state of shock and buzzing, he's talking but nothing computes, nothing is registering I've lost the power to speak.

Battered, buzzing like a kipper, I say, let's go to the pub and head for the door with black father Christmas and my auntie hot on my heels. I am wearing Rockport boots, white Armani Jean's a stone island t-shirt with silver rimmed diesel sunglasses. I set off quick sharpish making a be-line for the pub, thinking about that first fizzy frosted glass of beer and may be a nice fresh stick of wriggles.

The pub is packed, all my party people cramped into the small beer garden, pills and wraps are being passed under the wooden tables, people in and out of the toilets every 5 minutes. There's a buzz around the garden, its electric, sun shining on every beautiful face, chit chat, smiley friends chewing their faces off.

I'm handed a beer and a pill; I throw the pill to the back of my throat and knock it down with a slurp. It's a beautiful day but I'm not feeling the vibe. Father Christmas "Johnny" and auntie Stella rock up and join me at my table, budge up, room for a skinny one.

I'm trying to keep it together when Santa Claus "Johnny his is name" bends over towards me and whispers in my ear, how's it going, how's it going, really, how's it fucking going, how the fuck is what going. He then says stay off the drugs son, the first piece of advice given by a father as opposed to would you like a bed time story, milk and cookies before bed time, a back rub maybe. Stay off the drugs, I'm on the fucking drugs because I love them, it allows me to escape, escape reality.

I'm doing drugs because there is something very fucking wrong with what's going on inside my head. One of my friends asks me who am I with, and in slow motion I reply, this is my pops. She replies that's nice he's come to visit you on your birthday, I replay this is the first time I've meet him.

The beer garden falls silent, half my friends' jaws drop to the floor as shocked as I am "What a head fuck" what a fucking head fuck. So, your telling me this is the first time you've met your dad, YES, that first for me that afternoon was also a first for many of my friends, apologies if that afternoon messed your heads up as much as it did mine.

My thoughts are racing, there is no control of what I'm thinking, thousands of kids may never meet their real parents, but when they do they will most likely be better prepared than I was. I don't know if I'm coming up or coming down or going sides ways, I'm god smacked in shock, I whisper to a few friends that I'm going to take a walk, get me head together. I excuse myself from the table kiss my auntie Stella on the cheek shake Johnny's hand and walk away.

I head to the local park, walk to the biggest tree and sit underneath it, I sat there until the early evening staring into space trying to piece together what the fuck had just happened. I never spoke with my auntie about that day, we never sat down and discussed the experience, how I felt, if I did feel anything now that I had come face to face with my biological father.

I didn't feel anything, it was a blur, the haziness of reality, that period of my life I found it difficult to feel anything let alone love, or the love for a man that had just walked into my life. I wasn't prepared neither was he, but he could have been, he could have really got his shit together and tried, after all he knew way in advance he was meeting with me, but at the end of the day I'm just one in a dozen of kids he has spawned with I haven't a clue from how many women.

Waste of Time

Bottom line is you can be addicted to absolutely anything and everything, I suppose it depends how your brain is wired and who had done the wiring. I might have mentioned we can't choose our parents and it is in fact the parents who kick start our fuse box from day one.

Addiction, obsession, are they not the same, the more I'm obsessed with getting everything of my chest in writing my history I become addicted in wanting to finish the project. When you've been told by everyone, you'll amount to nothing repeatedly, put down, verbally emotionally abused something clicks upstairs. For me it was proving to everyone who beat down on me that I was going to do it, I was going to have the final say, but at what cost.

What was it going to cost me, really cost me, January 2020 I'm with my psychologist at the crisis centre, it had been about 2 weeks since my psychotic break down and I was barely stable. The question, the million-dollar question "WHY" why the fuck, an obsession had become an addiction and besides the drugs and alcohol this is one addiction that was truly in my shadow all along, it was with me all the way, from the get-go.

Walking through the streets on a sunny day with my kids making funny shapes with our bodies so we can laugh out loud at our shadows. Harmless fun, until you think about your shadow and what may be looking back at you. I see myself in the mirror, me, you, hello, but what you can't see or touch or have control over, that's the spooky feeling within.

I obsessed more about proving my family wrong, I had lost all sense of why I was doing the things I was doing and everything I had done. I moulded myself so tight not to be like any of them, but the identity, my purpose I was searching for wasn't even with in reaching distance.

I started living when faced with two end of line options, one, you ended it her today or two you let it all go. Let it all go, let it all go, let what all go? sounds simple right, wrong. When you've been clinging on to something, something I didn't have a clue what it was all bar the faces of my wife and kids, I realised, at the precise moment everything I was trying to prove wasn't for me, nothing had ever been for me.

I had wasted decades trying to prove to a family that didn't care if I was dead or alive, that I was going to make something for myself. Sucker, that's me, wrapped so tight I had been walking through my life blinded by the abuse I knew was always there until I had the balls to ask questions and speak out.

I suppose that's why everyone has fallen silent, they've all crawled back into their miserable pathetic lives knowing "I know", I fucking know. I stood so proud at my pass out parade without you there, I stood so proud at every chef's competition, I stood proud when our children were born, at our wedding, why, because I did in fact achieve something and I've got everything to live for, everything.

You may have wired my brain like a fruit kebab but my dance with you all is done, everything I do from this day forward I do for me, for my family, "my family" my wife and kids. You had your chance, I put it all on display for you all to see but your smiles and sarcastic remarks were futile, I can no longer be shammed.

I've fallen and risen more times than I can remember, I've battered my body senseless, black and blue. I have danced with the devil, been driven myself to the edges of darkness and there's still one thing I cannot deal with today no matter how hard I try.

Praise, when we praise people our kids, wife, family or friends, anyone, we release the feel-good vibe, a huge surge of dopamine followed by a smile from ear to ear. It gives our kids focus, motivation to do better to achieve more to want more of that feel-good vibe, but there is a flipside to praise.

If you're constantly putting your kids down, telling them they are useless a waste of space, constantly criticising them it gives the brain the adverse reaction, in other words a downer. Persistent criticism breeds resentment, defiance and totally undermines a child's initiative, confidence and sense of purpose in the world.

A great example of the feel-good vibe is playing with my kids, play wrestling, tickling, hide and seek, tag all those silly games that create so much joy. Giggling while running around the garden, falling over because your laughing so much it's the ultimate high for me these days.

Without a purpose in the world I felt worthless the only way to deal with this I became obsessed with proving my family wrong and where did that get me nowhere. Not being able to deal with praise has also caused issues in my life, nice chicken dish chef, thank you, and carry on about my daily chores. There's no surge of dopamine no smile from ear to ear I just crack on with what I've got to do, and then comes the criticism from others.

Did you see chef, how he dealt with that complement, he's so arrogant thinking he's better than anyone else, how far from the fucking truth. It's not that I'm arrogant I just shy away from praise, compliments seem to fly straight over my head.

Or there's the subservient smile, a smile with no emotion a smile to keep everyone happy an obeying smile. I had a full-blown argument with the wife years ago, I was writing out Christmas cards and she said, "babe you've got such nice hand writing" she stood there and kept watching me write these cards, I felt so uncomfortable I had to tell her to piss off.

I wasn't told I was useless a waste of space a few times during my childhood, I was crippled by it, I'm just trying to navigate my way through this complex world. I just try a little bit harder each day to be part of society "the social network" taking care, being mindful that my responses and gestures are appropriate.

If I happen to offend anyone then you can blow me, I don't have time to think what everyone else thinks about me today, the world is already way to offended "the offended generation" I wasted to many years orbiting Saturn oblivious to all the beauty around me, yeah, my bad, I'm just cracking on with living.

The Noxious Scuttlebutt and
the Inconvenience of Knowing

Truth can seem stranger than fiction.

The detritus you are about to read has been physically and emotionally draining as well having to deal the carnage done to myself. Unpleasant, inexplicable events that have gone on during the past two decades. All the troubles, interbreeding and inappropriate behaviour towards children that has gone on throughout the years, everyone seems to be totally ok with. It all appears to be natural normal behaviour. Done with it, over it, be there for someone today who didn't contribute to my well-being as a child. Why should I give them my time?

Mrs Jones

I receive a phone call late one evening, "no date required" I can sense by the tone of his voice he is over the moon with something. I thought he might have won the lottery or had my 18 years child maintenance he wanted to give me, slim chance of that happening. I didn't know that in today's modern era you can join a DNA club. You put your DNA, not my DNA online. If there are any poor souls out there who have been adopted or for any other circumstance want to reconnect with their biological parents. Hey presto, if there is a match with their DNA which they also must register the process begins, the sperm diners club.

Pretty cool if you ask me, but an emotional journey for so many. Johnny joins the DNA club because he is curious in finding out if there are any more souls out there, he spawned. For the record and the conversations, I have had with Johnny, this fella put it about back in the days. He shagged the living soul out of himself. The swinging "60s" and 70s, he carried on into the eighties. No wonder everyone who shagged during this decade will always say "the sixties, best decade ever". The seventies, single parents, mixed raced kids all living through one of the most racist decades in British history.

"Son, I've got a another" another what? another aircraft carrier. "Another son", another son, fuck me. "Yes, another son", I'm on the other end of the phone thinking what the fuck, who is this guy, he says he is my biological father but hearing this makes me realise I was never special. The lies, the deceit the agony some of his partners must have gone through is beyond me. I suppose its why I was abandoned, and Travis adopted from birth, "not special" just a human inconvenience.

"I've got another son", poor bastard, I was half-heartedly listening, drinking my wine tucking into to a delightful cheese plate. So, the ego stroking begins. "Back in the 90s I'm shagging this married bird. Smashing her back doors in and she's loving it, I'm all over this woman like a fox in a chicken couple, rampant".

"We are set to meet one afternoon, but she doesn't show" What like you and Missus, missus Jones meeting at that same café. Laughter breaks out, "yeah, just like me and missus Jones". Stood up by a tango dancing conquest. "So, so long story short, I hear she's gone back to Scotland, been kicked out by her husband, the banker".

Still stroking his ego, he mentions that there has been a match alert to his inbox from the DNA diners club. Bingo, child number got to be going on 19+ has grown up. Being the only black man in his family, village, town, city he decides he needs to figure one of life's little questions? where he came from. Travis has got questions and being a grown man the thirst for these answers is overwhelming.

Growing up without identity is crippling, not knowing where you are from, there are millions of questions that you cannot answer. For example, the most common questions are asked by your GP when going for a routine check-up. "Is there a history of diabetes in the family, cancer, high blood pressure, wankers"? yes wankers, lots of wankers.

Questions that cannot be answered, so you go looking for them yourself and it is only going to be you on this journey. The people that spawned you think you owe them something now that you have come into each other's lives. It hurts, it's not a journey I would want my worst enemy to go through, maybe one or two. The energy, the time spent contemplating alone causes so many issues, addiction, mental health issues, anxiety etc. The mental health addiction menu cannot be comprehended by anyone how has been raised within a wholesome, loving family unit.

"Listen son a match, a fucking match, I've another son", what a self-righteous selfish bastard. I have totally lost all respect, well what little respect I had for him. Not impressed, not impressed at all. Then the audacity of the man shone through. "You're the eldest son, so do some digging about, find out what you know about Travis and get back to me with the details". I mean really, what am I, am I this guy's secretary, Sherlock baby finding sperm doner club Holmes "His name is Travis, he lives in Scotland, he's on Facebook and Instagram".

Curiosity says let's check this guy out, that's exactly what I did, not for Johnny's sake, for me. Turns out this fella, my half-brother is a very cool dude. Surfs, snowboards, likes to travel, beautiful partner and a handful of close friends. Educated, raised well and a kick ass profession in IT.

A few months down the road I contact Travis in the form of an Instagram message. Hey presto he messages me back. We hit it off from the get-go exchange numbers and a week later we have an honest and down to earth conversation, which lasts almost 3 hours.

We talk openly about the challenges we have both had to deal with growing up. Mainly wanting to know our origin our identity who why what where when. There was one thing we both did agree on that both our biological parents were off the charts irresponsible.

Travis and I are still good friends to this day and continue to communicate. I'm closer to a half-brother that I am still yet to meet in person than I am with the brothers and sisters I was raised with. It's because we have a lot in common, I don't mean the same blood but other interests, common interests. The fact he hasn't tried to kill me is also a bonus.

You might be thinking that I've got nothing but hate for my biological parents. I documented a lot in beaten black and blue born into racism. There was a time when I had nothing but admiration for them both. As time passes by you learn, we learn, I have learnt the hard way that they are not the parents I can look up too, let alone call role models.

They say we can't choose your parents, but as we become adults, we can either choose to be like them or by the grace of God or a higher power we choose to accept who we are. Regardless of the damage, regardless of the scars, we move forward, start living our own lives and become the people some thought we would never become.

Proper Bonkers

Evelyn's ex-partner who she had two wholesome children with, she dumped him to have a relationship with her half-brother, yes, totally and utterly wrong. Doris felt sorry for Evelyn's ex-partner Blake, so she let the poor fella move in with her. Blake is also a premier league cunt. He was totally and utterly inappropriate towards Lyndsey who also lived with Doris at the time.

I will not go into the particulars, but during family get togethers if Lyndsey did attend which wasn't often for obvious reasons. No one could mention a certain name "Blake" because she gets upset. That is how they deal with this shit; they all make out its ok. "Yeah, it happened we cannot go back and change what happened that's all in the past now".

They move on and get utterly wasted. If the truth be told some of them are carrying a great burden which they were not responsible for. But they would rather take that shit to the grave and make out the perpetrators were the victims. Perfect example, huge family get together minus me and mine, Doris's side of the family plus Alfred's degenerates. They all meet early one Saturday morning. The booze is flowing at the crack of dawn, soon as the household awakes its beer on cornflakes and whisky in the porridge. Destination middle of nowhere, a rundown beat up watering hole for some seriously shady and shabby patrons.

Doris, Alfred, the SS leader, several of their kids and Daniel's two children. Obvious long story short the group are smashed before they arrive at the watering hole. The banter is loose and the booze if flowing harder than a packed walkabout during two for one student night. Someone looking in from the outside would most likely think "let's get involved". But a certain member of the party inside and Daniel's two kids are on the J20s.

Most of us have watched home alone. Crazy household, a crooked copper played by Joe Pesci. The entire household running around like headless what nots getting ready for their Christmas vacation. They all make a mad dash for the airport, the entire family are all on the jumbo and the irresponsible parent realises she has left the oven on, wrong. Yeah, you get it, she has left her child at home. For all young families living on the bread line, young families like 16-year-olds. Please do not watch this movie, make a crazy arse dash to Blackpool and forget the kids.

It will not go down to well in court, "I was motivated by home alone my lord, thought they might get by while me and Trev had a cheeky break for the weekend". "Well, there is no excuse as to why your house burnt down with your two children inside, Guilty as charged".

The party erupts, like Kevin's mum, no sorry let me rephrase, not like Kevin's mum on that jumbo jet, Armageddon. "Where the fuck is my daughter Sharon shouts Daniel, where the fuck is, she, what the fuck is going on, where has she gone". They also realise another member of the binge drinking party has also gone missing. I mean how paralytic do you have to be too realise your 6-year-old daughter has been missing and hasn't been seen for the best part of 30 something minutes.

Like a clan of intoxicated meerkats, they stagger and scatter from the pub. Searching in toilets, car park and the surrounding woodland. Several minutes after the initial nuclear strike, out of the wood's strolls Alfred's eldest, Fred and Daniel's daughter. Now this pair are not related at all, second uncles and all that crap, it's a load of bollocks.

A drunken coalition of family members who love being smashed. Fred casually strolls towards the mob of axe wielding lumber jacks' hand in hand with Daniel's daughter Sharon. If he had said prior to his disappearing act with a 6-year-old, "we are off to the park" then it would have been obvious, Daniel would have said, "you must be on drugs Fred, go fuck a tree".

Ask yourself, why would he disappear with her in the first place. For the record Evelyn did tell Doris years prior, "watch out for that one he is a pancake". Sharon runs towards here dad soon as she sees him. No questions asked, Bobby walks up to Fred, "sex predator" and knocks the fucker clean out.

Mad panic, Alfred's children all rally around this certain individual protecting him from the inevitable beating. "I fucking knew it, I fucking knew, you sick twisted bastard, what the fuck are you doing with my fucking daughter, you are disgusting fucking bastard".

They finally get Fred out of there, in a taxi and out of harm's way as Bobby and Daniel wanted to do a job on this fella. They wanted to fuck him up. The thing which strikes me as peculiar, one side of the party are screaming abuse and the other are protecting Fred. I asked a family member years later did they want to involve the authorities? they replied, "well you can't be sure, you know what he's like, it's not the first time something like this has happened, listen let's change the subject".

Well, this incident got leaked to Daniel's ex-wife. You see Daniel had the kids that weekend and when she heard of the matter, she crucified him, literally crucified him and I do not blame her. Which now brings me to the garnish for the final course. Doris's first marriage, the fella who thought I was his son was banged up for engaging in a sexual act with a minor, selling and supplying cocaine to his son. All of which seemed ok with Doris. It was just another thing that got swept under their carpet.

When I did turn to Doris to try and share my demons and addictions, I was brushed aside like a dead rat on the kitchen floor. She wasn't interested, Doris looked at me and said, "that's not my thing, I wasn't into that" She didn't care, she wouldn't give a fuck If I dropped dead. But I get it, I was the mistake that fucked her first marriage up, so why would she care.

My auntie Stella always knew something putrid was going on with the band living in Southampton. A pastor grooming his offspring to bread Hitler youth kids. During my time with Stella in the 70s and 80s she would often get incredibly angry and upset. She knew that entire family was all wrong.

At the age of 16 and pregnant Evelyn is booted out by Boris and Doris. After years of physical and mental abuse her first white boyfriend gets her pregnant. Its fucking ironic, do not date or hang around with black guys you'll be a no good for nothing bitch single parent whore. So much for boot polish black. Maybe it should have been furniture polish or white matt paint for what it was worth.

Two kids later Evelyn and Blake move down south as work Is fruitful. life is good, better than middle England. Well, it's not long before shit gets weird, the proverbial shit isn't a big enough cliché to describe what unfolds over the next few years.

Gut wrenching, wrong, surreal, warped, polluted, unnatural and totally incomprehensible. I get word from a brother from another mother that Evelyn is having a relationship behind the father of her children's back Blake, with her half-brother, her fucking brother. I didn't get wind of this, not until Evelyn gave birth to their first child. Which makes them both mother and father, auntie and uncle and I think maybe sister and brother to this baby.

Every half sibling, full sibling, uncle and auntie, grandparents and cousins are lost for words, dumbstruck. How the fuck could this have happened, apart from the obvious. The only person amongst all this chaos, the centre of this carnage that is not kicking off is Doris. "She's my daughter I have to stand by her and support her at every cost".

Gone are the days of the Roman empire, whereby future kings, princes are encouraged to smash their sisters back doors in to make a future heir of pure blood. First offspring of this Roman style incestual affair is born as all babies are bone, pure. A sigh of relief is heard across the maternity ward.

So, off the back of the first baby they have two more, if one wasn't enough, two more, really, three in total, talk about playing with fire. There is outrage within the ranks of the family, disgust, hate, displeasure the whole nine yards of bewilderment.

Blake finally moved out from the house that Doris built and is now shagging his best mates' wife Shirley. His best mate Randy by the way got thrown out a moving train. He survived being thrown from the train part, but as you can imagine he is proper fucked. This didn't stop Blake pumping two kids out from his penis into Shirley, friends no more, not even Christmas cards.

A full-blown incestual relationship with her hill billy blood brother, marriage would have come as no surprise. When the eldest turned 16 the sister brother relationship ended. Blake cheated on his sister Evelyn with a Mexican stripper. He packed his bags, moved out leaving his brothers and sisters, slash nephew's and Evelyn, mother, sister of his children in limbo.

Its fucking ironic because Doris proper kicked off calling him a waster, a wanker, how could he do that to his sister, useless cunt, he doesn't deserve her. I mean really, who has a head so twisted that they would say that in the first place. "The brother doesn't deserve his sister". Many years have passed and the incestual Roman style Chernobyl explosion shag feast is now contaminated history. But is it, the whole show has reared its smelly head? Children, adults, cousins, brothers and sisters want answers. Fuck trying to explain this one in the middle of Whoville with shotguns and crack.

For the record I haven't just made this up while I've been drinking a case of scotch shooting smack in my study, hiding form the world. No, I'm sat on my couch staring through the television contemplating. Is my cousin really my sister, was my late auntie really my mother, was my late uncle my dad, did I get swapped at birth, was my birth certificate forged. No, But I was abandoned for being a black baby, in a white racist household, savage.

No Title Needed

I thought I looked up to grandad as a kid growing up, but memories relating to those years back in the 80s on that god forsaken council estate have made me think otherwise. A wolf in sheep's clothing, a quite unapproachable man who wasn't loved during those years. You put two and two together as a child being a witness to countless arguments and domestic and verbal abuse its fucking obvious, he was just as bad.

It's unfortunate how he passed, I wouldn't wish that disease on anyone. There is one incident which stands out regarding him. Something so irrational, pointless and vindictive. Something so spiteful and terrifying for an 8-year-old kid, why?

Question if I may, what does an 8-year kid know about woodwork? unless he's the son of Noah. I knew nothing about woodwork, how to measure, saw, drill, hammer, glue, varnish, nothing. The only thing I knew was kicking wooden fences in.

Summer 1979 the Gestapo had moved to the estate we had just moved to. What I do not understand to this day if there was so much hatred why would families want to live near each other?

Why not just move to other ends of the country or corners of the globe if it's that bad and it was that bad. So, we are at the compound out in the garden drinking squash, grandad on the patio making something out of wood. "Oi crusty come here boy", yeah that's how they rolled, no first name just racial slur, "crusty". Racism imbedded so deep it was normal in society back then and still is today, in most degenerate circles.

"Ok, we need to measure this piece of wood and saw it in half, can you do that", I will try, "I will measure where we need to saw, ok", ok. He measures the piece of wood, marks where I need to cut with a pencil. "Ok crusty see that pencil mark, that line across the wood, that's where you need to saw, ok", ok.

Yeah ok, its where that pencil mark is? "Correct". A piece of wood no thicker than a rounders bat must be sawn into equal halves, my job to saw where grandad has marked the wood. I place the wood on a sturdy chair place one knee over the wood to support it, to stop it from moving about, or so I thought. There was zero fat on that kid back then, just skin and bone, a kid who dreamt about school dinners.

I turn and look up to grandad who was standing over me nursing a can of bitter. "Saw on the line crusty, chop chop, I haven't got all day". Haven't got all day for what? I mean really what has a retired fella got to do all day apart from terrorise kids and drink lash.

I begin to saw dead straight on the pencil mark, the piece of wood slipping and sliding beneath my knee. Hyperventilating like a kid in a toy shop, ten minutes later I'm through. Grandad grabs the pieces of wood from me as if I've just done something so stupidly outrageous. He puts the two pieces together, "what the fuck is this shit, are you fucking stupid"? The other runts stop playing in the dirt, it's all eyes on me. "Stupid", no I sawed on the pencil mark where you said to saw.

"Are you fucking answering me back boy"? Come here you little shit, I'm here I'm stood at his feet. He bends down and rests on one knee, eye bawling me. "Look at me boy, look at me do you hear me", my head bent down slowly rises, the look on this monster's face sends spine chilling stabs wounds through my frail malnourished existence. "What the fuck is this? I told you to saw on the pencil mark" I did, "don't you dare fucking answer me back". He pushes the two pieces of wood into my stomach with force, "do you see what you have done". One piece is shorter than the other.

"I wanted to equal pieces of wood in length, now I have one shorter than the other". I can clearly see the pulse in his neck, his blood boiling in the heat, he bends closer and whispers in my ear.

"Do you hear me inside that empty head of yours crusty, do you hear me"? I stammer out words yes "yes what, yes sir", yes sir. "I remember when I meet that pathetic excuse of a man called your father, a fucking disgrace to our family".

"The idiot did a handstand up against the living room wall wearing bright orange trousers, stupid monkey". "Anyways, you've messed up my project by sawing in the wrong place", I didn't, "shut your mouth boy".

"Can you run"? Yes, "yes what"? Yes, I can run sir, ", you've got 5 seconds to out of my face or else". Or else what sir, "well if I catch you, I will beat you within an inch of your pathetic little life". That is the only thing I remember about him, why cause so much trauma, the fact of being caught and beaten was nothing new.

It's obvious why he was screamed and shouted at during Christmas get togethers, get togethers in general. Boris pissing petrol onto the already monstrous inferno, "there all fucking different, not one of them the same, how does it feel".

Doris at the helm screaming "you fucking wanker get the fuck out of my fucking house", Boris behind her egging the rage on. It's clear as day that these two monsters had caused considerable abuse when they lived in Asia while grandad was serving in the military. If memory recollects, I remember an argument about a scalding bath, wooden stairs, a wire coat hanger and a bottle of whisky for a teenager.

Vodka and Stitches

It was just fucking madness. If it wasn't an issue involving a sexual predator or a full-blown argument regarding Evelyn having four children with her half-brother. It would most definitely be a full-on vodka-fuelled scrap, a battle to the death or thereabouts.

What can I say about Bobby? he is the personification of Boris and Doris. Now this would not be the first time we have had our ups and downs me and Bobby. We had mad crazy stand offs, fist fights, sticks and bricks thrown at each other. But the most memorable incident was when he almost split my head in two. It was attempted murder when you look at it.

A brick the size of a football launched into the back off my head when we were kids. I ended up with severe concussion, ten old school stitches and a day in hospital but this was not it. During my time in the military, we happened to be in the same place at the same time, we were both back at the mad house, the house of nightmares.

Like always loads of booze, myself and Bobby got talking, it would be the first time he would hear of the carnage that Boris bared down on me as a child. Bobby did not like what he heard; he did not like it one bit. I am square in his face pouring out every sick warped noxious experience.

Bobby and his girlfriend would be staying for the night plus some random baby crashed out in a highchair. We are sat around the breakfast table with Doris royally smashed hanging from the ceiling. So, nothing unusual so far about the everyday carnage that has been going on in the house for years. Bobby is sat opposite wearing fine designer clothes sloshed beyond measure. He's got that look in his eye, the omen look.

The conversation starts to fizzle out, so I decided to make a cheese toasty before bed as the kebab shop across the way had closed. Yes, a cheese and tomato toasty before bed, just what I need. "Bruv, do not touch the fucking cheese" screams Bobby from the breakfast room, "yeah don't touch the cheese shouts his girlfriend".

What do you mean don't touch the cheese I've touched it, better still I'm eating it? I walk into the breakfast room holding the packet of sliced cheese and ask what the big deal is. "That's his cheese", the baby in the highchair, you're saying that's his cheese, "yes". Well, the baby is asleep, I am hungry, I'm making a cheese toasty. "Bruv, you dare use that cheese or I will fuck you up". Hold on, your saying, shits going to hit the fan if I make a cheese toasty, "yes, it's going to go off, yes correct".

Bruv this is a slice of cheese we are on about, not a chocolate lobster, not a tin of Iranian caviar. Neither is it a cheese and ham quiche form Harrods, it is a fucking slice of cheese. So, I'm stood there in the doorway eating a slice of cheese then the place erupts.

The breakfast table gets turned the fuck over, the entire contents of the table flying. Bobby grabs the vodka bottle from the floor and attempts to smash the bottle with full force into the back of my head. I would not know this because I've turned around to exit the breakfast room. I have grabbed my stone island coat and walked out of the house for a stroll to get some fresh air.

It's where I stroll to which is bizarre. I end up standing outside the house I moved into with my sister, Boris and Doris in the early 70s. That crumbling rat infested house with the overgrown garden. The house of pain, hatred, anger, tears, abuse, madness that God forsaken house. I just ended up there hoping to see a plum tree in the garden. I had planted plum stones from a tin of plums back in the 70s.

I arrive back to the house hours later. Doris is sprawled out on the sofa, I haven't a clue where Bobby's is let alone his lady friend or baby. The kitchen is a mess, blood splattered walls, broken glass, the place is a horror scene. Fuck it, there is not a chance I'm cleaning this shit up. I head upstairs and crash out.

The following morning, I head downstairs, Doris has cleaned and tidied the place up all bar the blood splattered walls. Where's Bob, "he's in hospital you stupid bastard, why the fuck did you have to eat the cheese, you're a fucking wanker, a fucking arsehole".

"He had emergency surgery, you're a lucky bastard you are, a right lucky bastard, he could have killed you". What do you mean a lucky bastard, what do mean what do I mean, I don't mean anything? So, I'm lucky my half bastard shell shocked cunt of a brother did not kill me.

In his failed attempt to crack a vodka bottle over the back of my head, he misses by a whisker. If I had hesitated for a split second, a hundredth of a second, I would not be writing this today. He would have caved in the back of my head. He came off worse the silly cunt, he split three fingers clean open down to the bone. Tendons, muscle, flesh proper fucked.

I mean really, what do you say to someone, a supposed half sibling in later life that they did in fact try to kill you. You would think in later life both Boris's sons Bobby and Daniel would man up and get their shit together.

I mean how stupid do you have to be to fuck this all up. Married, huge house, three cars, inheritance to a fortune including racehorses. A beautiful wife, money in the bank, children doing well at school, healthy with the full sky package and broadband. To fuck that all up you have got to be bonkers, proper bonkers or just stupid.

Dirty web site for dirty people wanting to get their rocks off in car parks with other dirty people watching. Daniel logs in and starts the chitchat with aliens. He has all the above, what happened is a miracle its Hollywood magic. He's in chatting, so what does the stupid idiot do? He tells the other person on the other end of the cosmic highway his name.

One in a million that this carpark badger who is as mad for some car park dogging happens to be his wife's best friend. Well, it's obvious the chat was cut abruptly short, no one is getting a spanking in any carpark within walking distance of Daniels mansion that night. House phone rings within seconds on the disconnect. "Hi, Marlene, is that you"? "Yes, it's me" long story short divorce.

The yearly mash up is set, nice weekend together, Bobby, Daniel, their wives and children. A weekend away at Bobs townhouse. The usual bollocks, meet, greet presents for the rug rats and more booze to sink a naval destroyer. Vodka for you, Whiskey for you, screw drivers for the ladies.

Now I know this happened because cunt face, I'm going to smash a bottle of vodka off the back of your head decides not to attend my wedding. Why, let me explain, phone call comes in on my drive home from work two days before the big day. "Bruv, we can't make it to your wedding, me, (vodka bottle) we've all got colds and think it's best if we stay away and rest".

Three years before covid-19, really, I'm driving bruv, just finished work, take care speak soon, hang up, cunt. Well, when the invitations went out months before the big day, I receive a call from vodka bottle. "Bruv, just want to mention, please make sure I'm not sat next to that cunt (his brother) or his ugly cunt of a fucking wife". I can concur she is not a looker. Ok bruv consider it done.

My wife to be did not like this one bit, "it's our day babe, if they don't like the arrangements, they can go fuck themselves". I agree babe, seating arrangements do not change. They had every intention to swerve, fuck them both, lets invite Sharon and Domonic.

So back to the semi-sibling's wife children get together. Exchange kids presents, hit the booze. Takeaway, poker hit the booze harder. Kids are asleep on the floor, hit the booze even harder. The booze is now in the driving seat, the carnage bus has left the football stadium.

It's as clear as the fresh fallen snow that they have all got issues minus the kids sleeping on the floor. I will not go into the detail in how the bull fight started but it had something to do with Boris. Now, how can I put this into a black and white picture?

Take a fresh killed zebra leg, season with a wild African shrub marinade for a few minutes. Then throw it into a posse of deranged ravaged starving hyenas. I'm sure a few have watched David Attenborough documentaries. Please may I ask you to do the math with that scene. Well, these hyenas have west country accents, and they speak human. This is the carnage that ensued in that household on that evening with kids thrown in the mix.

Big boys WWE, two wives made in Chelsea, kids sesame street crazy. Phone numbers deleted, Facebook, Instagram deleted, there is no way on god's green earth that I will expose my children to that sort of madness. This is how it is; they roll this way and it's just another reason why Auguste Knuckles has decided to go it alone with me and mine. If the truth be told with a free bar, wine and vodka on the tables during our big day it was a blessing in disguise.

My Bookshelf

When I'm feeling low, depressed or just not in the mood for life, I go to beaten black and blue on my bookshelf. I pull out a copy and look at the cover, understanding my achievements with such a project. It gives me hope knowing it's a living object with so many flashbacks and traumas within its pages. It's been filed away, but I'm human and somewhat still vulnerable.

During the early years when Doris saved me from what seemed to be imminent death from whoever I was with at the time. My cousin would stay with us for long periods of time. The actual dates are hazy circa 1975, Boris and Doris fully fledged alcoholics. Both bringing pain down on the household.

The crumbling house was riddled with mice. They occupied upstairs, while downstairs in the kitchen, pantry and bathroom we had rats. Big, horrible rats, as a kid they seemed even bigger. After a day scratching around in the dirt at the bottom of the garden it's in doors for a dip in the dish water before bed. No cartoons, hot milk or a cookie, that was to lavish for us runts, up the wooden hill and into our scratchers.

I have no clue or can comprehend why adults want to cause such misery. The only thing I can surmise is that they personify evil. It didn't t surprise me when I heard Boris's brother was banged up for being a paedophile. It didn't surprise when I heard through the noxious scuttlebutt as a grown man that sexual predators were almost forgiven for being misunderstood.

Even after writing my first book, going back down flashback lane is never easy. I have had to walk away several times from my laptop to compose myself. Willing energy within to finish this chapter as there is still healing that needs addressing.

We would be woken by Boris in the late hours. Myself with my cousin taken downstairs through the living room and into the kitchen still half asleep. Wearing a pair of pants, cold, shaking, still half asleep.

Two vulnerable half-asleep children no older than 5, Boris would start the game, "who wants some sweets then", rubbing his hands, sick, perverse atrocious. Although we could not see the rats in the pantry scratching around for a morsel of food, we could hear them.

"There are sweets at the back on the middle shelf, if you want them go and fetch them". Only a mad twisted human could do this to children, this was happening, this was the nightmare, a nightmare with our baby eyes open.

Petrified shaking hyperventilating, I hadn't a clue what to do, is it a game, it can't be. I felt Boris's hand in the middle of my back trying to push me forward of the first step onto the pantry floor. Pitch black with a glimmer of the moon piercing a wooden board covering a space where a glass window used to be. My cousin grabs my hand shaking her head, "don't do it, don't do it, if you get bitten you will die". I'm given a smack to the back of the head and told to fuck off out of his site.

There is no emotion in my words, just trauma and flashbacks being filed away and shared with the world. I told you I had something to say. You might be living in your big house with Alfred and the SS Gestapo, but your probably so lonely it hurts. knowing the son, you neglected has made a life for himself and achieved the unachievable.

"I have got every goddammed given right to be fucking angry".

Frogs' Legs

48 hours in Paris sounds awesome right, epic in fact, food orgies, fingering fit French girls in doorways, French kissed by Michelin starred chefs then off to Buddha bar for tranquil beats and million-euro cocktails. Wrong, wrong on so many levels, 48 hours in Paris? Killing Zoe, the sound of music and Pulp fiction smashed into one wild weekend.

Roger Avary movie, 1993 Eric Stoltz professional safe cracker flies into Paris gets fucked up beyond madness with his college pal played by Jean-Hugues Anglade. Zed fucks the fittest hooker July Delpy then the mob robs a bank on Bastille Day hanging out their bum cracks like a mother fucker.

Well, I was not a safe cracker, neither did I rob a bank on bastille day or fuck a French prostitute. You may be thinking, a chef in France for a 48 hours. forty-eight Beautiful French hours one would most definitely indulge oneself with all the culinary wonders of Paris.

My 48 hours in France was spent with half a dozen Parisian locals who prefer the sleazy, electric under belly of Paris. Nocturnal animals with a lust for all things illegal and loud. Where would I meet such creatures and how the fuck did, I end up in the back of a van tripping fantastic for the duration of my visit.

Regardless chefs are chefs, it's that thing which makes us the individuals we are. Being a chef isn't a nine to five existence, it's a brotherhood which only chefs will get. We are in fact all fucking raving lunatics, the same. Or once was raving lunatics but still have that chef twitch.

I had spent a few weeks at the end of winter season working in the posh ski resort of Corcheval 1850. This resort is so posh they sell Krug, Dom Perignon champagne and Iranian caviar in the local Spar. Spar in 1850 resembled a mini-Harrods.

Easy money, spring snow, warm climate sunny skies in the mountains where the rich come to play. Private chalet chef back then 60€ per hour. The local seasonal bars were full of hardcore season airs getting juiced before the summer season. This is where I meet three lunatics who I would get to know during those few weeks.

During the short stint earning good bread I would also learn how to, prepare, cook and eat frogs' legs ala Pernod. That delightful aniseed drink the French like to consume by the bucket loads on Sunday morning before lunch. Weekly routine, work, eat frogs' legs, get smashed on all sorts of uppers and downers being stoned like a caveman in a cave on some very fruity skunk.

The date is set during one finger in the eye frog eating evening. I would visit my new French foreign legion friends in Paris for one hell of a weekend before I start my life as a chef in sunny climates.

"Last call Auguste Knuckles, last call to gate number 69 departing in ten minutes". I've never been late for a flight let alone had my name called over the tannoy. A sign of things to come, drunk before getting on the plane. More drunk in the plane. Paris was going to eat me up and proverbially shit me out.

Bee, Philippe and Bear picked me up from Charles de Gaulle airport. If I thought, I was drunk these three Parisians were peeled. Jean-Hugues Anglade in killing Zoe firing on all sorts of medications peeled. "Auguste my friend you made it" well I wasn't going to miss it for the world, "agh that's so nice, come on let's go".

My French was ok back then, I had managed French kitchens in the alps but this weekend I was going to get a crash course in French slang. "Espèce de conard français, va baiser ta souer". Meaning, you French fucker, go fuck your sister is what Bear screams out the window at a taxi driver who has just cut him up as we depart the airport.

MDMA is on the menu as we make the short journey into Paris central. Destination, techno DJs residence. No time for a quick stop at Bear's place to drop my bags off and freshen up. Oh no, the French live fast and live young. If they don't die, bonus.

We arrive at la Maison techno our jaws are grinding away. Quick introductions and its straight on the pastis. It's practically pernod, served with ice and water. "Cuisses de grenouilles tout le monde" merci beaucoup. Frogs' legs quickly sauteed with olive oil, garlic, cherry tomatoes and flambe with pernod.

Blaring techno, several people in a tiny apartment with a great Dane trying to fuck my leg. A bottle of pastis in and several beers down the day quickly shifts

275

to night. A dozen bombs of MDMA are dropped into shots of grey goose and passed around. "Sortons, let's go".

The Rex club in Paris two decades ago was the place to be. Pumping house and techno. Another bomb of MDMA 8 hours on the dance floor and its breakfast time. Not that I could manage breakfast let alone a croissant or pan au chocolate. Its hard liquor in the brasserie next door. That breakfast of hard liquor and coffee was the closest I got to nouvelle cuisine in Paris that weekend.

Next stop after hours party across town. Transport, back of a hippy's van smoking weed with Bear. Tabs of acid are passed around in the lift. In a random apartment rushing my tits off. My eye's balls are sat on the end of my nose. Bon Jour je m'appelle Beetle juice.

Random sex, random apartment, a bunch of frogs tripping in a confined space going bananas like it's the end of the world. 3 hours later I manage to freshen up as best I could with a random toothbrush and someone's flannel. Armpits, ball sack and feet, million-dollar makeover. "Let's go people", it's out the door for a Turkish kebab, cold beer and cocaine. The only drug which is going to get me through Saturday.

Last stop it is off to a boat on a river somewhere in Paris to see the techno DJ I meet yesterday. By the time we arrive I could have been on fire and I wouldn't have known it. Ten hours of sweat, grime, deafening music and copious amounts of alcohol it's time for me to drop dead.

I come to in the back of the hippie van being woken by the most seductive French woman. In the most seductive accent, she taps my passport on my nose and whispers "we go to airport". DJ shadow vibrating the van all the way to Charles de Gaulle. "Au revoir Auguste, I like you very much, bon voyage".

It took me several weeks to get my head straight and to process those 48 hours in Paris. Paris chewed me up and shit me out. The thought of Paris during those months of come down, I would shake my head look up to the sky and say, "thank you".

It would be many years later before I returned to Paris. Only this time I would not be molested for breakfast, shagged senseless in a van and shit out. Not that I minded all the above, it's how the Parisians got their rocks off. We fucking live well, so we can fucking die well.

Frogs Ala Pernod

One Dozen frogs' legs, 1 finely diced shallot, 1 clove of crushed garlic, 8 Cherry tomatoes cut in halves, few springs of chopped flat leaf parsley, 1 shot of Pernod, Olive oil, rock salat, crushed black pepper.

Method

Method is easy just do not burn the garlic or over cook the frog's legs.

The Mind of a Fruitcake

So, it's always been fascinating, the murky world that goes on behind sheds, in bushes, around the back, behind bike sheds. Annal sex has always fascinated me, from its humble beginning's way back when. Way back when I have no fucking clue when but be assured our shit does stink. Someone or something decided one day to stick its genitalia into a random bottom of a love baboon, some sort of orifice or maybe an ear, once you've had cock you go deaf.

This single passionate gesture may have happened millions of years ago. Or it could have been a huge fucking mistake. Maybe that penis or mating rod just happened to stumble headfirst into something warm, tight, dirty and smelly, maybe, I'm just surmising as I attend the executive management morning meeting. My eyes wonder around the table pondering who got smashed on cocaine this weekend or took it in the pleasure pocket of grime. It's just how the mind works when you live with irrational compulsive thought disorder. At least it's not a waking nightmare today. Death, destruction, madness. Not today, today its bum sex day, utterly bizarre. Auguste knuckles, trying to get my head around why we love the welfare canal. A smelly cavern of shit.

Now I guess gay dinosaurs didn't exist during those millions of years they roamed free. Free to be who the fuck they wanted to be. Badass dinosaurs. I cant imagine two T-Rex having a freaky fondle with their baby arms. Let alone going arse mental over some dinosaur glove box. I think we can wipe the slate clean with LGTBQ dinosaurs or dinosaurs who mistook the female dinosaur love box for anything else but supper. Doubt there was anything crazy enough to come on to a T-rex. "Hey Rex fancy some bum sex raaggghhhh". But like sapiens some dinosaurs were vegans, and some dinosaurs were wankers who loved a raw dino chop. I've never met a vegan that doesn't think a meat eater isn't a premier league wanker. Vegans marry vegans the rest of us are just meat-eating cunts.

From where I'm standing, I don't know of any other animals that are into ass. I've never seen two male dogs fuck, only sniff each other out. I've watched a cat lick its pussy but never the pussy of another cat. Maybe it goes on behind the sofa, whatever. Never seen a lesbian cat, two gay rhinos fucking in the zoo in front of Johnny Flipflop and Auntie Betty. Would they know they are LGTBQ rhinos? Never seen a camel smash the back doors out of another camel, and why the fuck don't animals' cross bread with other animals.

Dog on pigeon, it would be a bloodbath. Hedgehogs mad for badger snatch. Foxes going mental for some rat pussy. A male elephant coming into puberty ravages the back doors of a hyena. Would the hyena be up for elephant sized cock? Maybe if the hyena was a slag, staggering out the spoons after a few tequilas gagging for some elephant action. I'm sure that kind of behaviour happens somewhere, anal liquorice love lane here we go, that's us, mad for the backdoor bird box.

We fucking hate it when we wipe our arse after a mega shit, the toilet paper tears, shit on our fingers. Disgusting, its mayhem in the toilet it's a 10 man rave 6 by 6. Dare to smell those shitty fingers? Hell no. Scrub those pinkies clean. Changing a baby's nappy, projectile shits over you and a new laid carpet, shocking, but funny. But shit on your dick after a shit BBQ spit roast is kudos. Buff that chest "shit wings yeah". Not the easiest of shit treacle to clean up. Soapy sponge and hot running water, bonkers. Shit on a dick, never seen that in a porn movie. "Spring clean people, I want your farmer's love cul-de-sac squeaky clean, no shit on set today people". Am I seeing things? A clean dirt box, my dick, covered, covered in melted peanut butter, crunchy peanut butter, what am I doing wrong, porn studio here I come. Get me some professional arse fucking hygiene tips. "Welcome to today's course, arse hygiene level 4 for aspiring porn-stars, otherwise known as shit pickles".

And why don't Zebras fuck horses, same thing right. Like our insatiable lust for meat, we can't get enough of ass. Surely vegans must fuck and eat ass. Lesbian vegans are they truly vegan? eating a chicken breast without swallowing it. The whole fucking vegan thing, all agricultural animals are vegans. Grass feed until their untimely death. So why don't vegans eat grass, hay, and feed? Or if you're an ass eating terrorist, would you suck a brother's dick after being hip deep in the devil's pocket before blowing up an all-pork butcher shop? The whole world loves ass. Just a species of arse loving, all-inclusive buffet arse chomping back door addicts up the dirt box poop smelling bottom bandits. My wife walked into a halal butcher shop many years back and asked if they sold pork chops, life time ban right there, innocent mayhem.

Anyway, I'm going with the Romans. The Chinese invented pasta, the Italians took it to a whole different level. The empire killed billions basically fucking every country in the ass. The Romans put a stamp on shit and spunk, they own it. Now before I continue, bum sex isn't just for the homosexual community. No, no, no. Bum sex mania has been off the charts long before we learnt how to fly. Australian women love it in back burner back, "going further off piste here guys" those chicks down under love being smashed upside inside their welfare canal. Well, me being me I don't mind getting messy as a coal miner, going balls deep with my Cornish pastie to keep me fuelled. After all, I'm just the causality of my ancestors. Lord of the rings Frodo bumbaggins and no wiser than a dildo called gollum.

Anyways some shit from the internet by Joe Duncan. A Polish anthropologist by the name of Bronislaw Malinowski explored many cultures which have been encapsulated in time through their remoteness and lack of contact with other cultures. One of the cultures he wrote about, the Trobriand Islanders who live near New Guinea on a very remote island, had no clue how babies came to be, and it's likely that many older cultures were much the same. These people believed, quite simply, that a "ghost" (yes, an actual ghost) came and impregnated women, and thus the responsibilities of adulthood didn't belong to the father but the community, as they had no conception of fatherhood.

Imagine having no conception of fatherhood at all and an entire civilisation of people running around having whatever kind of sex they wanted with whomever they wanted the tribe communalised the responsibilities of raising the children while everyone else played. Human history was likely much more radical than you think, and an understanding of this ancient and prehistoric sexual liberty will shed some insight into other cultures who loved doing it in the backdoor long before we showed up on the scene. And that shit is research people, not my research but I did google, the origins of bum sex.

So back to me and back to the barbarian Roman I became. Oh, and just like the said civilisation above the Romans had an appetite for ass and I don't just mean sapiens ass. They personified sex with animals, sheep shagging, whatever, long before a lonely Welshmen fell into a bush with a sheep and ended up with his cock buried deep in a woolly sheep's bottom. Glad the Roman empire is done and dusted; I would be proper buried with demons fucked in the afterlife for ever days. Although I'm guessing cat ass, the Romans, not sheep. Or a catfish. Never come across a hieroglyphic of said mania. Must have gone on behind the pyramids.

With the amount of ass fucking around the world why haven't we invested more into bum products. It's just dildos and prostate ticklers. For example, imagine being balls deep in arse. Out of the blue you hear the same sound as a fanny fart. That same sound when you're hammering a vagina. That quintessential sound which cracks everyone up in the heat of passion. A farting vagina. Imagine the fucking mess from an ass if it began farting continuously while hitting the sweet spot. Hence bum products. We invented a wetsuit. Why not invent a shit suit, exactly a shit suit.

"Don't worry about being pebbled dashed in the face while out and about in your partner's bottom. Purchase an Auguste Knuckles pebble dash shit proof suit. Money back guaranteed. You can also upgrade for a few dollars more and invest in the Auguste knuckles snorkel protection shit mash, guaranteed to stop those shit pieces ending up in your eyes and mouth, visit our arse bandit store AKbackdoorproducts.com".

They say you can't smell porn but an hour inside the temple of doom it's going to get hell smelly. It's going to get sweaty and smelly. "So why not invest in Auguste knuckles ass potpourri for those savage bum sessions. Fill the bedroom with oak, cinnamon and lavender fragrances and be at ease with the smell of shit". Our love and devotion for the rusty sheriffs' badge needs more investment, invest with AK now.

Back to the down under relationship. The welfare canal was truly the 1st port of call during daily bondage under the duvet. My dick didn't have a clue what was going on. Well tell a lie it did know. I just made out that this sort of behaviour was totally acceptable between man and his penis. He thought differently. Being rammed senseless. Into the dungeon of doom, not good for morale. Only on special occasions did we go to that fluffy place. A place where his master would drink from. That warm velvety moist place, a willy wonka Alice in wonder place full of moist warm wonder. Wrong this cock is a dark side cock. "So why not invest in a tube of Auguste knuckles pussy-smelling cock cream.

Apply liberally to one's shaft or dildo before going balls or fist deep. AK cock cream comes in several fragrances, vanilla, strawberry, chocolate chip, tutti frutti, strawberry cheesecake and the top seller bubble-gum. AK cock cream stays on during the hardest of ass workouts. AK cock cream, out the bum straight into the mouth. No shitty aftertaste, AK cock cream guaranteed to taste like bubble-gum several hours after being in the welfare canal, or your money back".

And after a hard day on the back burner of bum madness relax in a hot Soapy bubble bath. I don't fucking think so, you can fuck right off. I'd rather be fucked by a three-legged two headed zebra horse inbred T-rex meerkat rhino.

"Out of sheer madness authors are born, madness out of authors who don't consider themselves authors sheer chaos is created" AK

21st Birthday Cocktail, the Aftermath

Lift off

Armed to the teeth with a goody bag full of magical treats which consisted of angel dust (PCP) an eight ball of cocaine, blotted sheet of banana splits "acid" 30 ecstasy tabs, several wraps of speed, more skunk and solid than a small festival, it was time to celebrate my 21st birthday.

This was going to be a private affair, only the head strong, the closest of friends. We drove back from Amsterdam and made our way to a beautiful caravan park outside of Hamburg. The brochure lived up to our expectations, our fully furnished caravan was a stone's throw from a beautiful lake.

Lush surroundings, enough space between the caravans so no chance of pissing our neighbours off. What a place to launch ourselves from the planet. There was Beanie the cat, Brummies' Pal, Cuthbert the posh kid, Dave Jumpers, ambulance bob, johnny 6 stickers, Jacko the smacko and me.

We had got to know each other well during the past few years serving in the army, in Germany with our regiment. Our brief to ourselves was simple, to celebrate my 21st birthday with soldiers we could all trust, them knowing I had their backs and vice a versa. The recipe for that evening was to get beyond fucked up. To travel to a place most humans will never experience, unless you have watched fear and loathing in Las Vegas or depraved as half a dozen squaddies in a yellow caravan.

Mise en place, 1 gram of PCP, 2 grams of cocaine, six love doves, 4 tabs of acid, 2 grams of speed, jack Daniels and tumblers. Grind all ingredients to a nice powder consistency. Sprinkle equal quantities of your space dust into clean crystal tumblers. Top the tumblers with Jack Daniels, say grace, salute one another, down the hatch.

Freshen up, change, head to the local night club which is highly recommended in our shiny caravan brochure on the out skirts of town. The excitement was electric, it felt like I was about to get laid for the first time, not laid as such but an orgy with angles doing a job on me. I had to crack one out before we departed. Extremely dangerous going out with friends on the same level, a body full of chemicals with a sawn-off shotgun in your pants. Not good for morale when the poison starts cursing through your veins and you have an Uzi pocking out from your waistline.

We were about to exit our humanly form, leave the earth's atmosphere and head on out into space. Buzzed, ripped, quivering, pickled, smashed, tripping, speeding, rushing, pulsating, peeled, trembling, orgasmic, inside out pummelled.

The drugs had started to work their magic, I cannot speak for my friends, but I was walking there passes in front of myself. I could see myself wrapped in psychedelic colours shooting off into space. Bright yellows and oranges zooming out in all directions. I could not feel the ground beneath me. I had left my shell in the caravan, what I had become was not off this world.

The boys are splotches of colour, their voices echoed through my skin, "auguste, get in the car brother we need to go". Fuck me did you fucking see that shit? Day had mysteriously turned into night, Apocalypse eerie, strange with a hint of paranoia and excitement. Inside the car I could feel everyone's electricity, If the car explodes, then it explodes.

Every movement was followed by thousands of bodily tracers. Guys stop fucking moving please, there are hundreds of us in this capsule. The drugs had ripped through us all sideways, we were now locked in, no way out for at least 24 hours.

I could not focus on anything, everything, everyone around me was trembling, vibrating, pulsating, zig zagging in and out of sight. My heart was sat on the tip of my tongue, my toes sat on my eye lids and my torso had twisted 180 degrees, front was back and back was front.

How the fuck are we going to get in anywhere in this state, it's a thought I had within a thought, within someone else's imagination. Did I just say that, or did I just think that or was it the purple cat sitting on the dashboard dressed as a punk?

Destination disco, we all slide from the car, I sink waist deep into fluffy bubbles then catapulted into the que in front of a bouncer the size of a furry bus. My senses had lost the plot, I was being tickled with a million feather dusters. My balls felt like they were being caressed by several beautiful angels. We are in the club, fuck knows how, were the house-sized bouncers as twisted, ripped as we were?

PCP, ecstasy, speed, acid and cocaine are now the driving force. I am just a passenger along for the ride. I am a beer sat outside drinking myself, millions of tracers as people move, dance, gyrate and wiggle about. Everything is moving around, tables, chairs, people are levitating. I see the boys in several different places at the same time around the club. Beanie is at the bar; he is on the dance floor and doing the spiderman thing on walls around the club that appeared to have no roof. A club with no roof, so why is my voice echoing up down and all around.

Brummies' Pal is wrestling six hairy German girls. Cuthbert the posh kid is sonic the hedgehog. Dave Jumpers is river dancing like fifty ladies, ambulance bob and Johnny 6 stickers are frozen in time. Jacko the smacko has no arms or legs, he's bobbing about the place like a psychedelic beach ball.

When you least expect things to get any higher, I'm outside on a car bonnet having oral sex performed on me. How I got there is still a mystery, to this day I have no clue if I was with a man or a woman, hermaphrodite, lady boy or bouncer. If the truth be told, I could have been with an alligator wearing an afro with pink lipstick.

The world explodes into a trillion colours, my body erupts and shatters like a glass on a marble floor. We are back at the caravan site, all sat by the lake with our feet in warm bubbling water. I turn to the boys; they are all sat in a deflated rubber dinghy fishing on dry land drinking champagne wearing pirate outfits. It is clear as the night sky they believe they are out on the lake floating around waiting for a yellow submarine to appear. Who was I to spoil the fun, it would have freaked them out if I were snorkelling around the dingy in lush green grass?

"Hey, you there, you, yes you, what's your name?" Who me? "Yes you, I'm talking to you". I am speaking with a fish dressed as Charlie Chaplin. "Auguste" what's up boys? "Please pass the oars, this dingy doesn't seem to be going anywhere", sure.

I turn back to Charlie fish Chaplin who is walking on water across the lake, with a fish wink and a nod he disappears. I fall back on the lush green grass, the sky is electric pink, stars, planets zooming across the cosmos. I awake on the floor of our caravan, eye lids as heavy as alloy wheels. The sun rays bursting through a razor slit in the curtains, I am staring at several empty tumblers scattered across the caravan floor.

We clean up, check out of the caravan site and make our way back to camp. As we drive through the gates, jolly green giants and purple monkeys everywhere with machine guns, eyes on us. What the fuck is going on boys? It appears we are still tripping in a celestial analogous biosphere still by our beautiful lake buried up to our waists in jelly next to our caravan.

"No one really listens today, they only hear what they want to, to really get someone's attention today, you have to hit them around the head with a sledgehammer".

What Goes Around, Goes Around

The consequences of one's actions will have to be dealt with eventually. A phrase proclaimed by so many "what goes around comes around". If I had known the magnitude of this meaning, I would have become a monk, fuck becoming a chef.

I was born into a generation during the height of so many social issues. But at the end of the day, it's just the same old shit, just at a different time, a different generation with the same social and economic issues packaged differently. It's just one gigantic merry go round of merry go round horse shit with social media added to the Dutch pot.

My first proper role as executive head chef came in 2007 when I relocated back to the UK from Dubai. During my interview I didn't sit opposite the GM or HR manager reminiscing my past. I had to sell myself and sell myself well to be the successful applicant. I did not discuss how much of a twat I had been during my younger years. As a matter of fact, I hadn't thought about my early career until I started working at an executive level.

"Auguste what do you like to do in your spare time"? Sleep with gas cookers and snort copious amounts of Nicky Lauder. Nobody needs to know about that shit. If the GM had asked "do you like to smash hookers and dabble in Pablo's lunch box"? I would have said no, not my thing. I am a god-fearing church going individual with strong morals. Returning from Dubai I was clean, I had dabbled with hard drugs once in almost two and half years watching Cirque du soleil out in Dubai of all places.

If the HR manager had said, "during your appointment every chef within the said kitchen is going to try their up most to break you". "They will call sick because that given weekend, they will have consumed to much cocaine and hard liquor, every Monday morning, leaving you in the shit". Would I have believed them? No, why would I? because we don't like to discuss the obvious. Everyone who has and is working within the hospitality industry, class A drugs for some individuals is like tea for others.

I was a liability, a fruit cake, a nut job only until someone mentioned the word mental health. I realised I had issues, issues that had manifested into life threatening problems. Besides the point during this new role managing at the top, the HR manager was correct. This team of thirty plus chefs, charismatic, vivacious, cannibalistic team of cannon ballers would fucking destroy me. I thought I partied hard during the 90s and the early years of the new millennium.

Half my team were aged between 18–25, the other half, married, stable, settled down family chefs ticking the days off until they retired. What I had done and experienced over the course of two decades was nothing compared to what these youngsters were going to do to me in the space of a few months let alone years. Hung, drawn and fucking quartered medieval nights templar savagery.

These cats were on a different level, I hadn't worked in the UK for the best part of 10 years all bar a little agency work in between seasonal work. For what it was worth I should have moved to Mogadishu to run arms for smacked-up lunatics.

The entire kitchen porter team resembled the slave workers I had witnessed in Dubai. Being ferried around the city in coaches with iron bars for windows. None of the kitchen porter team spoke English, they reported to the ringleader, the fat bloke from Mogadishu.

A man as crooked as al Capone who held their passports for two years until they had paid back their travel expenses. This came to ahead when immigration raided several hotels on the strip several months after I started. The following morning two kitchen porters showed for work. The rest of the 18-man kitchen porter team fled, the majority deported.

Back to, what goes around comes back around and hits you in the head with a submarine. There are way too many moments during this five-year posting, to many. These were and are the days you can't call a chef, "a horrible masturbating bastard" down the phone when they call in 2 hours before their shift starts to report their sicknesses. You would of cause be summoned to HR for gross-misconduct and most likely given a final written warning or sacked for such slur towards general staff.

The difference with this kitchen team I was in no position to be called a hypocrite. I really did have to manage with caution and empathy. An executive chef doing more cocaine than his entire larder section put together, one had to be functioning. One chef with no filter who now had to manage a dozen chefs who had never heard the phrase "no filter".

There are no excuses, but my war was kept behind closed doors during these chaotic years. Apart from looking like a walking zombie who worked out every now and then it was all behind closed doors. A functioning junkie who made everyone around him feel he was in control. What a chef gets up to outside of work, not my problem. What they did during work was my concern and problem.

Breakfast chefs dancing in the prep section at 10am in the morning wasn't of concern until one chef lost the tip of his finger slicing ham wasted on vodka and orange. Tommy came to work every morning plastered; he would leave work plastered. I know this because chefs would tell me he would share a bottle of whisky with them on the bus home.

During his disciplinary he confessed he was an alcoholic due to the trauma he was suffering from an abusive father. Case closed assigned to a company councillor until he went ballistic and attacked a guest at breakfast. I just had to manage accordingly up until the time he pulled out a machete.

One chef didn't even call in sick, they wouldn't show for two or three days on top of their two days off. They exhausted every excuse until they said their mum was dead. Mad crazy excuse to use just because you're a smack addict. Either that or they hate their mum, she never died she was just an evil parent to this chef from birth. Emotionally and physical abused for years.

Both my sous chefs, split shift, 2:30pm on the nose, both in the pub across the way on the Britney spears and Columbian cake frosting. I had to let Albert go after a heavy session in the boozer one afternoon. During service, the lunatic walked out into the restaurant minus his chef's trousers with his ass hanging out singing opera.

This chef had been banged up and raped. If you've watched the world's toughest prisons this chef had been there. He had done a stretch in Turkeys toughest hell whole. Dom had his arms put through a rock crusher. Off the sauce a diamond individual and an amazing chef. On the gear and sauce, Pavarotti no trousers.

Where do I start with Fred, OCD, asperge's, dyslexic with a stammer, an outstanding individual when you did have a one-word conversation with him. But like many chefs within my team, he had demons, a fragile quite individual who had the living life bullied out of him at school. All the professions out there he chooses to become a chef. I wonder why postmen choose to be postmen.

Accident hot line, "had a fall at work, lost your income due to time off with injuries, call today for a free quote". Wankers, health and safety was at the top of the agenda at every operational meeting. Staff just looking for that wonky step or that spillage in the middle of the kitchen.

If there is no sign, let's just throw my self against a work bench and onto the kitchen floor. Baldor the room service manager, the GM hated this employee. Why? Let me explain. This fool wasn't even a chef, he went out his way to fuck himself over to claim the big bucks from "accident helpline" they paid his mortgage off.

Winter 2007 room service is going off, 900-bedroom hotel, sky sports in every bedroom. Seven chefs working in the room service kitchen. I reported that the light to the entrance of the kitchen from the carpark needed changing. I also explained the steps down and into the kitchen needed gritting in the morning and evening due to the build-up of ice. "Not a priority" from maintenance, guests health and safety are my priority.

Baldor did the math, he assessed the severity of his potential injuries "death minimal, survival, absolutely". No grit, no light, blinded to the obvious calamity. Oops a daisy 35k for a broken arm. Made out his days of playing the piano, golf and the harp were over. Who must rewrite the entire risk assessment manual? Wankers.

It's not enough supporting and managing your full-time chefs, there is also the agency devils I would recruit for huge functions and Christmas. If it wasn't bolted to the floor, they'd have it out the back door. Stone heads, thieving little bastards. The only back they had was the back they were looking at while they were balls deep inside someone's ass.

I have seen more waiters concussed, bleeding because they have gone ass over tit. They think it's ok to wear the wrong footwear during a busy shift in banqueting. But it's ok, chef will deal with it, he looks after health and safety. Unless someone died during a shift front or back of house "chef will deal with it". Layers upon layers of issues but could you call someone a stupid cunt or tell them to fuck off for coming into work smashed or wearing the wrong footwear, no.

I had my issues, but being a selfish bastard, my issues came last, my concerns were the wellbeing of my chefs no matter the cost. Even if the fuckers didn't want to be there. Company values came first. Chefs sleeping on the changing room floor during split shifts, nope I had a day room in the hotel for chefs to have forty winks. Although I did catch a few sleeping in the room service lift, sleeping or smacked up I can't be sure.

I've had chefs on the phone during my days off telling me "I'm going to blow your car up". I've had chefs calling me from house parties at 4am in the morning, "chef my car broke down I can't come in today". I knew they could have taken public transport. I could hear the grime music in the background. Chefs entering the kitchen wearing jeans and trainers because they are too smashed and paranoid to go to the laundry to collect fresh whites.

I put out more kitchen fires in the space on five years than the local fire brigade. Chefs turning on brat pans. Adding oil to heat up before they add their ingredients for a chicken chasseur. The only issue is they fuck off for a cigarette, five minutes later the brat pan has exploded. Oven fires, waste bin fires on the loading bay, I've got no issues with putting out fires today, fireman fucking Sam that's me.

The injuries I've had to deal with because chefs are in a world of there has been one inch from surgery. Substance abuse, an alcoholic off to HR to be assigned a support worker. A few chefs were just genuine cunts, and they will always be cunts, and there is a few out there. One chef confessed that he purposely stitched me up for no apparent reason.

Our paths crossed a decade after our brief stint working together. We both attended the Birmingham hospitality awards. Long story short at the bar, he confessed "chef I'm so sorry I tried to fuck you over back then" why? "I don't know chef my head wasn't in the right place". Endless disciplinary hearings a grievance garnished with a warning all because he assumed, I had beef with him. The only beef I had was a medium rare forerib five bone out on the Sunday carvery each week.

The idiot is still a sous, a sous chef for the past fifteen years who has pulled the same stunt on several other head and executive chefs. How do I know? Yeah, it's a small industry. One chef, after their orientation came into my office during his first shift. Closed the door behind him, squared up to me and asked "chef, have you ever met a Rasta man before"? This chef then gave me the run down on his religious beliefs. "Chef during my break I will leave the kitchen to go smoke my weed chef". I replied if you break is your contracted break that being 30 minutes and the weed doesn't affect your work, I shall turn a blind eye.

This certain chef filed a grievance against me because I addressed his food hygiene, that it needed immediate improvement. He ended up with 8k from the hotel plus 2 months paid leave while the grievance took place. The emotional roller coaster I had with human resources was mind bending nonsense. Chefs are a different bread in today's hospitality industry.

You say boo to the wrong individual in today's world guaranteed it will end in tears. The only back I didn't have back then was my own which at the end of the day came at a great cost. What goes around sure fucking comes around when it comes to that shit sandwich.

Betty, the Rabbit Lady

Brown envelopes, I remember my first week on the job in London when I relocated back to UK, executive head chef. Big title, generous package and a huge team to manage. I started this role when brown envelopes were still apart of the hospitality industry. Brown envelopes for switched on chefs doing the underground handshake with suppliers. New chef at the helm, suppliers flood through the back doors wanting to meet the new chef who is going to continue in making them a ton of money.

Sat in my new swanky office minding my own business getting used to the procurement system, T&A (time and attendances) forecasting, budgeting plus a dozen other systems to assist me with making my life easier. As chefs we all know this is bollocks, half a dozen systems to make your life easier. If that were the case, why not have one system that does everything?

Shortly after the management morning meeting I find a shady looking fella taking a casual stroll around my kitchen. Well-dressed this fella, a dapper dan. "Good morning, you must be the new executive chef", yes that's me Auguste Knuckles please to meet you. "A pleasure to meet you also sir, please may we talk in your office chef"? certainly. I'm ushered into my office, the door closed in a hurried manner. "For you chef" the first brown envelope.

No small talk, a cheeky reach around, brown envelope, full of crisp fresh wonga. "Chef I've been working with the hotel supplying fresh fruit and vegetables for the past decade". "I would really appreciate if we could continue this respectful relationship under your esteemed management"? I peer inside my envelope, £350 for a handshake, I'm sure we can continue this relationship. Continue using a nominated supplier, why the fuck not. Money for old rope, winner winner chicken brown envelope dinner.

This was only one supplier, I was using a dozen, free money and free booze, decent booze. What's not to love about my new role, fucked if I'm leaking this cash cow during a morning or ops meeting.

293

As we all know, nothing lasts forever 2008 the Lehman brothers crash which was felt across the globe. Massive cutbacks within the hospitality industry due to the downturn in revenue coming through the doors in the form of guests. Not that it concerned me with transient foot fall, most of our revenue was generated through the new conference and banqueting centres. Meeting and events revenue also contributed to my department achieving its forecasted budgets.

Small businesses like my Brown envelope man were pushed aside by the big boys bidding through purchasing limited systems for our trade. I wasn't concerned with no longer receiving my pocket tickler because I was about to receive a ton of dodgy cash via the used oil boom. Three kitchens, 10% of my menus, went through the fryer due to the amount of room service we churned out. Chips, fried, brownies, bhajis, veggie sausages, battered and breaded items. Onion rings. Spring rolls, prawn cracker and poppadom's. Eight double burning gas fryers blazing away 8 hours per day.

I was going through 20 × 20litre drums of oil per week. I didn't have to reach out to any company. The size of the hotel gave it away with the size of culinary department I managed for potential used frying oil barons passing by buy. I will skip the meet and great, you scratch my back I'll scratch yours. £4 for every drum of used oil, 90 drums of used oil every working month. See no evil speak no evil, what the general manager does not know, doesn't hurt. Not a bad brown envelope every month.

There are a few lessons in life that I have learnt the hard way, it's not all about free money in your pocket. Not that I'm any good with money, I'm useless when it comes to cash. My wife looks after the cheddar under our roof. Considering I had a £1500 month cocaine habit during those days I needed those brown envelopes to pay the bills.

Anyways this little chapter isn't about the dodginess of the average dodgy kitchen two decades ago. It's about the warm kindness of an elderly Italian lady who I befriended in northern Italy years before my brown envelope days in London. By the way nothing sexual happened with me and Betty, she was old enough to be my great, great, great granny. I mean after all I wasn't breeding rabbits under my floorboards; this old lady was. Breeding rabbits all year round then selling them to dozens of chalet and hotel chefs throughout the winter season.

Betty had been breeding rabbits and selling them throughout this beautiful Italian resort for decades. Long before and long after I was blessed with this stunning resort's natural beauty. My first day in resort Betty arrives at the chalet where I am head chef, unannounced early doors, wading through three feet of fresh snow. "Buongiorno capo cuoco mi chiamo Betty" Buongiorno Betty mi chiamo Auguste. "Chef per favore posso avere il tuo vecchio pane". Sure, you can have my old bread, per che cosa, what for if I may ask? "I miei conigli", Rabbits yes sure ok. "Grazie chef torno domani, grazie mille", Prego.

This is how our little friendship started before she tried to blow me up, yes, you read correct, blow me and my kitchen up. Unlike the brown envelopes later before I found my way back to the UK. This transaction was me giving Betty all my leftover bread to feed her rampant bonking rabbits. In return up until that fateful day I received nothing in return. Just a grazie in the early hours of the morning. It wasn't about me skimming a few pennies from the economy of this beautiful ski resort or requesting money for old bread. It was about me being part of something that had been going on for years and being respectful.

The season flew by, I felt blessed beyond measure to have worked with such amazing produce cooking authentic Italian cuisine. Authentic Italian cuisine from the region of Piedmont. A chef with a love for Italian food, in this region of Italy immersing themselves during the peak of their career. When in Rome and all that bollocks, I cooked like an Italian or thereabouts. Rustic cooking using nothing but the best and freshest ingredients. I learnt the basics and spoke as much Italian as I could muster which gained a lot of respect with the local chefs and bar staff in resort.

I always adopted this mentality, while working in the French alps and Corsica. Today I find people utterly disrespectful if they cannot manage a few basic words when holidaying on the continent. It's just fucking bizarre why anyone would want to blow my kitchen to kingdom come.

I had dined out in all the best restaurants up and down the valley, drank Italian wine fit for a king. Enjoyed 5hr long tasting and wine menus. Snowboarded on the glacier next to Mont Blanc, rode the most insane off-piste and watched a good friend helly lifted of the mountain. Story long short, blue skies, up early to ride deep fresh snow before I start my day in the kitchen. My snowboarding skill set back then out of ten was ten.

I didn't know that several chalets' boys had followed me across a ridge to ride an untouched mountain face opposite Mont Blanc. I dropped into between two rock formations then rode 500 meters of fresh snow. Being mindful of the mountain I knew where the snow had been windswept and shallow. I turn to admire my fresh tracks and notice three boarders about to drop in.

Screaming was futile, I hand gesture them to follow my tracks as best as possible. Too late, Ronnie is the first to drop in, he carves a magnificent left turn but not reading or understanding the snow fall he fails to carve back to follow my line.

His board catches the rocks beneath the shallow snow, Ronnie starts to cartwheel, not wearing a helmet his head takes the full force of the mountain. After tumbling and cartwheeling more than 50 meters down the mountain, he final lands lifeless snow soaking up his blood. He's suffered life threatening blood loss; Ronnie's head looks like it's been scalped in several places.

Barely breathing he cannot be moved knowing full well he's also suffered an horrific spinal injury. We can only keep him warm until the medical helicopter arrives to air lift him to the hospital down the valley where he will spend the next two weeks fighting for his life in critical care.

I can see Betty through the steamed kitchen windows in the distance crunching through the morning snow. I great lady rabbit with a bag of old uneaten bread "grazie chef". Betty hands me a two-litre bottle of grappa, grappa ala Betty and heads back through the village to feed her rabbits. I doubt Betty intentionally wanted to blow my kitchen up, such a sweet old lady.

I suppose being a grappa imbecile not knowing were to store such a large bottle of liquid dynamite. After several large shots with my kitchen team, I store the bottle on the metal shelving unit above the eight-ring gas burner. It's not funny at all what happened, well it is now but it fucking scared the living shit out of us all working that evening. "Check on chef, one porcini risotto, three wild boar and polenta, two pasta fagioli, BOOM". In the heat of the kitchen just above my eyesight the bottle of grappa explodes.

The entire eight ring gas burner ignites while I'm finishing a porcini risotto, half the kitchen engulfed in flames sleeves on fire I make a Husain Bolt dash grabbing both chefs heading for the back door to douse my arms in 5ft of snow before returning to the inferno to extinguish the fire with a fire blanket. No time to dilly dally, I need to get this show back on the road. The hairs on both arms have been singed away, my eyebrows have singed a nutty orange colour. My heart pumping over time when the hotel manager walks into the kitchen half smashed on local chianti and asks, "chef where is my risotto"?

During that season close friends in resort always warned me about the dangers of the mountain, snowboarding off piste. They would always mention close ones who had persisted, I listened and processed their advice accordingly. I suppose it's why I'm still here today, because half the time I do listen, even if my wife doesn't think so, what's that babe, sorry.

Nature had run its course; spring was in the air. That final evening in resort before heading home was spent eating out with the head ski instructor from the ski school, various bar and restaurant owners including my hotel manager. Our meal was finished downing several shots of flavoured homemade grappa. I mentioned the incident with Betty and her grappa.

"Dio mio, non sono sorpreso quella dinamite ti ucciderà" that is so fucking hilarious. You have warned me regarding the dangers on the mountain all season but failed to warn me about Betty's exploding grappa dynamite, that's funny cheers guys. Betty's grappa was as famous as her rabbits. I guess I missed the 'molto forte" and "non mettere vicino al fuoco", basically translated, it is extraordinarily strong, don't store near fire.

Good old-fashioned respect for traditions is the lesson I learnt that season. The fact I nearly killed myself again in one of a dozen kitchens during my incomprehensible career, was a stern warning from the grappa gods. Do not try and flambe a risotto with two litres of Bettys grappa, that style of cooking will fucking kill you. Amen, lesson learnt, cheers Betty.

The Astronauts

A lot of things that happen are not for us to understand. 1997 I woke to a nation in mourning, Princess Diana had been killed in what can only be described as an horrific car accident. I was lost for words, gutted and saddened by her passing. She was a beacon of light and hope for humanity.

An icon of her day and still as iconic now as she was back then.

Early 1997 I had been arrested, banged up and charged with a crime. The cultivation of cannabis act. Some nosey neighbour had seen my cannabis plants on my balcony, busted and cautioned. I was also in a dead-end relationship; we were both party animals. Our relationship had died months back, neither of us had any trust for each other. Young enjoying our hedonistic lifestyle. If I can be brutally honest the 90s and 20s relationships all though I tried were futile.

I had planned to leave the UK and move out to Australia a few friends had flown out that summer. My intention was to save money and fly out just before winter. A good friend of mine had taken my resume out with him and circulated it throughout Sydney's dining scene.

The plan was soon as I had an offer for work, he was going to send me a postcard which was the green light for me to fly out. A few months had passed, I had heard nothing from Jamie.

November had arrived, I had given up on my dream of living and working in Australia. The contract on out one bedroom flat was coming to an end so I started to clean the place up ready for a move. I removed a box which was sat on top of the wardrobe in our small bedroom. Within the box was a crumpled postcard. The postcard was from Australia, on the front was the Sydney opera house. Jamie had drawn an arrow pointing to the opera house with a short note, "pack your bags, book your flight you have got a job here, see you soon".

The postcard had been posted in August; it was now November. I was gobsmacked, my girlfriend had obviously seen the postcard in the mail and decided to hide it from me. Well, this didn't go down to well when I confronted her, I kicked off like a bull in a China shop. I was livid, I was beyond gutted, frustrated and angry. I packed my bags and moved out.

I moved in with my cousin across town, I made a few calls about seasonal work, two interviews later I was packed up and heading out to St Anton in Austria "Ibiza in the snow". That season I would meet and work with three awesome fellas although they are not fellas today. We see each other as brothers. What I was about to be introduced too would change my life for the foreseeable future.

I arrived in St Anton, after an arse killing, back breaking, morale murdering 18hr journey from London. We are separated into our groups, ski guides, chalet boys and girls, bar staff, chefs and pizza chefs, I was one of four pizza chefs.

Darren from down under, otherwise known as NASA (nice and safe attitude). Desmond was from sunny Guildford also known as Lè Demon. Sparky the one eyed scouser, known as sparky the one eyed scouser and me who would be known as the Astronaut. A scouser, an Ozzy, a wide boy from Surrey and an ex-soldier with a love for everything illegal. A proper motley group of lads, who would go down in St Anton seasonal history.

The best ice breaker when one embarks on seasonal work weather be winter or summer is alcohol, and fuck loads of it. A few drinks I was introduced to, the flugel, slippery nipple, B52, traffic lights, TVR, and green beer all off which have gotten a few seasonairs including myself into a shit load of trouble.

I should also mention the Olympic drinking game "dirty ashtray" a game which isn't played while one is sober, a game which is only played when all parties involved have lost all morale's and who are beyond saving.

Its without saying we the pizza chefs bonded from the get-go, our seasonal goals are all identical. Fuck, drink, dance, drink more, shag harder and become lunatics of the piste. The thing was, I hadn't skied or snowboarded. Easy option when you are working with three snowboarders. They decided I would also snowboard, excellent.

Kitchen set, pizzeria set, hotel ready, restaurant set, cutlery polished, fuck buddies sorted we are ready for our first guests arriving 1st week of December. All I was missing was my gear, a short stroll through the resort, into Endless winter to get fitted with my starter set of snowboarding clobber.

Looking back at the gear and snowboard I purchased that 1st season; I sort of looked the part but not the case being all the gear no idea. I had some gear and no idea, but it kept me warm. The following morning, we were issued with our ski passes and headed out onto the mountain. Pumped, buzzing, ready to smash it. I had skateboarded as a kid so this snowboarding thing, balance etc no fucking problemo.

Positive vibes and loose chit chat on the cable car up the mountain, the view was epic, the piste freshly groomed motorways. "Ok guys Its the Astronauts first time on a snowboard so let's stay together". Everyone made out it was there first time on snowboards also, we were all in the same boat or so I thought, wrong.

We exit the cable car, make our way out onto the piste, red run to boot. We step onto our boards strap ourselves in. The group fly down the first section with me still at the top. How hard can this be, two feet I catch an edge, fall flat on my face and break a rib. As I look up to see where the group are with a face covered in snow it's obvious, they've all fucked off and left me on the mountain.

4 hours later I make it down the mountain, in pain, in tears, soaking, freezing cold with no love for snowboarding whatsoever. Late for my first shift as I've had to pop to the medical centre to get myself sorted out with some fruity pain killers. Fruity with a few pints of Austrian beer.

The following morning bruised and shamed I decide to head to the nursery slope on my own to give snowboarding a good crack. It wasn't long before I started carving, Christmas had come and gone. I was steadily cruising down red runs, I caught a few edges, and I did go on to crack two more ribs, but I was hooked.

Snowboarding all life long, fuck yeah, talk about a new addiction, this was mine. Four pizza chefs working that season were by far the best pizza chefs that had ever graced Scotty's bar. Our shenanigan's on and off the piste had also started gossip, and rumours that we were four of the craziest bastards in resort. I had designed a t-shirt which went on sale in one of the local souvenir stores. We had gained a bad boy reputation for being totally off the charts reckless when we went clubbing. Chalet girls smashed like the world was coming to an end, what is there not to love about this time in our lives.

Life was fucking awesome, snowboarding after breakfast, back in the kitchen at 4pm to start our prep and service. I must mention we did have an awesome boss, the restaurant and bar manager André who kept us in check as best as humanely possible. It was André who made the four of us pizza chefs famous, yes famous. Emma Harrison the larger-than-life neighbours star at that time in the 90s was hosting and filming a new and one of the first reality TV shows in resort called showgirls.

The producer from Granada TV asked Andre if he knew anyone who wanted to appear in the show, showgirls over a few pints of green beer. "Absolutely he replied", he had four pizza chefs who were all equally crazy. The evening before the eventful morning André asked us all before service if we wanted to be on TV? The one condition we must snowboard naked down the James Bond run, the most famous ski run in resort. James bond had skied down it, well not James Bond, his stunt double skied down it in the movie, from Russia with love.

The following morning up early hanging out our arses. A mad night in Scotty's had by all including Emma Harrison. We meet the film crew at the top of the James Bond run. Its minus twenty with fresh snow on the ground. We hadn't thought about what we were going to do, let alone say, we just blagged it. Quick pep talk from the film crew, there was no turning back, camera, action.

"So, boys tell us why you like to snowboard naked"? we all kind of jump in over each other nature, feeling free, the buzz the rush of cold air on our skin. "Awesome, ok, let's see you boys in action". A crippling, cock freezing, ball aching minus twenty. We all strip, stark bollock naked, my balls had shrivelled back into my body. My cock resembled my belly button, but not demon he was hung like a reindeer.

"Ok boys off you go", one eyed sparky sets off, not even ten meters he's caught an edge and wiped out into a Christmas tree the size of a house, buried and naked. NASA follows, he makes it halfway down the run. For some stupid reason he decides to ride switch, he also catches an edge and ends up under a Christmas tree buried in snow. Lè Demon also perished at the first turn, it's down to me to make it to the bottom.

I slide past Sparky and Darren who have dug themselves out of a snowy grave, Lè Demon is back on his board. I make it to the bottom of the run followed by my fellow three astronauts. We were not told this by the film crew, but at the bottom of the run waiting eagerly was loaded magazine, the daily mirror, a dozen journalists, more film crew and Emma Harrison.

Four stark bollock naked pizza chefs heading towards a crowd of cheering new fans, "yes boys absolutely awesome" shouts André. All I can say, I am a grower not a shower, I was not impressed with what was between my legs at this point neither was NASA and Sparky.

We are stood in fresh fallen snow with giant snowballs covering our frost-bitten parts being interviewed for the best part of an hour. Soon as the interview ended, I'm off to nurse my manhood back to life. I had to sit down for a week to take a piss, not good for morale, wounded. The season was full off shenanigan's and hardcore drinking, drinking that would put the hardest of Wetherspoons drinkers to shame.

As mentioned earlier dirty ashtray is not a game for kids, it is not a game for adults either, it's not for anyone. Anyway, for a pissed horde of 360, back flipping, bone crunching marmots it's like playing connect four. Participants, anyone who is wasted and has a cast iron stomach. Take one pint glass, fill with top shelf shots and a mixer of the barman's choice usually milk or cream. Cover the top with a servette and hold it in place with an elastic band, place one coin in the middle.

All participating, light their cigarettes and the game begins. Each player takes it in turn to stick the tip of their cigarette into the servette. The unfortunate soul who makes the coin drop while sticking their fag into the pint glass drinks the contents. A game of skill and luck depending on where you are sat at the table. I have witnessed grown adults' vomit at the thought of drinking the contents of the pint glass, even though the coin has not dropped in. After ten minutes of dirty ashtray the pint glass in the middle of the table looks like an alcoholic, medieval, ashtray swamp.

Game over, a 4ft nanny from the creche, un-fucking-lucky. A few piss heads and spectators cringe at the thought of her task in hand. Some remove themselves from the table to vomit outside the bar entrance. She calmly looks around the table, one eye on the pint glass, one eye of the lamp hanging from the ceiling above the table.

Chloe draws the glass towards her. Sticks her middle finger in to give it a quick mix and downs the entire pint of gunk. I and two others dive under the large round table to empty the contents of our stomachs onto the bar floor. Chloe stands up, removes herself from the table walks not but five steps and projectile vomit's the entire drink over several patrons sat at the bar, wounded.

The season is almost at a close, we get word that showgirls is going to be aired during the final week of the season at cartouche, a bar slash night club. Hundreds crammed into the cartouche ready and waiting eagerly to see if their half suntanned faces have made it onto the show.

Opening credits, the show starts with the four pizza chefs snowboarding down the James Bond run with me at the helm. No way are they going to show my belly button dick. I am square on in the camera's lens. No please, this cannot be, no way, the picture is frozen. Me wearing an afro with showgirls spread across my hips. The show begins, the DJ drops smack my bitch up by the prodigy, cartouche erupts.

We all received copies of loaded magazine, newspaper prints signed by the film crew and Emma, legends that season, and icons today. Besides the copious amounts of cocaine, shagging, debauchery and drinking. A dozen of the original team that arrived at the beginning of the season had been flown home with broken bones. The four astronauts, the craziest lunatics that went larger, bigger for longer depart in one piece for the journey back to the UK as brothers.

After a few crazy years of traveling and working abroad, I return to St Anton 2004 as the executive chef for the hotel Rosanna and Scotty's bar. I decided my last stint at seasonal work would be back where it all started. I had all the gear, head to toe in Burton Ronin snowboarding clobber. I exit the cable car for my 1st run of the season. The same piste I attempted back in 97. LTJ Bukem full volume on my discman.

Top to bottom ten minutes, several 360s, a dozen method airs, endless tail taps, and a few floating back side 180s, the Astronaut had returned. I ended the season in crutches, ruptured ankle ligaments. Not sustained by my shenanigans on the piste. Playing fucking football in the hotel car park pissed on flugels.

Dedicated to my brothers, Darren, Desmond, Mark and not forgetting Boss man Andre and all who partied hard, skied, snowboarded harder and lived like there was no tomorrow. Hotel Rosanna, St Anton 97 and 2004, the astronaut.

Bull Fight in Majorca

The most barbaric fight I've ever witnessed looking through spread fingers. A memory that has stayed with me until this present day. During my time on the beautiful island of Majorca, running a beautiful beach restaurant and snorting copious amounts of cocaine, we decided to indulge ourselves in one of Spain's sporting traditions.

The bull fight, not for the faint-hearted, not for vegans or for anyone wearing sandals and socks. But, when in Spain trying to pass for a Spaniard and I don't mean Russell Crowe in *Gladiator*, a proper Spaniard, one must indulge in all things Spanish. Women, drugs, alcohol, food, evening snoozes and a must once in a lifetime massacre of the toro negra.

History. According to "Former's Travel Guide", bullfighting in Spain traces its origins to 711 AD, with the first official bullfight, or "corrida de toros", being held in honour of the coronation of King Alfonso VIII. Once part of the Roman Empire, Spain owes its bullfighting tradition in part to gladiator games.

Bullfighting is a physical contest that involves a bullfighter and animals attempting to subdue, immobilise, or kill a bull, usually according to a set of rules, guidelines, or cultural expectations.

There are several variations, including some forms which involve dancing around or leaping over a cow or bull or attempting to grasp an object tied to the animal's horns. The most well-known form of bullfighting is Spanish-style bullfighting, practiced in Spain, Portugal, Southern France, Mexico, Colombia, Ecuador, Venezuela and Peru. The Spanish Fighting Bull is bred for its aggression and physique and is raised free-range with little human contact.

The practice of bullfighting is controversial because of a range of concerns including animal welfare, funding and religion. While some forms are considered a blood sport, in some countries, for example Spain, it is defined as an art form or cultural event, and local regulations define it as a cultural event or heritage. Bullfighting is illegal in most countries, but remains legal in most areas of Spain and Portugal, as well as in some Hispanic American countries and some parts of southern France.

Enough of the cut and paste pretentious historical history lesson back to the carnage. After18 days on the pans and a sleepless nights drinking beer and snorting Majorcan cocaine we decided we would hammer our marshmallow brains with culture. Sitting here a little wiser but as equally stupid it wasn't the best idea. But at the time fuck it, I want a golden unicorn that's shits money.

Drugs, money, shades, shorts, flip flops and more drugs we pack ourselves into cars and speed off to Majorca central, Muro. Sundays are the best days to take off on the beautiful island. Several stops along the way for tapas. Carrilladae, jamón iberico, boquerones en vinagre, albóndigas, patatas bravas, croquetas, garbanzos with spinach and mini black pudding sausages served with lashings of epic local wine and estrella served in frosted glasses.

The whole day is a festival of celebration, friends, family, drunken coked up expats and one negra toro whose life will inevitably end at some point during this day of days. The standard bullfight typically lasts about 20 minutes and is often described as a tragedy more like a fucking blood bath in three acts. These acts called tercios principally consist of picadors, banderilleros, and the matador's killing of the bull.

Before the fight, workers rub petroleum into his eyes of the toro to obscure its vision and beat the bull's kidneys repeatedly. They give him tranquilisers, laxatives, and drugs that induce paralysis or a hypnotised state hours before the bullfight. With all due respect all the above is what we did to ourselves throughout the course of the morning hours before we set off, bonkers.

The stadium is jam-packed with faces of thousands. The atmosphere is electric, a Coldplay concert with a bull. Booze vendors quench the thirst of many hangovers. Snacks and nibble vendors, cold boxes full of gastronomic wonder fill the air with food napalm.

I'm not going to document the whole day of madness. I'm going to revisit this one fight. A fight like no other, whatever they did to this magnificent species before the fight only those who administered whatever it was and that beautiful bull will know, the bull obviously taking it to its end of days butcher shop window.

The matador wasn't any old matador. This fella was the Mike Tyson of bullfighters. The Gordon Ramsey of the stadium that given Sunday two decades ago on the seductive island I called home for a hazy few years. The matador

Tyson Ramsey bloke no taller than 5ft 6". There is no small man syndrome with this fella. Small yes, but anyone whose about to take on king fucking bull Kong with one-meter elephants tusks sticking out from the top of its head, in my books is mustard.

Screaming, jubilation, women's underwear thrown into the arena, men's boxers and G-strings too. If half the arena could have jumped atop the wooden fence separating him and us, they would have, and they would have fucked this matadors slim frame into oblivion. "Sex bomb, sex bomb you're my sex bomb" you get it. Before I continue, I must add I knew nothing about bull fighting before this eventful day, absolutely fuck all. One toro negra verses one Harry Potter-sized Spaniard, "let's get ready to rumble". This fight will not begin with thousands of the rambunctious hoard singing "show me the way to Amarillo".

I've never witnessed such a beautiful animal run out into an arena pumped on all sorts of uppers downers and sideways'ers. This toro negra must have stood at least 7ft tall, the length of an F1 race car and as wide as two telephone boxes. If I was a beating man Harry Potter is about to get bull raped big time, several times over big time. Harry matador Potter centre arena toro negra on crack charges like the fast train to Paddington. "Please stand clear of platform two, this bull does not stop here, I repeat this bull will not be stopping here".

Twenty minutes of British bulldog this fight has already broken records. What the fuck is this shit, three more Harry matador Potters appear with miniature spears "picadors". Pica-fucking-dors gobsmacked I assumed this was one on one. My mate the bull obviously needs a break but no time for oranges and a steamed jasmine hand towel, its picadors and spears. Several spears pierce the bulls' shoulders. The main matador tucking into local wine and a seafood paella on the side lines, "cunt". Blood bath central, I've never witnessed an animal lose blood so fast.

The arena now resembles a battlefield, trenches, IED'S, body parts splattered across the arena. A fucking war zone, gulf war Majorcan zone. The mood within the stands has changed from admiration to unease. The mood has changed; the screaming hoards are now in the bull's corner. Bottles, beer cans, scraps of food are being launched towards the matador.

The picadors have done a proper job on the beautiful specimen of a toro negra. Proper fucked, 40 minutes into a battle with one inevitable outcome. Myself and my party are battered, booze and cocaine cursing our sun-tanned bodies. When we thought it couldn't get any worse a fucking horse with body armour with the assassin atop branding a huge fucking spear. The bull charges, connects and throws the assassin off his armoured tank of a horse.

Cheers, missiles thrown into the ring. All bar a few hardcore Spanish bull loving dicks the crowd are fighting alongside our friend. The assassin back atop his Sherman tank spears the bull a dozen times within the course of twenty minutes. Fucked, battered, staggering around the arena after almost an hour the matador reappears. There's no love for Harry matador Potter. The entire length of the matador's blade penetrates between the bulls' shoulders. Brown bread dead silence for a few seconds then the entire arena erupts. There's only love and respect for the bull.

Its tail and ears are swiftly removed as souvenirs and its body dragged out of the arena. Last stop butcher shop. The love the Spaniards have for such a barbaric sport is off the charts bonkers. The bull that day was the undisputed winner in many eyes. With regards for my quench, we battered our bodies senseless for the remainder of the day as we drove back to our beach side villa. Cocaine, strippers, hookers and local wine until the sun came up. Zero sleep and it's back on the pans.

Slurping Oysters

I've started so many new chapters in my life without finishing quite a few. So many stories to tell, but this little chapter I must write. All though my first experience with food wasn't as exotic as this one, it's up there with godliness.

I spent two months during springtime 98 in New York with a girlfriend I had meet In Val desrè working in a small ski chalet. Blessed beyond measure two months in Queens experiencing all of life not as a tourist. I was a local, so when In New York act like a New Yorker.

Charlotte gave me some great tips when out and about in the city and the boroughs. I had plenty of time to cruise all over New York and that is what we did during those amazing two months. Another crazy drunken story which stands out, making slippery nipple shots for a bar full of marines in a funky little hideaway of 5th avenue. I suppose the fact I'm an ex-squaddie and was wearing a pair of desert storm camouflage combats gave it away.

The time I was asked by two pizza chef brothers in the Bronx if I knew the queen was hilarious just because of my British accent. Visiting the World Trade Centre, looking out across New York and the five boroughs at the top was mesmerising. If only I had known of Les Halle's ran by Anthony Bourdain, we would have had a long lunch there.

I had secured a summer contract working as a head chef within a beautiful beach side hotel near Ajaccio on the Island of Corsica. Such a beautiful and diverse Island which offers so much beauty. The food produce is on another level not compared to any other Island within the Mediterranean.

The team of chefs working that summer were knew to me and me to them. They had flown out to Corsica a week earlier during my last week in New York with Charlotte. The brief from the hotel manager to my team in Corsica, "chef has managed some big hotels within the estate, so make sure when he arrives next week the kitchen is set, I want to make a good impression".

Maybe so, yes, I had managed the bigger and prestigious hotels within the group during winters and summers, but I also came with baggage. The kind of baggage a magician would carry around entertaining children. It's one thing working with a team you haven't meet or do not know because you can forge new relationships and evolve.

One thing I did know, anyone doing seasonal work has an element or behavioural likeness to that of myself. We all want to have a good time and push our luck. I flew into Ajaccio airport to be meet by Rob the hotel manager. Nice touch that we played a cheeky 9 holes of golf before arriving at the hotel.

From the get-go it was obvious this was going to be a cracking summer. Not only did we have a party animal managing the hotel we had several staff members who had done previous seasonal work in Ibiza. The ice breaker Rob had organised that evening, drinking games. Basically, to weed out the light weights and to get a better understanding of his team and the ones who could be potential casualties during the season.

The evening kicked off with simple fare cooked by Bill my sous chef served with local wine and lots of it. The team totalled roughly thirty staff members spread across the relevant departments. Kitchen, front of house, hotel, reception and beach. For Bill, my sous chef, the season almost ended during that first night of carnage.

First night two finger drinking game, boozy giant Jenga, six teams. Once all teams have removed a wooden piece everyone downs two fingers of their drink. The team that toppled the Jenga must down all drinks including a shoot of absolute.

Talk about the kitchen team being shit at giant Jenga we toppled the first four games. Vodka for the non-vodka drinking chefs and kitchen porters went sideways. I myself loved vodka, most of the kitchen team where beer drinkers including Bill. Dancing, drinking, snogging ensued. Bill however wanted to see which one of us had the bigger dick in the kitchen that season. So, let's see who passes the fuck out first.

We end up outside walking up the main drive near the cliff face overlooking the bay of Ajaccio. "What an amazing evening", Yes, it is Bill, I projectile vomit first which kicks starts a reaction. Two chefs who have just meet each other vomiting over the cliff with Ajaccio in the background.

I would say it's a twenty meter drop down to the beach. The rock face was sandy with lots of bushes dotted about with several huge rocks at the bottom. Both chefs pissed, cocks out pissing into the ocean.

I turn to Bill, the fucker, he's disappeared, where the fuck could he have gone. Back to the hotel maybe, why didn't he piss on my foot before he departed to say he was walking back to the hotel. Smashed, pissed I walk sideways back to the hotel bar. Has anyone seen Bill? "No chef he's with you isn't he"? ugh, no he's not with me. "Well, he was" then Bill has just disappeared into thin air or worse been kidnapped by Corsican mafia from right under my ball sack. "Thin air chef"? oh fuck me.

Several pissed managers stagger sideways up the driveway trying to dodge our vomit. We peer over the cliff face. "Holy fucking shit, fuck me, are you ok down their Bill"? shouts Benjamin. "Help" Bill cries from the bottom, "help, someone please help". After several frantic minutes, we manage to get Bill to safety and in need of some serious first aid.

Falling that far down a cliff face onto rocks with the waves breaking hard isn't good for anyone's morale. The hotel first aid kit, well it's like trying to put a plaster on a bullet wound. This cat needed hospital and off he went.

My first evening, not even a full wholesome day in the Mediterranean I've almost killed my number two. Well not as such as killed him as it wasn't me who pushed him. Bill informed us on his return from hospital that he fell headfirst over the edge. It's a fucking miracle he didn't kill himself or our season might have been short lived.

Like previous seasons there has been carnage, chaos, relationships, alfresco sex, broken bones and near-death experiences and it wouldn't be any different that season. My highlight during that summer wasn't me dressing as Pocahontas having prehistoric caveman sex with a dozen hotel guests during those hot long drawn-out summer evenings, no.

Neither was it entertaining my two best friends for a week in the hotel who had flown over from the UK to relish in Corsican sun and shenanigans. Neither was it crashing a car into a tree or swimming with dolphins let alone cooking a BBQ blind folded in front of a packed hotel.

The highlight that season was free diving with Ozzy Dennis. Free diving isn't something you can just do off the bat. I spent a week working with Ozzy Dennis during my free time on breathing techniques. Once I had three minutes down we were ready.

Free diving for oysters on boat moorings six meters down was the pinnacle of the season. Regardless of all the local food and wine. Regardless of the sex and parties on tap, this was it. This was me diving down to that coach floor back when I was mind fucked by such a simple gesture.

Early evening, we make ready, oyster knives, flippers and snorkel. We had set up a wooden board, Corsican lemons and ice-cold Corsican rosé on the beach waiting for us on our return. The bay was so calm that evening. The sea, like glass with dolphins playing in the bay, what a place to free dive.

We collected a dozen medium-sized oysters from two boat moorings. The viability six meters down was out of this world. You could see 100 meters 360 all around. We swam back to shore with our stash of Corsican oysters. A few hotel guests had joined us on the beach. Kneeling with waves lapping around our waists we poured ourselves a large glass of rosé and started to chuck our oysters.

Still in the Mediterranean Sea, drinking the most amazing rose sharing and slurping the sweetest oysters splashed with a fresh Corsican lemon, with a warm sea breeze all around. listening to a cafe Mambo compilation was as pure and sweet as the oysters themselves. Regarding my fondest memories as a chef there is no better memory than that, well maybe that and the memory on that coach floor.

Cognitive Behavioural Therapy

It's not easy trying to eat your own head, it's far from fucking easy knowing you are an abandoned child. I totally get it, a new born baby fresh from the womb and put straight into adoption. So many reasons to mention. Groomed, stupidity, rape, abused by a family member, an incestuous fuck. Straight into adoption, through the system, nine times out of ten raised by a loving family. Please don't quote me on those statistics it could be fifty fifty.

Knowing I was abandoned out of pure hatred, disgust and racism is a pill stuck at the back of my throat broken in pieces. It chokes me every moment when I'm silent in thought. it's a pill that is going anywhere. At 11 months, having suckled from her breasts, connected with all five senses, I'm handed over by a woman with no face to a man with no face who is as selfish and pathetic as they come.

As a middle-aged man today, I have flashbacks and nightmares of that moment. Although too young to remember, I've relived it time and time again. Piercing baby screams that stop me in my tracks, not wanting to leave her skin, her smell, her voice. That moment has caused extreme mental health issues in later life.

I find it hard to trust people, I feel separated to this day, disconnected from my emotions. Grown adult mothers who abandon their babies out of hatred, racism and family pressure do not deserve to be called mother in later life when they want closure in wanting to be close to that abandoned soul. The lost soul who has grown into adulthood with children of their own, is closure neither shall be blessed with.

The emotional pain is overwhelming, but I shall not falter again and turn to drink and drugs. I shall rise, I shall rise above you all to be the best father I can be regardless. My children are my soul, they are the air I breathe, my heart, flesh and blood. The love I have for them cannot be quantified. I rise for them not you anymore. All of you are no more.

The moments we have spent together, I've been a ghost to you, a voice amongst unwanted spaces, that dead guy in the room no one notices. A has been, a junkie, an addict, a tornado of self-destruction, a nobody, a corpse amongst soldiers. One in a billion spawned.

I have never lived with you; I was never raised by you. I never felt your love because you never gave love. You were and always will be that organic vehicle that made it possible for me to come into this world, you are and always will be, people without faces.

Some days it does not even feel like I'm here. In the physical form It's like I'm dead, a long time dead and I'm just living out a sick twisted dream spiritually. The miracles around me viewed from a distant vantage point not of this world. Everything is beautiful, it's all fine, is this what it would be like if I was here.

It's not easy living with the proverbial fact that you would be better off dead. Brown bread dead in a box in the ground looking around your plush coffin hoping you'll wake up. Those whose minds are wired and organised like they should be will never understand those whose minds are wired like a giraffe putting stickle bricks together.

How can, and who do you tell, that you've had back breaking burnt alive thoughts that you've just sliced your child's face off with a box cutter while making their breakfast. These thoughts are the blinding realities of obsessive-compulsive irrational thought disorder. The cherry on the cake, you step out in front of that speeding train. "Please stand back from platform two this train does not stop here". I bet it will stop somewhere down the tracks if there are human remains splattered across the windscreen. People don't want to die this way let alone end their own lives.

Some days these thoughts can be multiplied beyond measure. Razor blades trapped within your own thoughts, slicing, slashing behind your eyes. You add failure, neglect, abandonment, uselessness to this recipe regardless of what you have or have achieved. The battle is gargantuan, but this might be a good day.

A bad day, well the razor blades slashing your thoughts to pieces stepping out in front of a speeding train day isn't bad compared to setting fire to your own house on Christmas day watching everyone cook inside while standing in the back garden wearing fluffy slippers sipping a large gin and tonic.

It's a bull fight inside your chest. Picadors, banderilleros, and the matador's killing of the bull which is basically your heart. Trying to breath while all this is

313

going on I'd say it's easier to walk on water but you're on the seafloor miles down where light has no say.

The cold dark blanket of suicide wrapped so tight. Blinded by blackness with the weight of the oceans breaking bones like a child snapping candy cane. Deafening screams of children being burnt alive, flesh popping like popcorn in an overheated pan of oil. The scariest thing is, this is all going on while you're into a sixteen-hour shift on the pans in an all-day fine dining restaurant with a dozen clowns in your face barking in several languages.

I've seen things, I've seen what a broken mind can conjure. I've had my flesh peeled from my body and fed to dogs. Eaten alive by rats, been pulled apart like an unwanted Christmas present. I realise the cashier is asking if I have a reward card. Beads of sweat pouring off me, paralysed, with fear I manage to summon the word, No.

And there's the dreams, dreams so vivid the woken mind can't figure out if you were asleep or awake. Its constant, awake or asleep it doesn't matter. Your mind is a pinball machine day and night with a speed freak on the buttons. Dealing with the side effects of powerful anti-psychotic anti-depressants medications is as welcoming as having your head put through a meat grinder. Bleeding gums, bleeding from your arse. Weight gain, full body aches, palpitations, drowsiness. But compared to what the mind is like without such medication they are phenomenal. Few beers and its cloud nine.

Peoples who commit suicide aren't self-indulgent wasters. 9.5 out of 10 have most likely exhausted all options. But the living will never know the facts, the whys, I don't believe it, Only the tormented will rest in peace knowing that hell is the life they leave behind.

I'll always be in and out of therapy. I'll always be on groovy psychotic drugs. It's been almost a decade since I feel asleep naturally. Well fell asleep after passing out after a 48hr cocaine hard liquor session. All I remember and know now is that its medication, little funny tablets that put me to sleep. When I wake up, another fruity psychotic drug to keep the sledgehammer skull smashing thoughts at bay.

Its fucking scary when I wake and think I've taken the bedtime pill for breakfast. The drive to work would end with me sliced up, splattered across the M25. I could live with that, which doesn't make any sense at all. The thoughts I have today said in the first chapter to this mini narrative "I can live with". They're just passing thoughts that are managed through mindfulness and grounding techniques. Or is that just what my therapist tells me, "Passing thoughts". Is that what I need to be told? absolutely.

It's what I've accepted today. Passing thoughts, that's all they are and that's what it is. Death is a welcoming comfort to the horrors of mental health. "Let's break the stigma" the stigma that it's normal to be mully mushed in the head. "It's good to talk". "I would rather hear your story than attend your funeral", really? If I had confessed to only half my irrational thoughts during the height of addiction, I would have been banged up with nurse ratchet.

Some choose for their stories not to be heard, I can empathise, sympathise the whole "I get it". Walking through life knowing your mind is utterly and truly shattered, sometimes I wish the dogs would have ravaged me as a baby. Pain I wouldn't have to endure today, we cannot feel the pain of yesterday, we only live with the mental trauma scars. The dead feel no pain, the dead know only one thing, they are dead, they are free.

Trying to summarise this narrative, my life's journey is an ongoing battle with accepting the fact it needs to end for me to move on. To say the least it's somewhat fucking challenging. Frustrating, move on knowing they live amongst me, protecting their parents and loved ones from shame.

Nightmares, flashbacks of being sexual abused. Thrown against a wall. Dogs barking around me in a state of madness wanting to tear me from limb to limb. A baby left for hours in a highchair soiled. Screaming because of a severe nappy rash. No one is around just the silence of an empty house. No one's baby in no one's house, duty of care didn't mean shit in the 70s. Duty of care doesn't mean shit to all those vicious vermin who choose to abuse and neglect children.

Everyone knew I was being abused, physically, sexually, mentally. The thoughts of that night being rescued by him and her with my kid half-sister on the back seat. Bite marks, beaten, bruised, half alive. These thoughts will be with me forever.

When someone, anyone, a brother, sister, family member or a friend says they're having a good day, give them a hug, a loving squeeze, hold them close for a moment. Look them in the eyes and tell them you are there for them today and forever. Why? because a good day compared to your bad day is living hell.

Here we go again 2nd round of CBT (cognitive behavioural therapy). It's not even been a year since my last course of CBT plus new improved anti-psychotic medication. My first session of CBT was to process and store all the detritus going on inside my watermelon head. Living life with my adrenaline on a slow drip. Hypervigilant, hypertension, hypothyroidism every hyperfucked plus paranoia. Let's just say the five months of therapy first time around saved me.

A new man, a new me so to speak. Born again, free from hyperfuckedness. You know as well as I do that once the brain is free from your current addiction, illness, whatever it has a miraculous way of finding something else to play with. I have learned to live with complex post-traumatic stress disorder, but I had no clue my childhood would start playing out in an unfinished symphony.

I don't mean joyful, playful, blissful daydreaming wonderful jelly and ice cream memories. Skin peeled from you flashbacks, walking nightmares. My brain had somehow found within the complex multiverse of my coconut head the images from a baby child's eyes. Out of the blue I'm starting to relieve these haunting episodes of abuse. Just another dick punch after dick punch.

Trauma untreated never goes away, never, regardless it is always going to be there. We may think we don't remember traumatic incidents that happened way before potty training. Every microsecond flashback that fires off in your adult brain is a memory working its way out of hell to haunt you.

I started to slip back into a flow I had left behind many years ago. Cocaine excessive alcohol consumption ensued. Before I fell back down to rock bottom I reached out to my wife after driving home from a party totally blasted. I reached out to my closest friends who knew I was going sideways. All their suggestions lead back to one solution to deal with a man about to go pop again. Time to check in again with talking Therapies before I go full relapse and end up in a ditch.

"Good afternoon, can you hear me loud and clear? Auguste, I think your speaker is on mute". Yes, my bad, just getting used to Microsoft team meetings, there you go, can you hear me now? "All good my end, we are good to". No, we are not good to go, not my end, not good at all. I'm about to explain over again what I have written about in hot Soapy water to a stranger.

During 10 days of isolation, Austin Macauley publishers were doing their first proofreading of this book you are reading. I thought to myself why not write about that first CBT live video session specifically targeted at childhood trauma. Why? because what was echoed by my therapist was something I thought would never hear even after all these years.

"Let's begin, firstly this session is confidential, we will contact your GP stating we are having this, these sessions, but the content of said sessions will not be disclosed unless you give consent. So, Auguste where would you like to start"?

I've always been concerned how sexually promiscuous I was from such a young age. Something doesn't sit well with me even to this day. The things I did at infant school I can remember so clearly. I can only describe these incidents as sexual advances towards several of my class even my teacher. Fondling girls in the cloak room. Snogging, if you could call it that. To me it wasn't behaviour that a child aged five should do let alone even know about.

Playing mums and dads on the playground, hiding away doing stuff a child shouldn't be doing at that age. I remember losing my virginity aged 11. Masturbation was an evil act, it plagued me. I was seen as a dirty horrible bastard. "Stop playing with it you little shit, it will drop off". No advice during puberty but protection and silence for the vermin. Did they really believe it was ok, anger and frustration? I remember hearing my auntie screaming "doesn't she know she's being sexually abused by her biological father". I guess having three children with her half-brother, brother, and no one batting an eyelid was a sign something was wrong, and the majority were ok with it, not me.

Is this a sick and twisted way of regret knowing abuse was rife? Turn the other way and make out its ok. The stupid fucking mind games played out for years by everyone including my half siblings. The deafening arguments we had to endure from the top of the stairs or shivering with fear in hiding places. Fucking idiots, they all were, it's obvious they underestimated the power of memories. All the years of lies deceit. What else will they take to their grave knowing their silence is guilt.

Do you mind if we take a minute, please? "Please take all the time you need Auguste". Sorry but talking about the causes of trauma, going back down memory lane is a head fuck beyond all proportion. "I know it's hard but expelling all these negative thoughts will help the healing process".

"Auguste, a child, meaning you who is acting like that at such a young age are the characteristics of someone who was sexually abused, do you think this to be true, that maybe you could have also been sexually abused during those early years of abandonment"? There have been sexual predators within the toxic family I was raised in, I know this to be true, I know this. Many years ago, while I was in the presence of certain individuals, they spoke about certain incidents that should not be shared or spoken about with others. But to them it felt so normal to share such verbal dog shit.

Hearing, "fucking dirty bastard liked me to piss on him", by your biological mother made my skin crawl. Being told "I love it when he comes on my face and neck" that person being her brother is south of the border wrong. Hearing of distant uncles who were paedophiles, banged up for the obvious. But they seemed totally ok with sharing this, totally ok. There have been situations where I've been repulsed. There's a certain uneasiness, eeriness which hasn't and doesn't sit well with me about sexual incidents that have been brushed under the carpet like its water of a ducks back.

"Do you believe it's possible you were sexually abused also?" The carnage I was subjected to, yes, I believe how sexually misguided I was, sorry rephrase that last bit, misguided. Assuming that my behaviour was acceptable, but how does a 5-year-old know what is or was acceptable when it came to what I was doing and the memories I have. Yes, I believe it to be true. "So do I Auguste, it's common for you not to fully know or understand what you were doing unless you were in fact playing out what you were subjected to obviously thinking its ok".

"Would you like to discuss your stepdad Boris"? A hairy ape of a man, a bully, it's disgusting thinking about what he did. Doris stood on his dead shoulders for years blaming him for the worst outburst. The rage, the beatings, Boris was just as bad, even worse. She must think I'm stupid, I felt her fist as much as his. The last time I was in the presence of Boris must have been two decades ago at a wedding.

I had just flown back from Vancouver; cruise ship madness. "Who's wedding was it"? Boris's son, 100% bling, no expense spared. We all arrived at the church waiting for his son's meal ticket. "Meal ticket, what's that"? The bride, I remember clearly as the driven snow walking over to the boys and Boris. A frail man half the size riddled with Parkinson's disease.

"Auguste, you're good at doing ties, sort dads tie out for him". Sort dads tie out, what a cheek. This being was as far from my dad as Jesus was to James Brown. I looked at him square in the eyes and began to organise his tie. He fucking stood there trembling, not a word. I could have strangled the bastard right there on the day of his son's wedding. There you go Boris, there you go and patted him on his shoulder. A man riddled with such a disease deserved to see his son's big day as opposed to me in a tuxedo strangle the last few years out of him. "Cheers crusty" were the last words I heard him speak. The cunt couldn't even say my name.

A mental deep dive with a therapist trying to repair the damage of abuse you have only just become acquainted with got to me. They care about you, they empathise, they listen so well taking in your body language they start to piece together memories, a journey you chose to bury a long time ago during childhood. Child trauma therapy I never knew existed until I hit the bottom of the universe ready to end my life.

"Auguste, would you like to contact the police, because what we have discussed, if certain peoples are around children, what's saying those children will not be sexual abused today"? No, the individuals responsible, who stood by and let the abuse happen have become silent. I am here today to sort out my scars. Certain individuals have done time, sexual offenders they are today. Certain peoples have long passed away. I was threatened sometime back saying there would be consequences. "Do you feel threatened now". I no longer feel threatened.

I'll never know the true extent of my abuse so will so many adults spawned in the 70s. It seemed to be the norm. Emotional, physical, mentally and sexual abuse seemed the norm. "It never was and never will be the norm Auguste, where beauty lays there will always be predators, my work is to help heal the victims so that they may lead a positive and normal life, as best as possible".

"Let's wrap this session up for the day, we've gone over your risk assessment, gone way over our allocated time, but before we end, do you feel like ending your life anytime soon or self-harming?". No, regardless, I have everything to live for. "What plans for the rest of your day". I'm going to post a note to the house of Doris. A spiritual note which will end all communication from my side on my terms and let her know I solely blame her, her and Boris for the abuse I endured. Only this spiritual letter isn't going to be burned for me to let go of the past. She can own it, own the damaged caused.

Hot Soapy Water

Raped By A Bar Of Soap

My wife loves a bath, full to the brim with hot soapy water. Me personally unless I'm in a Turkish sauna which is never then its showers all day long. Something in me just doesn't register when it comes to having a bath. Not even a well-deserved soak after a shift on the pans., smelly candles, Barry White playing, Bliss, no, not bliss.

I've mentioned already that everything was different for Boris, he got the first-class treatment and we got what was left over, the scraps and on many occasions his dirty bath water to wash ourselves in before bed.

My auntie Stella hated him, absolutely hated him because she knew what was going on she knew everything. My auntie always knew who my biological father was, baffled to this day all my summers in the switch he was just down the road.

It was decided between Boris and Doris, regardless that "I", would have nothing to do with him my biological father Johnny, Boris would raise me as his own that was the deal. I would be kept away from him and wouldn't be told anything, not even his name, not his background where he was from at all costs.

Raise me as one of his own, why would someone who painted my sister with black boot polish, raise a half breed as one of his own. A kid growing up with no soul, no purpose, no direction no ambitions, no one interested in my wellbeing apart from my auntie Stella the phenomenal woman.

She could see the pain in my eyes, the hurt but couldn't do nothing because mother wanted it that way and forced my auntie not to say shit. My auntie could only give me the love the same love she gave to both her kids my cousins during my time with them. It was priceless, it's probably what kept me alive knowing the 6 weeks school holidays we spent together, and then the odd half term break would recuperate me from the carnage only until I returned to no child's land.

Going back, back to my first memories as a child one memory like a few others always stands out. Walking to school at the age of 5 or 6 was the norm, well it was the norm for me because I didn't remember any other kids walking alone without their mother or father one of them was always there with them as they walked hand in hand around the block to school.

Even my pass out parade from the army I was the only soldier whose parents were absent. Good thing about the army it gave me something I had never experienced before, belonging, 3 seriously good meals per day, structure and the ability to believe in myself. The fights I had, the bumps and bruises, the scrapes sustained during infantry training my sergeant major screaming at me every minute of the day wasn't nothing I couldn't handle, standard procedure.

I remember walking home from school one grey cloudy day, it's funny because it always seemed grey in middle England, always grey. I had soiled myself, a squelchy mess in my pants, I even remember the colour of the pants I was wearing that day a purple pair in the style of a stringy vest, lots of tiny little holes in them. I Walked all the way home with my pants full of shit, I must have smelt proper bad, I was caked in it.

I arrived home, no hello, nothing like that Boris had just finished an early shift I know this because he was in the bath it would have been around 3pm. The next thing I remember, and this is a memory clear as the driven snow before I know it, I'm sat in a bath of cold dirty water, his dirty water covered in shit.

Doris couldn't even be bothered to wipe me down first, clothes off, shit clung from my ass down my legs straight into his dirty bath water and left me there for the best part of an hour. By the time she pulled me from the swamp Infest putrid bath water I must have had early systems of hypothermia. I remember being wrapped in something resembling a towel and left in front of the coal fire shaking uncontrollably.

There's another reason why I don't do baths today because of soap, soap on a rope, no fancy products back then like you have today. If you name any brand of perfume or aftershave there's a brand of beautifully smelling shower or creamy bath moisturising foam. Organic or vegan cream, bath bombs and spray foam, I don't care who's made it regardless I don't use soap especially if it's on a rope, I don't care if Hugo Jesus Boss had designed it's just not happening.

Soap made from whale flesh or whale oil it's a smell you don't forget, you'll never forget that smell. It was most likely in every school back in the 70s and

80s accompanied with tracing paper for bog roll, wipe your arse shit halfway up your back.

Today I've heard it's good for you, great for your skin they say but it's not good for you if it is rammed up your ass, not for a small child with constipation, not good at all. So, unless I am missing out on something here maybe a Fanny Cradock remedy in the good housekeeping guide in one of her many cookbooks for small children then I guess it's some sort of twisted medieval wicked witch of the north thing to do.

Constipation, my guess a poor diet not enough fibre, fruit vegetables etc, now knowing today how twisted and tormented Doris and Phillis were, it most likely started with a phone call to SS headquarters from the pay phone on the corner of our street, because it wouldn't have been a mobile not in the early 70s anyways.

He's been constipated for a while now, what do you suggest, now before I continue, Doris is having a confab with the SS leader who didn't want me anywhere near her Gestapo bunker when Doris first took me there.

Constipation is it, nanny Phillis is most likely thinking what sick and twisted remedy can she conjure up, BINGO, have you tried inserting a piece of soap up his bum? Now why didn't she consult with our GP or took me to A&E it was that bad, a child laxative, anything, or maybe a telephone conversation with someone less twisted like my auntie or our neighbour next door

I'm a massive believer that the smallest slightest thing can trigger a flashback which can transport you back to that very moment. What triggers this memory is a bath, a fucking bath, so I'm led into the bathroom. I remember the bath being downstairs near the kitchen because the radio was on, and the radio was always kept on the kitchen. Until one-time king Kong Boris launched it up the garden, kind of a radio vacation outdoors for the electrical device.

The pain was excruciating more painful than any hiding I had experienced white pain. As a bit of a plonka I'm my late 20s and early 30s anyone who knew me, knew I was mad for snowboarding. With such an extreme sport which I loved comes consequences, concussion, sprains, broken bones and in extreme cases death.

If you've broken a collar bone, you'll know what white pain is, its decapitation with your head still attached to your body, not for kids. It stung, it stung so bad, if felt like I had a dozen hornets in my arse. Tears pouring from my eyes but unable to make a sound as I had lost my breath, I had rigor mortis, I was being soap raped. This wasn't some old housewife's remedy for constipation this was torture at the highest level. A nice soak in the bath after a hard day's work with Barry white playing in the background, nice smelly candles, you can fuck right off, go fuck yourself some more, bath time lovers. The crazy mad thing was every time I farted, I farted soapy bubbles from my baby arse for the best part of a week.

Just a gentle FYI I am not a bath homophobic type person. I don't have anything against baths in general. So, if I have offended anyone who doesn't like dick heads like me writing about bath time "trauma" then try sticking a bar of whale soap in your arse the size of a fucking house brick.

Mandingo

"I fucking hate you with pure vengeance, you're a spineless scumbag. I hate every bone within that pathetic body you call a man. Auguste fucking wanker Knuckles I will never forgive you for what you have done to mum, do you know what I mean". No, I don't know what you mean. Have you ever sat and thought to yourself why I have chosen to hang certain peoples dirty washing out for public view? no. You contact my wife with a drunken fuzzy head claiming that all this is a play on words and that somehow, I have made all this up?

Delusional is what you are, a mindless fucking dick head banging away on your smart phone. It is obvious you are getting a kick out of someone's struggles. A perverse kick knowing someone is struggling with their mental health and childhood trauma. You are afraid of what you do not know. Two stupid dick heads who are as thick as pig shit. If the truth be told you don't know the difference between chicken shit and chicken salad. And because you don't know what you should know having been in my shadow for so long you act like a pair of immature childish morons who have just discovered their lip stick. Fondling yourselves with your dick beaters. It's savage to imagine you both giggling like two hyenas praying on the misfortune of others through your smart phones.

A handful of lost souls have the courage to go out into the wilderness to face those unknowns, to conquer, overcome the not knowing. The detritus that has been orated by a bottle of whisky on a wet windy rainy boxing day is pure and utter gable. You must think a slapped bottom and being sent to bed with no super is child abuse.

I should move on, grow a pair, be a man, be thankful and grateful for what I have. Such big bold masculine words mate. It must piss you off knowing you're reading my narrative rather than attending my funeral. Fact, your parents are child abusers. The abuse I suffered happened way before you were born. The abuse I'm talking about is something you'll never get your head around. I Have no intention in wanting to educate you on what has been written. You need to do this yourself, look at the big fucking picture. Why have I done this?

There are no long words, no colouring or popup sections. It's a book, it's a story, it's one in a million. Obviously not aimed at someone who has lived a wonderful loving life with amazing parents, beautiful memories, holidays with racists. Another fact you need to digest, your old man was a racist pig. He battered your sister in front of my own eyes for dating a black boy on that estate they dragged us up on. Rubbed black boot polish on her face, "you want to be with those black fuckers you might as well be black. Guess who sat there and let this happen? Your mother, just sat there with her nose in the air and let this abuse happen. How dare you question me in the matter of the fact your parents were no fucking angels when it came to mental torture. Yet again you have no fucking clue what or who you are comforting".

You think, you assume you know Doris, you're a keypad warrior giving yourself comfort off the back of others misery. You have no clue who she is, let alone the abuser she was. Remember I witnessed first-hand the abuse she dished out to her mother who was in her care. Abused her own mother of 90+ years with dementia. Drunken verbal and physical abuse, what person would do that to a vulnerable old lady regardless. Who made sure this abuse stopped? Me, I put myself between them both during a drunken onslaught. Passed away in her sleep, I hope she did go peacefully and not at the hand of some deranged drunken lunatic wielding a pillow.

Do any of you even grasp the years of abuse dished out to Alfred. The pain, the grief she has caused him. An evil individual you claim to know but like all those looking on with rose tinted glasses you are all fooled. There's a reason why half her spawn has turned their backs on her. The kid with silver spoons up his arse will never know, will he?

Your comments, gash, dribble is a wonky knee jerk reaction to the noise I have created. You have heard nothing but noise, noise, barks by vermin who are bewildered by such courage and achievements. Read and educate yourself on the truth, not the fake smiles and lies you have been poisoned with. I assumed you were smart, eloquent, a better man but reading back on these trailer trash WhatsApp message responses you obviously know nothing about me. You might think a handful of gatherings this past two decades, the majority ending in fist fights and rage, is enough for you to say, "he's my brother".

You don't know me, but you believe you have the right to judge me. You're broken just as I was many years back. "I hate you for what you have done mum". Let's just put the brakes on there for a moment, Mum. I don't think so mate, my mother no more. I didn't ask to be abandoned; I didn't ask to be beaten within an inch of my baby life. I didn't ask Boris to beat down on me as a five-year-old.

I own my past as a drug addict, but this individual is a recovered addict. There is nothing you can hurt me with. There is nothing which hasn't been documented in my work. It's all there. As I mentioned, you bark off the echoes of others. I don't hate you, I'm over you. A question if I may? How do you live with the fact that during a debauched evening after time had lapsed you noticed your daughter was missing? Your sister knew he was a paedophile. No one did nothing when everyone knew she was in harm's way.

"Lies, cheating, the drugs, the money I borrowed, the fights" you say, making out I'm a monster. Remember the messages and the conversations of your dogging days. Running off behind your wife's back. Fucking random strangers in dim lit car parks. Trolling numerous sex sites for your next victim. Only the one in a million subscribers you happened to fool into a potential alley way orgy was your wife's best friend. "Cheating" you claim. Can't you see, hasn't it registered within that blindfolded vision that you were vermin to your first wife. "My life is wonderful" fair dinkum mate, you must look at your partner with a certain sense of regret knowing she will never be your first love. Please don't throw accusations at me as if you've done your research on my life.

Absurd stupid little prick. The shit that has poured from your forehead must be flowing straight into your eyeballs. Talking of balls, Inappropriate balls. The time you made my wife watch a porn video of some stupid cunt having his balls kicked repeatedly by two midget female porn stars. Do you think that was appropriate? And when shit couldn't get any worse you showed my wife a picture of your dick. I mean really who the fuck do you think you are, Mandingo?

You vomit dribble, such a sad day that you have spent your Christmas discrediting me. It was only this summer passed that you wanted to reconnect with BBQs and ball games. In tears, but I refused knowing you and the deceit behind your intentions. You're as cold as your old man, calculated and evil like the cunt you fell from.

Our time has come to pass mate, blocked, deleted for good. Enjoy the fact when you wake from that dragon you sleep with that it must have taken a weekend boozing for you to muster the courage to vomit into your smartphone o contact my wife to get to me. Such a brave boy, Dutch courage is like wearing a condom with the tip snipped off hoping for the best. Just know the fact, the one act you cannot hide from regarding the number of books I write. They abused a child, they abused me. Live with it, own that fact.

I'm somewhat taken aback by the hatred which I can see and hear as clear as the driven snow within your writing. Farting from that thing you call a mouth, burping verbal diarrhoea making up stories that I laid with the only person I call a sister. The closest person to me, someone I was raised with because your parents couldn't stand the fact, I was in your family circle. That bastard child. The kid beaten black and blue, that child your father had no love for whatsoever. Sent away every holiday, every chance they had to get rid of me so that they could have their white family. You must be confused with your sister who had three children with her brother. Did you kick off when the first inbred was born? No, you all rallied around at the baby shower with gifts and support. You have the audacity to conjure such lies mate. Sad, sad day it must be for you to go so low.

They have been and will always be closer to me than you could ever imagine. You're a weak individual without thought for the big picture You're the child within half a dozen who was his prize trophy. The golden child who had life served on a silver platter. The truth hidden from your cotton wool ears. And now you fall like a new-born lamb because of her tears and anguish. You've obviously got your back up, "how dare you do this to my mother". They wrote their own futures; they cemented their history when they did what they did. It's so concerning knowing how easy you have fallen to a handful of drunken emotions, anger and twisted weekend banter. Even you should know there are two sides to every story. You have chosen the side that bares no weight, content, moral compass, compassion, empathy let alone integrity whatsoever.

Tread carefully little one. Names, dates, locations etc have been changed to hide those abusers and ones who have committed unthinkable things. To go down this path by threatening me will only lead to you opening dead ends. A dead end I closed years ago with heavy road works and high walls to move forward and heal the scars of trauma. Read the content, educate yourself then maybe one day we might have a friendly beer or two but please don't be a cunt passing judgement from the putrid noise of others trying to save face.

There is absolutely nothing you can hurt me with emotionally, verbally, physically or spiritually. There are places I have travelled to. Dark cold places filled with fear, torment, suicide and addiction. Places you'll never ever comprehend, places that you never know even existed. Take your worst nightmare multiple by a grown-up number and you'll still never understand the journey taken to be where I am today.

Go look in the mirror and ask yourself how you live with the fact you left your child, rephrase that, you were all so drunk that you hadn't even realised your baby daughter was missing with a known sex predator "paedophile" that had been protected by his own. Do you think what

happened that eventful evening, that you, you alone have caused irreversible damage to your own flesh and blood. You are so concerned with baloney obviously blinded to the truth knowing all of you have stood by individuals who have caused horrific abuse to others. Individuals who could in fact be imprisoned for their crimes.

My name, what's with you and conspiracies? I changed my name because you believe I was running away from something, what was I running away from? Please shed some light on this overwhelming belief for conspiracies. Fact and thought for you. Do you believe I wanted the surname of a sex offender? A surname that has absolutely nothing to do with me all bar the fact that this surname was on my birth certificate. Bit of a shock when he noticed the afro and a shade not that of white. You guessed it, not his baby boy he was expecting. I chose this name because it's the beginning of my children's heritage and the end of a lifetime of lies.

If my words, sentences, chapters, books have offended you. My actions towards those you claim to be my parents then it truly is a sad day in your household because you are just as poisonous as those who have crawled under their rocks knowing I live and breathe amongst you all. I have become someone I am someone, I've crawled out of hell to turn my life around and it's obvious it bothers you all that the little bastard nicknamed crusty stands tall knowing the truth, knowing the evil inflicted upon me is the past and the future is bright. Thank you so much for giving me the verbal shite to write another chapter within this biblical account of my humble journey thus far.

So, as I've said before if you want to go down this road of discovery, slander disingenuous and corruption then it's your call. Don't get child abuse and my pubescent immaturity as a lost soul drunk on drugs and distraction to the fact of trying to discover his identity. Two different things, not even the same ball sport. It's all there documented within pages upon pages. I'm hiding nothing, it's a roller coaster train wreck, a nuclear bomb fired into a volcano narrative and I'm guessing that you have no clue what that narrative is, that's why you're afraid.

You would both be surprised, very surprised in what I know about you. It's bonkers how neither of you are humble nor wise knowing the damage you both caused your previous partners is beyond forgivable. Allegations of rape, in and out of court with restraining orders against you. A man who kicked the mother of his child out onto the streets. A man who wanted the mother of his children sent to prison because she wanted to be free from the verbal abuse you caused.

I've sat down many nights alone thinking about my life and the chaos that was a lost cause. All I wanted to know at the end of the day was who I was and where I was from. When those facts have been hidden away, locked away for decades one becomes a savage animal. I just need to be told the truth.

So, before you call the pot black maybe sit down and ponder, "why am I here and what is my purpose"? If the answer is doing this, then do it to someone who gives a fuck. Laugh, laugh out loud about my stupid little books. Big things have small beginnings, and I don't mean your dick mate. Really, what headspace were you in? Were you expecting a blow job from my wife?

The Key

This key held within your hand has been in my possession since the day you smashed my head to pieces. "I abandoned you". Now, I don't want you to think that one day I'm going to use that key to open your front door with flowers and wine and pretend any longer that I'm such a brainless individual. I know the facts, the particulars, the truth. A spiritual letter I was going to post without an address or stamp.

What use would that be? It's about time you own this symbol of security before I turn this corner. I criticise you, you alone for the abuse and damage caused to me as a baby as a child. It was that single choice you made. You put your racist parents before me. I have no regrets, I live with the trauma, I own the content within these pages, I own the years that have made me and almost killed me. I have made my peace with those who have passed. Today I make my peace with you.

Painted Hearts

What do I become, where will I be?
Empty cupboards, mouldy bread
Water on Weetabix, just another morning in a beat-up house for me.

Told he is smarter, much smarter than me
Look at him, how beautiful he is, so smart
Am I not worthy, of course I'm not
I'm your mistake who you begrudge in raising.

I'm not strong, I am weak, so you say
The word manifestation does not compute
You look down on me, wanting to be beat down guilt and frustration
You wish me dead, you and him, I'm a child not worthy of love.

A rusty bike, a holiday alone with my neighbour
Cold mash and lumpy gravy, a jam sandwich if you're lucky
What do I know about identity?
I'm black, I'm white, I'm a child lost within misery.

Jerk chicken was a delight
You broke me down, shamed me, jerk fucking wings
Vicious, spiteful, empathy, what the fuck is that
A black child raised a slave in a white household

Subjected to blinding racism, a sister beat because she sort friendship with boys like me.
Drugs, alcohol ensued when I sought direction in the army
Barmy army an institute for grown men not boys

Drug smuggler, addict I soon became
I didn't care as it was the norm, just a surname and number, private junkie

I have more love for animals than I do you
You love animals more than me
An expression of waste, who would not become someone that anyone would discard in the grass.
I write because it heals me, I heal because I'm writing
My children will become angels of steel
My time is more relevant with them than you.

A product of an organic 70s love vehicle
My name was never my name
My name was never my name
But you decided to hide the truth
You chose to hide everything from me

I'm Auguste Knuckles a demonstration of my doing
House music food music French classic cookery Frankie Knuckles Auguste Escoffier
Top shelf mixers cheap booze and easy scratches
I rise, there is no higher I can go, is there?

My children are me; I am them; we are one
One love, blessed beyond measure
Blessed beyond belief.
No love lost, no shame lost, love was non-existent
One didn't search for love; love was moon distant
Did I mention I'm from there?
Certainly not here

At the end of the day the day is night
Every day seemed like it would never end
Half breed like you, no one like me
Somewhere out there an angle watched down on me
My story is a puzzle, a Rubik's cube I could never solve

A broken vase in front of a giraffe
A mind skewered like a fruit kebab
I've realised this gift was passed down through ancient wisdom
You'll have no kudos from this child called me.

Nothing but love for friends and kin
Friends and kin will come and go
Smiles and laughter fade like the morning dew
My love for my children will live through the ages
The ages of me painted in their hearts.

AK

The soldier I left for dead in the desert of Iraq was Pte Twyman.

Ingram Content Group UK Ltd.
Milton Keynes UK
UKHW020902230523
422206UK00004B/20

9 781398 468559